Religious Diversity and Civil Society

Religious Diversity and Civil Society

A Comparative Analysis

Edited by

Bryan S. Turner

The Bardwell Press, Oxford

Published by:

The Bardwell Press
6 Bardwell Road
Oxford OX2 6SW
www.bardwell-press.co.uk

British Library Cataloguing in Publication Data
A catalogue record for this book is available from the British Library

ISBN-13: 978-1-905622-11-5

Typeset by The Bardwell Press, Oxford, UK
Printed in Great Britain by TJ International, Padstow, Cornwall

Contents

Acknowledgements

The majority of these chapters were originally presented at a conference on Religion in Industrial Society, which was organized by the Islamic Religious Council of Singapore (Muis) in August 2006. The editor is grateful to Muis for its generous support of both the conference and the book, and especially to its President, Haji Mohd Alami Musa. This co-operation is one indication of the importance Singapore places on inter-faith dialogue and public discourses on religion. The ideas and views expressed in this publication are, however, those of the authors alone and do not necessarily represent the views of Muis and its members. Finally, I am grateful to Professor Tony Reid, the Director of the Asia Research Institute, who has made the study of religion an important part of the research of the Asia Research Institute.

Bryan S. Turner
National University of Singapore

List of Contributors

Gary D. Bouma is Professor of Sociology and UNESCO Chair in Intercultural and Interreligious Relations—Asia Pacific at Monash University. His research in the sociology of religion examines the management of religious diversity in plural multicultural societies, postmodernity as a context for doing theology, religion and terror, inter-cultural communication and missiology, religion and public policy, women and religious minorities, and gender factors in clergy careers. His *Australian Soul: Religion and Spirituality in the Twenty-first Century* was published by Cambridge University Press in 2006.

Noorhaidi Hasan is an Indonesian scholar of political Islam who received his MA from Leiden University (1999), MPhil from the International Institute for the Study of Islam in the Modern World (2000) and PhD from Utrecht University, the Netherlands (2005). He has been affiliated to Sunan Kalijaga State Islamic University of Yogyakarta, Indonesia, since 1995. Currently he is a post-doctoral fellow at the Asia Research Institute (ARI), National University of Singapore, doing research on the making of public Islam: piety, agency, and commodification on the landscape of the Indonesian public sphere. He has published *Laskar Jihad: Islam, Militancy, and the Quest for Identity in Post-New Order Indonesia* (Ithaca, New York: SEAP Cornell University, 2006).

Julie Chernov Hwang is an Assistant Professor in the Department of Political Science at California State University-Fullerton. She successfully defended her dissertation entitled, "What Went Right: Political Participation, State Capacity and Peaceful Islamic Mobilization," in 2006 at the University of Colorado-Boulder. She is also published in *Nationalism and Ethnic Politics*.

Kuah-Pearce Khun Eng obtained her B.A. degree at the University of Singapore and Ph.D at Monash University, Australia. She is currently Associate Professor and Head of the Department of Sociology and Honorary Academic Director of Centre for Anthropological Research at the University of Hong Kong. Her primary areas of research include Chinese diaspora and transnationalism; Chinese women and their network capitals; and religion (Buddhism) and politics. Publications include sole author books: *State, Society and Religious Engineering: Towards A Reformist Buddhism* (2003); *Rebuilding the Ancestral Village: Singaporeans in China* (2000); edited books: *Voluntary Organizations in the Chinese Diaspora* (2006); *Chinese Women and Their Social and Network Capitals* (2004); *Where China Meets Southeast Asia* (2000) and guest editor of *Locating the Self in the Chinese Diaspora, Asian Studies Review* (2006) vol. 30(3).

Gabriele Marranci is an anthropologist by training who teaches the anthropology of Islam at the University of Aberdeen, Scotland. His research focuses on contemporary aspects of Muslim communities, as well as identity, gender, social policies and religion. He is the author of three monographs, *Jihad Beyond Islam* (Berg), *The Anthropology of Islam* (Berg) and *Understanding Muslim Identities, Rethinking Fundamentalism* (Palgrave MacMillan), and also several articles and book chapters. He is the founding editor of the new journal, *Contemporary Islam* (Springer) and co-editor, with Prof. Bryan Turner, of the forthcoming book series *Contemporary Muslims in Global Society*. His most recent research, funded by The British Academy, has centered on the experience of Islam and identity formation among Muslim prisoners in the United Kingdom.

Amyn B. Sajoo lectures in international affairs at the University of British Columbia and Simon Fraser University in Vancouver, Canada. He has served as a policy advisor with the Justice and Foreign Affairs

Departments in Ottawa, and as a Canada-ASEAN Fellow at the Institute of Southeast Asian Studies (ISEAS) in Singapore. Dr. Sajoo has held visiting appointments at Cambridge and McGill Universities, and the Institute of Ismaili Studies (IIS) in London. His books include: *Pluralism in Old Societies and New States* (ISEAS, 1994), *Muslim Ethics* (I.B. Tauris, 2004), and the edited volumes *Civil Society in the Muslim World* (I.B. Tauris, 2002) and *Muslim Modernities* (forthcoming).

Li-ann Thio Ph.D. (Cambridge); LL.M (Harvard); BA (Hons)(Oxford), Barrister (Gray's Inn, UK) is currently Professor Faculty of Law, National University of Singapore. She was chief editor of the *Singapore Journal of International Law* and on the advisory board of the *New Zealand Yearbook of International Law and Human Rights*. With Kevin Yl Tan, she co-authored *Constitutional Law in Malaysia and Singapore* (1997).

Bryan S. Turner was a professorial fellow of Fitzwilliam College at Cambridge University and is currently a professor of sociology in the Asia Research Institute, National University of Singapore. He recently edited the *Cambridge Dictionary of Sociology* (2006) and published *Vulnerability and Human Rights* (2006). He is the founding editor of the journal *Citizenship Studies*.

Foreword

Mohd Alami Musa
President of the Islamic Religious Council of Singapore (Muis)

In August 2006, the Majlis Ugama Islam Singapura (Muis, the Islamic Religious Council of Singapore) organized an International Conference on "Religion in Industrial Society". The Conference was part of a continuous effort by Muis to contribute to a substantive understanding of the global forces shaping contemporary discourses on religion, the issues facing Muslims worldwide within a complex international environment, and the state of the religious life of Singaporean Muslims.

In publishing this volume, Muis is extremely privileged to be able to collaborate with Professor Bryan Turner from the Asia Research Institute, National University of Singapore. It includes all the papers presented at the conference, as well as three additional contributions commissioned by Professor Turner.

The chapters in this volume seek to raise several issues, among them:

- How does one envision religious diversity and civil society?
- How should faith communities cultivate a civic identity with their fellow citizens of different faiths while at the same time cherishing a distinct religious identity?
- What is the role of religion and civil society in the public sphere?
- How can we reach an equilibrium in positing religion's appropriate role in emerging advanced industrial societies?

Policy-makers, opinion-shapers and community leaders generally have to grapple with these difficult questions as international migration trends and massive social transformations occurring in both post-colonial industrializing as well as more advanced industrial societies inevitably create a profound impact on nations, social groups and ethnic as well as faith communities. We live in an age where politically assertive religious movements, for example, Pentecostals in Brazil, Hindu nationalists in India, Buddhist revivalists in Sri Lanka and Muslim radicals in Egypt play increasingly visible and public roles. Such a phenomenon makes political and civil society dynamics all the more important in order to promote trust and civic harmony between the state and civic communities on the one hand, and among various social groups, both indigenous and diasporic, on the other.

Modern conflicts involving race and religion point to the need to foster a deep commitment to civic sensibility which would enable ethical tenets to find concrete expression, not only as formalistic legal obligations, but also as everyday socio-culturalized ethical norms and values. It is such a shared humane sensibility made flesh, in a manner of speaking, which would form the cornerstone of mature citizenship.

Muis hopes that the collection of papers in this volume will help to enrich the current discourse and provide concerned policy-makers, opinion-shapers and community leaders many useful perspectives in formulating effective social policies and solutions to concrete problems and issues faced.

On a personal note, I would like to thank my colleagues, Bohari Jaon and Zalman Putra Ahmad Ali, who played a key role in conceptualizing the intellectual structure of the International Conference. I would also like to record here my thanks to Alfian Kuchit and Asri Aziz who have been involved in every stage of this book's production from its inception. Finally, thanks are due also to Juliana Johari, Mohamed Imran Mohamed Taib and Fa'izah Ahmad for organizing the International Conference.

Bryan S. Turner

Modern social diversity has in large measure resulted from international migration and in turn migration has created greater religious diversity alongside greater cultural complexity. The issues surrounding religious tolerance have, therefore, been produced by globalization. Religious diversity has become a political issue, because we do not, in general terms, appear to have robust social policies and institutions to manage the social tensions that flow from cultural complexity and the conventional liberal solutions, especially the legacy of the Treaty of Westphalia of 1648 which is the foundation of modern liberal policies in the West, appear to be in crisis. The chapters in this collection point in various ways to the increasingly difficult problems of multiculturalism and religious diversity in relation to the state and the law, especially after the international crisis created by the terrorist acts of 9/11.

The labour markets of advanced economies depend on high levels of international migration because they have ageing populations and because their own labour force is either insufficiently mobile or reluctant to take on unskilled or low-paid work. Global labour markets need migrants, but democratic governments, often responding to electoral pressures and negative media campaigns, cannot be seen to be overtly lenient towards unrestrained migration. After 9/11, there has been an unfortunate tendency to conflate three categories of mobile persons: migrants, refugees and asylum seekers. Conservative or right-wing governments have successfully mobilized electorates against liberal policies towards labour mobility and porous frontiers, but even the social democratic countries of Scandinavia and northern Europe have faced acute political difficulties over migration as we have seen in Denmark and the Netherlands. While migrants contribute significantly to economic growth, they are often thought to be parasitic upon the host society. They do not fit easily into a welfare model of citizenship and contributory rights. These problems are endemic, as the various contributions to this volume demonstrate, and violence towards migrants can flare up in Canada and Britain as in Australia and Indonesia.

In this volume, various authors argue that offering citizenship to migrants may be one step towards reducing the likelihood of civil conflict. However, governments have been reluctant to give citizenship status to migrants without stringent criteria of membership, and naturalization is often a slow and complex process. The United States, Britain and the Netherlands have all been discussing the desirability of increasing the difficulty of tests relating to history, law and language which migrants would be expected to take as a preparation for citizenship. Furthermore, dual citizenship is often regarded as an anomaly and there is, as a result, an increasing level of social criticism directed against quasi-citizenship, dual citizenship and flexible arrangements, because these forms of citizenship are thought to undermine the hegemonic model of traditional political membership.

How does religion fit into this scenario? The globalization of the migrant labour market, as Professor Bouma shows, has been one cause of the globalization of world religions, especially Islam, and the creation of new diasporic religious identities. Religious identities tend to be transnational, and offer alternative matrices of self definition that are not state based. There is, as a result, a tension between the transnational identities of neo-fundamentalist religions (Christian, Muslim, Jewish, but also Hindu and Buddhist) and the state-based identities of national citizenship. In the traditional American pattern of assimilation, Protestant, Catholic and Jew became alternative identities within a common pattern of civil religion. There is little indication as yet that "American Muslim" will be an acceptable cultural identity providing full cultural assimilation. In Europe, there is no tradition of civil religion as such to which Muslim Europeans or Christian Europeans or Hindu Europeans could become attached. The idea of European common citizenship has been, at least for the time being, shattered by the rejection of the Constitution in the referenda in France and the Netherlands, and by the failure to agree on a common economic budget in 2005.

The long-term solution to social conflict in culturally diverse societies must be the creation of a common legal and political framework, namely citizenship. Arguments in favour of flexible or global citizenship are problematic, unless they can resolve the relationship between rights and duties, namely the nature of social contributions. While human rights offer some protection to minority groups and to migrant workers through the Convention on economic, social and cultural rights and through such institutions as the International Labour Organization, ultimately human rights (including freedom of religious expression) require the backing of states that promote active citizenship. The framework of citizenship is an important mechanism of democratic education and protection of rights. The paradox is that citizenship is, in one sense, an exclusionary institution, but the erosion of citizenship is also a threat to multiculturalism and cosmopolitanism.

Much of the negative view of cultural dialogue has been shaped by Samuel Huntington's article on "the clash of civilizations" in *Foreign Affairs* (1993). In the post 9/11 world, Huntington's bleak analysis of the development of micro fault-line conflicts and macro core state conflicts has influenced the interventionist assumptions of western foreign policy in the era of the "War on Terror". Huntington, of course, believes that the major division of civilizations is between the Christian West and the Muslim world, but recently he has even more openly outspoken about "the age of Muslim Wars" and widespread Muslim grievance and hostility towards the United States (Huntington 2003). Any attempt to engage with Islamic civilization is set within the context of the war for Muslim minds.

Although Huntington's thesis might be seen as an extreme position, what seems to be beyond question is that cultural and religious complexity resulting from both legal and illegal migration creates new challenges for the state, because religious complexity creates new burdens on civil and political structures, and is a major test of the robustness of the institutions of social citizenship. Cultural and social diversity, including a trend towards legal pluralism, requires a vigorous defence of the rule of law if societies are to avoid social conflict and ultimately violence. There are many possible strategies for the management of ethnic diversity, but passive tolerance of migrants and arbitrary exclusion of asylum seekers does not constitute an effective political option.

Let us start then with two controversial propositions: (1) societies that are culturally and ethnically diverse are more difficult to govern than societies that are culturally homogenous. Heterogeneity creates significant political problems that require explicit, decisive and sophisticated solutions; and (2) globalization, especially the globalization of religion, makes these problems increasingly endemic, global and potentially catastrophic. The growth of fundamentalism and neo-fundamentalism in Islamic, Christian, Jewish, and Hindu traditions makes this political problem—how to sustain civil society in a context of religious diversity–increasingly difficult.

If these pessimistic views of globalization are valid, then there is an important research agenda to consider what political and social measures might be explored to understand the conditions under which modern societies might be able to embrace multiculturalism without running the risk of communal violence, that is the conditions under which they might be less precarious, and the lives of individuals less vulnerable. The chapters in this collection represent an attempt to consider such measures.

Social and political approaches to cultural complexity cover, historically-speaking, a wide spectrum of political strategies. At one extreme, fascism assumed the position that ethnic diversity undermines the quality of a population and the coherence of society, and hence degenerate and deviant elements must be expelled or exterminated. At the other extreme, one might regard the liberal Westphalian strategy, as developed in recent political philosophy by John Rawls, as a solution that regards cultural differences as simply personal attributes that should not intrude on the public space, believes that the market can act as an arbiter between competing social groups and values, and seeks to create a consensus over liberal values. In the chapter by Bryan Turner, the liberal option of Rawls is explored at some length. Rawls's argument concerning an overlapping consensus of opinions can only work if the liberal consensus of opinion is underpinned by an overlapping network of social groups. The liberal response to ethnic difference in Britain can unfortunately be characterized as a matter of benign neglect rather than one of active and positive multiculturalism. The everyday difficulties of British Muslims are explored by Gabriele Marancci in his discussion of what we might regard as "ordinary racism". We must also recognise, as Professor Li-ann Thio warns us, that the Westphalian liberal solution can also constitute an intolerant exclusion of religion from the public domain by secularists who happen to be intolerant of religious belief.

Contemporary social and political theory has been divided between a politics of difference that encourages us to recognise and accept cultural hybridity resulting from globalization, and a theory of global governance that attempts to identify new patterns of social solidarity. The emphasis on difference typically celebrates the diversity of cultural identities in a fragmented world by abandoning a strong commitment to principles of equality. Any emphasis on social equality—the basis of the Enlightenment tradition of citizenship—preserves some element of universalism in order to defend an idea of justice, but it has correspondingly great difficulty in formulating a satisfactory view of tolerance of difference. French republicanism was based on a formal principle of common citizenship, but the French tradition has run into difficulties over universalism in its confrontation with the Muslim community over the head scarf. The politics of identity implicitly abandons the emphasis on justice and equality in the republican notion of citizenship, and at the same time the idea of human rights is often perceived as inevitably western and indifferent to local and specific demands for recognition and respect. Any sociological account of rights, migration and citizenship must grapple with the problem of cultural differences and recognition, on the one hand, and the quest for justice and equality in the conventional discourse of citizenship, on the other.

Because ethnic and religious conflicts in the modern world are exacerbated by globalization, social philosophers have engaged in debates about how tolerance and cosmopolitanism might be promoted. These concerns have spawned a rich ensemble of theories and concepts—cosmopolitan virtue, care, tolerance, and recognition theory. Although these ideas are useful in the formulation of ethical orientations, they do not easily or immediately lead to empirical research strategies or to effective social policies. However, two authors have been widely debated as offering intellectual solutions that can be translated into practical strategies. These are Will Kymlicka who has developed a number of approaches to group rights as compatible with liberal constitutions, and the other is Robert Putnam whose notions of social capital and trust appear particularly relevant to the questions I am addressing.

Robert Putnam (1993: 172) provides four reasons why general reciprocity has beneficial effects in terms of enhancing social co-operation: it increases the costs of defection; it fosters norms of co-operation; it improves communication; and it embodies past successes of collaboration, providing a model for future co-operation. More generally, economists have argued that social capital (or trust) reduces transaction costs. Social capital theories are attractive to sociologists because they show how voluntary associations and local NGOs can make a significant contribution to making the social glue that holds societies together. Philanthropy is not only good for recipients but also collectively for society as a whole. This aspect of social capital is explored by Professor Kuah-Pearce Khun Eng in her analysis of Buddhist philanthropy in Singapore, where a mutual partnership between state and religion contributes significantly to the creation of a civil society. These theories of social capital have however been criticized because they, like the functional theory of social integration in American sociology in the 1950s, suffer from a functional circularity. Because the importance of reciprocity is explained by its effects, these theories do not provide an antecedent causal account of changes in social reciprocity (Knight 2001).

Critics of Putnam's social capital theory note that value consensus is not characteristic of modern societies, in which increasing social diversity destroys the cultural homogeneity of traditional societies, and where value diversity erodes social cohesion. It is useful to distinguish between sharing a common set of beliefs that are positively valued, and knowing about the beliefs that provide common expectations. In the cognitive sense of sharing, "co-operative predictable behavior is guaranteed by the existence of mechanisms that converge expectations toward actions that satisfy the requirements of mutual benefit" (Knight 2001: 358). Co-operation with social norms affects an individual's attitudes towards how other people will co-operate, and in turn these expectations influence assumptions about future behavior. This argument has been developed to make sense of Putnam's observation that social capital is a resource that increases with use. The growth of generalized trust is a function of everyday compliance with norms. Quite simply, the more individuals cooperate with each other, the more they trust one another. Past experience of reliable co-operative interaction tends to increase our general sense of the trustworthiness of others in the community. Conversely, lack of reciprocity tends to deflate trust. In societies with many transnational communities and many diasporas, if there is little reciprocity between social groups then there will be low trust, and consequently greater scope for misunderstanding, mistrust and conflict. The growth of mistrust in the face of growing competition between secular nationalists and Muslim parties has been characteristic of post-Suharto politics according to Noorhaidi Hasan.

In this pessimistic viewpoint, social diversity undermines community and the erosion of common values and shared sentiments undermines trust (Lukes 1991). Because ethnic and multicultural diversity is an obvious feature of most advanced societies, trust in such societies is difficult to sustain, because there are important differences of interest, of basic social ends, and of social beliefs and values. In culturally diverse societies, social groups will employ strategies of social closure to secure access to resources against outsiders who are seen to be competitors. Informal social regulation is unlikely to work effectively in social environments where social equality and fairness are manifestly absent. The greater the inequality in resource allocation, the greater the propensity of disprivileged groups to disrupt existing social arrangements. The greater the disadvantages, the greater the incentive on the part of disprivileged groups to distance themselves from dominant groups. The greater the relative deprivation, the lower the probability that marginalized groups will respond positively to normative motivation to comply with existing social norms. Religiously diverse societies will become conflict ridden, even with adequate legal safeguards, if material wealth is not only unequally distributed but perceived to be unjustly allocated. Corruption in public life is thus a major factor in social unrest. The history of South African apartheid would be an extreme instance of injustice and relative deprivation, where the legitimacy of the system was constantly questioned, but social conflict between groups on the basis of ethnic classification and associated material inequalities remains an all too common aspect of political violence in contemporary societies. In recent history examples of ethnic conflict and ethnic cleansing are unfortunately both numerous and spectacular: Rwanda, Kashmir, Chechnya, Tajikistan, Sudan, Myanmar, and so forth. However, in this volume we are more concerned with the more humdrum ethnic and cultural conflicts that characterise most, if not all modern societies. The post-Suharto situation in Indonesia as described here by Noorhaidi Hassan is perhaps more typical, at least of religious conflict in modern Asia, than more extreme examples from Darfur or Somalia.

Many of the chapters in this volume, such as the chapter by Li-ann Thio on modern Singapore, explore the role of law in sustaining or aggravating social order. The task is "to construct a conception of the rule of law in a socially diverse society that satisfies the requirements of social order and co-operation and, as a *possible* by-product, creates the conditions for the emergence and maintenance of informal mechanisms like trust" (Knight

2001: 365). Achieving this desirable outcome is not easy. A pragmatic perspective treats the rule of law as a mechanism for satisfying the interests of different social groups in a differentiated social order. In order to accommodate the different interests of culturally distinct social groups, the law must develop a range of mechanisms that are not unduly conflictual and divisive. Legal proceduralism as a juridical principle underlines the importance of overt and predictable legal processes in the resolution of conflict. These legal procedures include adjudication, mediation, managerial discretion, contract, and legislation, all of which can contribute to social co-operation. Pragmatism suggests that legal decisions have to satisfy a condition of equal respect and treatment for members of different social groups.

In my view, we need to see the rule of law within a broader social and political framework, namely of social citizenship. The institutions of citizenship have been the principal mechanisms of social inclusion in contemporary society, and citizenship has played a major role in mitigating the negative consequences of income inequality and economic disadvantage in societies where markets are unregulated. In particular, social citizenship is important in containing and reducing the negative consequences of social class differences in capitalism. In British society, citizenship evolved through the nineteenth and twentieth centuries as an amelioration of the negative effects of social class and the capitalist market. Citizenship provided individuals and their families with social security. One tension in British citizenship is that it assumed significant state intervention in the regulation of the market, but also emphasized individualism, initiative, and personal responsibility. In the United States, where there has been political resistance to the growth of a universal welfare state, citizenship is associated with political membership, racial equality and individual freedoms rather than with social rights. The lack of centralised, bureaucratic government in America encouraged the growth of individual initiative and voluntary associations rather than state intervention to solve local community problems. While citizenship is often seen as a solution to social divisions, it is important to bear in mind that citizenship can assume many different forms.

One conclusion of this discussion of values or more generally cultural consensus as a foundation is that a legal framework, contrary to most sociological approaches, is a necessary pre-condition of social stability. Social capital may provide the glue of reciprocity to overcome ethnic division and conflicting interests, but social capital may also need the backing or precondition of formal rules and structures. How can states provide rights regimes that are sensitive to the (often conflicting interests) of minorities and majorities? Let us consider another set of arguments relating to rights. Will Kymlicka (1995) has defended the idea of group rights and cultural rights within a liberal framework (as a policy that has specific reference to multicultural societies like Canada and Australia). Kymlicka (1995: 26) argues that liberal democracies that have accepted some form of multiculturalism typically make adjustments or accommodations to cultural pluralism through the mechanism of what he calls "group-differentiated rights". These are divided into three types.

First, there are rights to self-government. In multinational states, the component nations may demand some level of political autonomy or territorial jurisdiction. The right of self-determination has been sanctioned by the United Nations' Charter—"all peoples have a right to self-determination"—but the charter does not define "peoples". In some societies, the demand for autonomy may lead to secession, but one common institutional response to the demand for autonomy has been federalism. In some respects, Kymlicka's argument may be specific to Canada, where federalism offers some solution to the demands of the Quebecois within a federal structure.

The second accommodation is through the development of poly-ethnic rights. At a minimal level, these are merely rights to express cultural differences without exposure to prejudice. These rights are often expressed against so-called "Anglo-conformity" which has involved the dominance of Anglo-American values in the public domain, relegating minority cultural practices to the private sphere. More radical demands for these rights may entail the exemption of ethnic groups from laws and regulations that are seen to disadvantage them. The most obvious example has come from the Sikh community in Britain and Canada, where Sikh men are allowed to wear turbans as part of their official dress in public roles in the police force or military or schools. The point of these rights is to promote integration, whereas self-government rights are to secure self-government.

Finally there is the creation of special representation rights in which minority or oppressed groups are given automatic or guaranteed representation in parliamentary and other democratic institutions. These rights can be regarded as a form of affirmative action, but they tend to be temporary. They are "kick-start" devices to ensure an evolution towards adequate participation and they are subsequently abandoned once minority groups have entered the mainstream of the host community.

The theory of differentiated rights, while considered as a general legal framework, is often in practice specific to Canadian history and society. Canada is federal, and as a white-settler society it has first-nation communities with a problematic relationship to Canadian history and sovereignty. In addition, Canada has a substantial French-speaking community in the state of Quebec. Some aspects of the argument however can apply to Europe, where federalism could be a useful principle of accommodation. In addition, poly-ethnic rights already apply to certain social groups, but not to others. The case of the head scarf in French schools is the obvious illustration. However, one criticism of Kymlicka's general approach is the absence of any significant discussion of law. There is no attempt to connect legal pluralism with group-differentiated rights. Kymlicka's rights are, in fact, primarily cultural rights and hence the problem of legal sovereignty is not adequately broached and yet as various chapters in this collection demonstrate the legal framework is a crucial ingredient of social harmony.

This contribution to liberal theory implies that societies can survive as effective democracies provided they are able to accommodate divergent cultures and identities. Other writers have been far more pessimistic about sustaining social order in the face of social diversity. As we have seen, Jack Knight notes that cultural consensus in modern societies is unusual, because increasing social diversity undermines the cultural homogeneity of traditional societies. Co-operation with social norms affects attitudes towards how other people will co-operate, and in turn this expectation shapes assumptions about future behavior. Knight develops this argument to make sense of Robert Putnam's observation that social capital is a moral resource that increases with use (Putnam 2000). The growth of generalized trust is a function of everyday compliance with norms, and the more individuals cooperate with each other, the more they trust one another. Past experiences of reliable cooperative interaction tends to enhance our general sense of the trustworthiness of other people. In short, trustworthiness routinely generates trust, and conversely lack of reciprocity tends to deflate trust.

One consequence of cultural pluralism might, therefore, be legal pluralism. If legal pluralism is an inevitable consequence of multiculturalism, it suggests that Kymlicka's group-differentiated rights are at present underdeveloped because they do not recognise the importance of legal self-determination. Legal pluralism would thus stretch the assumptions of liberalism to their limits. For example, the right to join or to leave a social group is central to liberalism. But in Islam there are traditional views that regard the right to opt out as parallel to apostasy and they could not easily permit such arrangements. The notion that individuals can opt out of their own communities is therefore perhaps the most problematic aspect of individual rights. In the case of minorities, the survival of their cultures and traditions requires continuity of socialization and transmission—a process that has historically depended on women. Hence, women are typically subject to excessive (and at times brutal) subordination to group norms. But this fact offers no normative reason for supporting gender inequalities.

What is to be done? The social policy implications of these chapters are numerous but also relatively simple. Professor Amyn Sajoo provides an excellent summary of such requirements in the conclusion of his chapter. A successful society that is diverse and complex requires a strong legal framework and the institutions of citizenship to create a public environment in which overt racism is not tolerated and where assumptions about diversity are core elements of government business. Governments need such overt and explicit policies that convey to the public that the government does not favour one group over another, and hence minority rights are protected. Secondly there must be sufficient economic growth and an adequate taxation system to redistribute wealth in such a way that second-generation children of migrants are not systematically disadvantaged. Educational policies are therefore fundamental to success. Thirdly, there must be social arrangements that allow for inter-marriage, reciprocity and the growth of intermediate associations (clubs, churches and voluntary associations) to build up social capital as the underpinning of liberal values. These overlapping social groups are the supports that make possible an overlapping consensus of opinion and belief. Finally, there must be cultural events such as sport and general values such as patriotism that will counteract the tendency towards group loyalty, tribalism or sectarian solidarity. Despite these arrangements, to quote the Scottish poet Robert Burns, the best laid schemes of mice and men tend to go awry.

Given the ubiquity of social conflict in the modern world, a pessimistic scenario of failing states and failing societies is common place. But pessimism is probably a poor premise for social policies which by their nature are oriented towards changing societies to improve them. Several authors in this collection have developed valuable arguments supporting diversity and pluralism as viable bases for social cohesion. Julie Chernov Hwang shows how educational policies in both Indonesia and Malaysia can contribute to social progress and civic harmony, while Gary Bouma reminds us that societies like Australia and Singapore have been relatively successful in embracing social diversity.

References

Huntington, Samuel P. (1993) "The clash of civilizations," *Foreign Affairs* 72(3): 22–48.

—— (2003) "America in the world," *The Hedgehog Review* 5(1): 7–18.

Knight, Jack (2001) "Social norms and the rule of law: fostering trust in a socially diverse society" in K. S. Cook (ed.) *Trust in Society*. New York: Russell Sage Foundation, pp. 354–373.

Kymlicka, Will (1995) *Multicultural Citizenship. A Liberal Theory of Minority Rights*. Oxford: Oxford University Press.

Lukes, Steven (1991) "The rationality of norms," *Archives Européennes de Sociologie* 32: 142–149.

Putnam, Robert D. (1993) *Making Democracy Work: Civic Traditions in Modern Italy*. Princeton and New Jersey: Princeton University Press.

—— (2000) *Bowling Alone. The Collapse and Revival of American Community*. New York: Simon & Schuster.

1 The Challenge of Religious Revitalization and Religious Diversity to Social Cohesion in Secular Societies[1]

Gary D. Bouma

Introduction

Religious life in the twenty-first century has taken on a renewed vitality that was unexpected and which many fear threatens social cohesion and civil society. The global movement of people, capital and culture has produced higher levels of religious diversity in many societies and has unexpectedly led to increases in religious practice, the salience of religious identity and the involvement of religion in politics. While the beginnings of these changes can be seen to be at work from the mid-1970s, their effects were brought into sharp focus in the twenty-first century by the events of September 11, 2001 and subsequent religiously motivated violent attacks and conflicts.

As a result of the revitalization of religion many societies are re-thinking the roles of religion in their civic life. As they do this, the idea of what constitutes secularity is reconsidered (Fenn 2001, Martin 2005) and the philosophical foundations of secular society re-examined (Milbank 2006). Revitalization and diversification of religion in a society raises issues of the role of religion in politics, the management of conflicting demands stemming from purity codes, and decisions about forms of education necessary for civil life. This chapter reviews the current situation and explores issues of conceptualizing the current relations of religion and society as well as exploring some of the policy issues.

Religious Revitalization

The evidence for the revitalization of religion is now overwhelming and incontrovertible (Thomas 2005, Berger and Martin 2005, Bouma 2002, 2006). While particularly evident in Africa and Latin America evidence of revitalization pours in from Asia and even Australia where the secular press has been doubling the coverage of religious issues annually since 2001, and some political leaders are open about the religious bases of their politics. Revitalization can be detected not only among Christian and Muslim groups but also Buddhist, Hindu, Sikh and others (Almond, Appleby and Sivan 2003), to say nothing of a burgeoning array of spiritualities (Bouma 2006) and within Christianity the Mega-church phenomenon (Connell 2005, Chavez 2005). Muslim societies such as Indonesia and Malaysia as well as those in South Asia and the Middle East experience increased rates of religious practice and calls for the imposition, or stricter enforcement, of Shariah law (Hassan 2007, Khatab and Bouma 2007). The fact that Europe appears to be an outlier as it persists in its particular form of secularity has been discussed (Davie 2002, Martin 2005).

This wave of religious revitalization is the product of several interrelated factors. Some people are reacting against the failure of otiose secularized liberal and formally organized forms of religion to meet their religious needs. This is a familiar pattern in the history of religions. For example, the early 19th century witnessed such a reaction against The Church of England in the Oxford Movement and the rise of evangelicals. At the same time many new religious groups and movements emerged, for example the Church of Latter Day Saints, the Disciples of Christ, The Brethren and the Churches of Christ. Religious revitalization and innovation also occurred in other parts of the world, for example in Iran this period witnessed the rise of the Baha'is. A second source of religious revitalization is found in continued failures in each society to deliver universal justice and to achieve a fair distribution of goods and services, including food and health. In such circumstances, some people react against the failure of the secularist humanist paradigm to deliver its promises of peace and prosperity with justice, or to provide satisfactory explanations for evil, inequality and pain.

Meanwhile migration moves people and with them religions and religious ideas around the globe. Some migrants use religious organizations to assist them in settling (Bouma 1994, Ebaugh and Chafetz 2000). Migrants also tend to be more religious than those they leave behind, and more traditionally religious. Migration has dramatically increased religious diversity of many societies and as a result has increased inter-religious contact. Much of this migration has been voluntary, but some has involved less voluntary forms of population resettlement bringing religious groups into conflict over land tenure and use as in the case of the Maluku (Stern 2003: 70–74).

The forms of this religious revitalization or revitalization found in each of the Abrahamic faiths and in others include increased intensity of commitment, increased salience of religious identity, the rise of puritanical extremes (Almond, Appleby and Sivan 2003, Antoun 2001, Porter 2006) and a return to political engagement to apply faith whether by establishing Shariah Law in newly Muslim majority countries like Malaysia, promoting the teaching of Creation Science in the USA, or condemning particular patterns of sexuality (Bates 2004). Revitalization often brings conflict between the more liberal and more conservative or fundamentalist positions within religious groups, as seen in the history of the Southern Baptist Church, and now among Anglicans, but also within Islam, Hinduism and Buddhism (Almond, Appleby and Sivan 2003). Revitalization is also associated with more emotive and charismatic forms of spirituality and worship, particularly in the West where it forms part of the reaction against rational, cerebral and propositional forms of Christianity (Bouma 1992, 2006).

All of this religious revitalization runs strictly counter to mid-20th-century secularization theory (Berger 1999, Martin 2005). Religion was supposed to become increasingly private, less engaged with political issues and decreasingly a force in both society and individual lives. An echo of this expectation that religion would fade away can be heard in some multicultural policy orientations to religion which seem to expect that religious difference should not, and with proper management will not, make a difference. There is a revival of interest in and respect for religion in social theory (Derrida and Vattimo 1998, Berger 1999).

Secularity itself is undergoing a long overdue deconstruction as scholars are confronted with the fact that secularism is a committed viewpoint with its own metaphysical assumptions (Stark 2003, Sommerville 2006). The idea that secularism provides an objective, value neutral position for the development and enforcement of social policy with respect to religion is becoming increasingly difficult to sustain as the ideological foundations of this perspective becomes clearer (Stark 2003, Martin 2005, Berger 1999). The reactions of those who work hard to exclude religious variables from explanatory frameworks make it clear that secularity is not a neutral, or objective position, but a committed anti-religious standpoint, a belief system in its own right with consequences. Milbank (2005) calls for a remembrance of the ontological foundations of all social thought criticizing those in the Nietzschean tradition who claim to be able to establish deontological bases for values and social order.

For Fenn (2001) and others, secular societies are not irreligious but societies where the religious and spiritual are no longer under the control of religious organizations such as churches. From the Peace of Westphalia in 1648 which ended the European wars of religion in the West and by imposition in the former colonies of western powers the religious has been directly under the control of religious organizations which are themselves "organized" through proclaimed allegiance to the state. In the secularization of the 20th century, religious organizations lost their capacity to control the religious and spiritual such that they are now "free".

The Diversification of Religion

Four forms of differentiation have radically transformed religious life in secular 21st-century societies. First, the West has witnessed the decline of the power and membership of what were mainline religious groups. But this decline has masked another more profound change. Religious and spiritual life has slipped out from the control of once hegemonic religious organizations. As a result, it is now freely available in myriad forms requiring much less commitment and taking often much less organized, or very differently organized forms.

Second, migration and conversion have brought unfamiliar religions to many places, putting religions that previously dealt with each other only as stereotypes into direct relationship. At the same time, global communication technologies have brought the widest diversity of religious teaching and practice to every corner of the world. Not only are there now more religious groups in many societies today than ever before, but also each group is much less homogeneous than it was before.

Third, there has been an increased differentiation between religious organizations and the state. Take the example of Osama bin Laden. In this case religious action has had global consequences without the offices or agency of a state. Religion has become a force outside the structures of statecraft, effective without the trappings of the state. In many societies, religious groups have moved further from direct association with government while at the same time religious welfare organizations have become largely dependent on state funding as the state has chosen to channel funds through "faith-based" organizations.

Fourth, there has been a decline of national or regional organizational religious structures to pattern religious belief and practice. Separate congregational organizations with limited networks and no collective organ of responsibility are replacing once strong and vertically integrated Christian denominations. Of course, religious groups like Muslims, Jews, Buddhists and others have long lived without the kinds of organizational structures that characterized Christendom.

The diversification of religion has also been occurring within religious groups. During the late 20th century this process has gone so far that religious diversity is often found to be at least as great within religious groups as between them. Some refer to this as the death of denominationalism. For example, the internal diversity of Anglicans is legendary, even if stretched to the breaking point by current debates. The Charismatic movement has cut across denominational lines as have liberalism, social concerns, and evangelicalism. It is no longer possible to speak of the Anglican, or the Uniting, or the Catholic point of view. But within-group religious diversity is also evident in the different ways Muslims give expression to their faith in the one God, or the differences in the practices and theologies of Buddhists, Hindus or any other religious group.

The consequence of the diversification of religious groups has been to render them much more difficult to manage by those who would promote healthy inter-religious relations and reduce conflict. For example, Australia's religious organizations have become so diverse that religious diversity is much less able to be managed by this society than it once was. In 1947, the Prime Minister of Australia would have had to make only two phone calls to speak with religious leaders who represented over half the population and one more would have enabled him to reach nearly 70%. He would now have to make many more calls and none of those whom he called would be able to speak clearly about what their people believed or did. This story can be repeated among the nations of the Asia Pacific. Diversity within and between religious groups has greatly reduced the capacity of these older structures to deliver social cohesion.

Increased diversity by itself does not pose a threat to a society. I have been studying the management of religious diversity for over three decades. What has become clear to me is that religious diversity is not a disease to be overcome, but a cultural resource that can be used to enrich the capacity of a society to operate effectively in a global context. In addition, religious diversity is not a problem needing to be transcended by finding something everyone will agree to, or by showing that there is great similarity among the beliefs of different groups. First, the differences between groups are real, not to be trivialized and can become sources of conflict. Secondly, those who think they have transcended religious differences in fact are proposing yet another religious perspective, belief system or group and are increasing diversity, not reducing it.

Finally, it has again become clear that not all expressions of religion are "moderate," innocuous or, for that matter, even safe. Some forms of religious expression found as minority perspectives within some religious groups can be considered socially "toxic" as they reduce the humanity of some groups in the society, erode human community and impair the ability of different groups to live together in peace and mutual respect. It is naïve to ignore the possible harm some expressions of the religious life can have. Since the notion that religion is withering away is no longer tenable, the management of religious diversity becomes more critical.

Increased Religious Competition and Conflict

A direct result of increased religious diversity and religious commitment and practice will be an increase in religious competition. The increased number of religious groups in a society can, and often does, lead to competition (Finke and Stark 1988, Finke, Guest and Stark 1996, Thomas 2005). Although Finke and Stark focus on the impact of competition on religious life, the nexus between religious plurality, competition and religious vitality is complex. Certainly in Australia plurality has led to an increase in vitality and following the increased vitality an increase in competition. Although often confused with each other, competition is different from conflict and clarifying the differences helps to sharpen thinking in the area of managing religious diversity (Bouma 2006). Religious conflict is treated here as a subset of religious competition. Competitors recognize the legitimate existence of each other, most actually respect each other, and accept the principle of the right of free choice in the market. In competing, religious competitors often learn more about their own positions and approach to their faith thus increasing the commitment of members and the salience of their faith. Religious conflict, in contrast, does not proceed on this assumption, but actually seeks to overcome, eliminate, or convert the other to extinction. With increased diversity, increases in competition can be expected, whether this competition will flow on to conflict depends on how boundaries are defined and how these boundaries are viewed by social policy makers.

Religions can play a role in interstate conflict. For example, the Cold War had a strong religious dimension—Christian Democracy vs Godless Communism. The rhetoric of the Cold War was redolent with religious imagery and the threat of communism was not just to a capitalist economic system but to Christian society as expressed in Western Bloc democratic nations. This major global polarity with clearly drawn boundaries easily depicted on maps produced a common external enemy which in the West had the effect of promoting a more open interpretation of the boundaries between their religious groups which resulted in a more generous sense of "us" against "them". "Those for us, or who are not against us, are us". Communism as a global threat and common external enemy facilitated the rise of ecumenism as the internal tensions in Christianity were reduced. There was a denial of difference, as we stand together against them, whoever they are. Thus in the USA there was a ready hearing for the contention of Will Herberg (1955) that Protestants, Catholics and Jews were all American. It was not until the ending of the Cold War that the Christian right began its revitalization and involvement in social issues.

Following the Cold War, most violent conflict in the world has also had a religious dimension. Some of this conflict has been the result of the passing of heavy-handed regimes that had repressed religious groups and in so doing also prevented conflict between them, for example in the former Yugoslavia and in some of the former Soviet republics. After the Cold War no simple bilateral polarities could be sustained, even though Huntington (1993) tries to construct one between the West and Islam, or the West and the rest. The lines of this conflict are not able to be drawn on a map, the boundaries are not clear, do not stay stable, are not able to be visualized or identified geographically. They are boundaries between ideas, images, and beliefs not geopolitical realities.

There are several sources of post-Cold War religious conflict. The conflict between Israel and Palestine is over land, access to resources and fundamentally the right to exist. Each side includes both those who seek accommodating peace and those who seek the removal or annihilation of the other. Theological and biblical passages are used to defend Israel's right to exist. The fact that this position is adopted by conservative evangelical

Christians in the United States as well as some Jewish groups indicates the theological underpinnings of this conflict. The claim of Palestinians, particularly Muslim Palestinians rests on historical possession and the importance of Al Quds/Jerusalem to Muslims.

Conflicts between Christian and Muslim groups in Nigeria are over the implementation of their religious ethics in social policy and the religious tone of the nation. The violent conflict between Christians and Muslims in the Indonesian province of Muluku has been over land and social position prompted in the 1990s by the migration of Muslims into territory that had been controlled for several centuries by the Christians who had been put in leadership positions and favoured by the Dutch. The Christians massacred Muslims and burnt mosques, and then the Muslims retaliated. Later a peace was brokered and the religious divisions removed as cooperation emerged (Stern 2003: 70–4).

Much of this increased religious competition and conflict arising from increased diversity and religious revitalization also involves internal conflicts within religious groups. Revitalization brings new life and with it internal differences that lead to competition for the resources of leadership positions, adherent support, and the capacity to define both the direction of the organization and its public perception. The organizational weakness of many religious groups prior to the revitalization reduced their capacity to manage internal diversity in creative ways, to socialize newcomers into the dominant ethos of the group and to train clergy effectively. This has resulted in unproductive internal conflict rather than creative competition, or dialogue among those holding different views. In addition, the fact that many religious groups, like their societies, have lost the threat of an external "other" has decreased tolerance for internal difference as the "other" is found within and sharp conflict ensues.

Key examples of conflicts occurring within religious groups include "the clash within civilizations" literature describing in particular the clashes among Muslims over degree of strictness, political involvement, appropriate forms of political order and theology (Hefner 2001, Bilgrami 2003). Conflicts between Shi'a and Sunni Muslims are largely over theological and ritual differences but take on political dimensions when territory is shared and questions of access to power emerge, as in Iraq (Nasr 2006). These conflicts are also deeply rooted in history as well as in recent violent clashes such as the Iran–Iraq war of the 1980s. These differences are also found within diasporic Muslim communities where they are not usually associated with violent clashes. Further examples are provided by internal wrangling in Christian denominations over the election of an openly gay Anglican bishop, gay and lesbian marriage, abortion and church planting (Wallis 2005, Bates 2004 and Porter 2006) and the emergence of the conservative evangelical Christian denial of "belief in one/same God" for Jews, Christians and Muslims (Cimino 2005).

The forms of post-Cold War religious conflict have included inter-religious violence in Bosnia, Nigeria, Indonesia; attacks on places of worship in India—Hindu attacks on Sikh shrines, Indonesia—burning of mosques and churches. Religious conflict takes the form of religious vilification in Canada (Regina v. Harding Ontario Supreme Court—Provincial Division June 19, 1998) and Australia (Islamic Council of Victoria v Catch the Fire Ministries, Victorian Civil And Administrative Tribunal, Human Rights Division, Anti Discrimination List, VCAT reference No. a392/2002). The law has been used to limit rights of particular groups to practice, attract members or build places of worship in Greece, Malaysia and Australia, and to deny the rights of certain religious groups to exist, for example, Falun Gong in China and Scientology in Germany, France, and Switzerland (Boyle and Sheen 1997, Richardson 2004a and b).

Religious Diversity, Conflict and Social Cohesion

Many fear that increases in religious diversity combined with religious revitalization will undermine social cohesion. I take social cohesion to refer to the ability of a society to so coordinate its resources as to produce what it needs to sustain itself including reproducing itself. How societies hold together sufficiently well to enable them to be sufficiently productive to survive and reproduce themselves and their way of life has long fascinated social theorists and shapers of social policy. History reveals that many social forms have achieved this—hierarchical, diverse, monocultural, monarchical, democratic, totalitarian, egalitarian, small and large. History reveals that no particular instance of social order persists forever. Moreover, history reveals that the role played by religion in holding societies together has also been variable, from social glue to being a potent source of conflict and division. While some forms of social order may be more desirable than others to some members of a society it is not clear that one form is more prone to be socially cohesive than another, and there is no form of social order that persists forever.

Most European social theory presumes that a society with one, preferably official, religion (such as France or Sweden or Italy) will be more cohesive than one that has a diversity of religions. Since the end of the wars of religion in 1648 with the Peace of Westphalia, each state was to have an official state sanctioned and supported religion, which was the decision of the prince. Religion was to be supportive of the state, providing an overarching integrative meaning system that linked all citizens into a single unified religiously legitimated culture and social structure, praying for the success of its ventures and legitimating its actions. In exchange, the state supported the church financially and by warding off competitors through the provision of a monopoly. One of a citizen's responsibilities was to identify with and use the state church for their religious and spiritual needs and to mark their rites of passage. Religious diversity was seen as a source of division, evidence of weakness and something to be overcome.

It has become clear that it is necessary to examine the particular and complex roles of religion in producing or reducing social cohesion in each society. The roles will be shaped by the history, demographic composition, religious composition and the particular issues confronting the society. For example, Australia is a society comprised of many groups, organizations, persons and religions. This has long been the case. Pre-colonial indigenous Australia was culturally, linguistically and socially diverse. No single culture or religion unified the many nations into a single social entity. Each group may well have been quite socially cohesive and their very survival suggests they were adequately cohesive. Religious diversity was a characteristic of the first fleet and the society that has emerged in Australia. Australia has also been very cohesive in that it is a successful society quite capable of producing, reproducing and of responding creatively to change.

What holds such societies like Australia or Singapore together? Australia is not, and has never achieved cohesion by similarity. It is not a society that enjoys mechanical solidarity. Rather, interdependence has required each group and individual to make place for the other, to tolerate and even assist the other, because without the other, self or society would not survive. This was very true in the convict days and given the very low unemployment rates until recent years has been true for most of post-1988 Australia. This foundational social fact qualifies and inspires any and all rhetoric about social cohesion. Australia is a congery of groups, organizations, and persons held together by interdependence. We simply need each other.

Singapore is also religiously and culturally diverse. Muslims live together with Buddhists, Confucians and others in a very densely populated urban setting. Again interdependence is the glue. No one group can say of another that it is not needed to produce the essential services and keep the economy vital. Living together raises issues as mundane as the discomfort produced for Muslims by neighboring Buddhists who have dogs in their homes as pets. Singaporeans tend to turn to regulation and state intervention to sort out such conflicts involved in managing the purity requirements of its several religions.

Social cohesion is most threatened where one group convinces itself that it does not need another. In such cases, social conflict, including religious conflict, can reach levels that tear the social fabric to shredding point. Examples of this include Nazi Germany, or the Middle East today where religious and state groups seek the annihilation of other state and religious groups, or in the case of religious fanatics who dehumanize those who take different views.

Conclusion

Religious revitalization and increased diversity have produced a situation where religion and religious differences have become more salient in personal and public life. These changes have increased the incidence of religious competition and conflict and have reduced the capacity of religious groups to work together to be agents of reconciliation and social cohesion. Societies are also less able to use the familiar 20th-century mechanisms to manage religious diversity.

Note

1. The research for this paper has been made possible by grants from the Scanlon Foundation. Portions of this paper have been published in P. Beyer and Lori Beaman eds., *Religion, Globalization and Culture*, Leiden: Brill 2007.

References

Almond, Gabriel, R. Scott Appleby and Emmanuel Sivan (2003) *Strong Religion: The Rise of Fundamentalisms Around the World*. Chicago: University of Chicago Press.

Antoun, Richard T. (2001) *Understanding Fundamentalism: Christian, Islamic and Jewish Movements*. Walnut Creek, CA: AltaMira.

Appleby, Scot (2000) *The Ambivalence of the Sacred: Religion, Violence and Reconciliation.* New York: Rowan and Littlefield.

Bates, Stephen (2004) *A Church at War: Anglicans and Homosexuality.* London: Tauris.

Berger, Peter, ed. (1999) *The Desecularization of the World: Resurgent Religion and World Politics.* Grand Rapids, MI: Eerdmans.

Bilgrami, Akeel (2003) "The clash within civilizations," *Daedalus,* Summer: 88–93.

Bouma, Gary (1994) *Mosques and Muslim settlement in Australia.* Canberra: Bureau of Immigration, Multicultural and Population Research.

—— (2002) "Globalization and recent changes in the demography of Australian religious groups," *People and Place* 10(4): 17–23.

—— (2006) *Australian Soul: Religion and Spirituality in the 21st Century.* Melbourne: Cambridge University Press.

Boyle, Kevin and Juliet Sheen (1997) *Freedom of Religion and Belief: A World Report.* London: Routledge.

Chavez, Mark (2005) "All creatures great and small: megachurches in context," RRA H Paul Douglas Lecture, Annual Meetings of the Religious Research Association, Rochester, New York, November.

Cimino, Richard (2005) "'No God in common:' American evangelical discourse on Islam after 9/11," *Review of Religious Research* 47: 162–174.

Connell, John (2005) "Hillsong: a mega-church in the Sydney suburbs," *Australian Geographer* 36: 315–332.

Davie, Grace (1994) *Religion in Britain Since 1945: Believing Without Belonging.* Oxford: Blackwell.

—— (2002) *Europe: The Exceptional Case, Parameters of Faith in the Modern World.* London: Darton, Longman and Todd.

Derrida, Jacques and Gianni Vattimo (1998) *Religion.* Cambridge: Polity.

Ebaugh, Helen and Janet Chafetz (2000) *Religion and the New Immigrants.* Walnut Creek CA: AltaMira.

Finke, Roger, Avery Guest, and Rodney Stark (1996) "Pluralism and religious participation: New York 1855–1865," *American Sociological Review* 61: 203–218.

Fenn, Richard (2001) *Beyond Idols: The Shape of a Secular Society.* Oxford: Oxford University Press.

Finke, Roger and Rodney Stark (1998) "Religious economies and sacred canopies: religious mobilisation in American cities, 1906" *American Sociological Review* 53: 41–49.

Hassan, Riaz (2007) *Inside Muslims' Minds: Understanding Islamic Consciousness.* Melbourne: Melbourne University Press.

Hefner, Robert (2001) "September 11 and the struggle for Islam" http://www.ssrc.org/sept11/essays/hefner.htm.

Herberg, Will (1955) *Protestant–Catholic–Jew.* Garden City, NJ: Doubleday, Anchor Books.

Huntington, Samuel (1993) "The clash of civilizations?" *Foreign Affairs* 72(3): 22–49.

Martin, David (2005) *On Secularization: Towards a Revised General Theory.* Aldershot, Hants: Ashgate.

Khatab, Sayed and Gary Bouma (2007) *Democracy in Islam.* London: Routledge.

Milbank, John (2006) *Theology and Social Theory: Beyond Secular Reason.* Oxford: Blackwell Publishing.

Nasr, Vali (2006) *The Shia Revival.* New York: Norton.

Porter, Muriel (2006) *The New Puritans.* Melbourne: Melbourne University Press.

Richardson, James, ed. (2004a) *Regulating Religion: Case Studies from Around the Globe*. New York: Kluwer Academic.

—— (2004b) "Regulating religion: a sociological and historical introduction" in *Regulating Religion: Case Studies from Around the Globe*, James Richardson, ed. New York: Kluwer Academic, pp. 1– 22.

Sommerville, C.John (2006) *The Decline of the Secular University*. Oxford: Oxford University Press.

Stark, Rodney (2003) *For The Glory of God*. Princeton: Princeton University Press.

Stark, Rodney and Roger Finke (2000) *Acts of Faith*. Berkeley: University of California Press.

Stern, Jessica (2003) *Terror in the Name of God*. New York: Ecco.

Thomas, Scott (2005) *The Global Resurgence of Religion and the Transformation of International Relations*. New York: Palgrave Macmillan.

Wallis, Jim (2005) *God's Politics: Why the Right Gets It Wrong and the Left Doesn't Get It*. San Francisco: Harper.

Yinger, J Milton (1947) *Religion in the Struggle for Power*. Durham NC: Duke University Press.

2 | Citizenship and Its Discontents: Public Religion, Civic Identities

Amyn B. Sajoo

I

ivic culture in occidental constructions of modernity is tied to a secular public sphere in which religion and its ethical claims are privatized. The institutions that underpin legitimacy in this civic culture—from the rule of law and independent media to associative freedom—are posited as autonomous from the control of State and Church alike. Hence, in Ernest Gellner's influential articulation (Gellner 1994), a commitment to a modern pluralist civil society is incompatible with a public affinity to a community of virtue, such as the Muslim *umma*. Citizenship in this liberal perspective is about membership in a civic sphere that is distinguished by its secular identity (Janoski 1998, Heater 2004, Lister 1997).

This picture is usefully complicated by José Casanova's sketching of public religion and its intertwining with the political and civil spheres (Casanova 1994), together with the communitarian ethic of Amitai Etzioni against liberal atomism (Etzioni 1995). However, the events of September 11, 2001 have reinforced the discourses of political modernity as, in essence, being about a commitment to secular liberal citizenship that is equal, inclusive and rational. Yes, the secular may accommodate assertive public religion—as in the United States, where it finds its way into crusading polemics in domestic as well as foreign policy. But this occurs in the context of an underlying constitutional separation between Church and State, anchored in a Euro-American ethos that harkens to the post-Reformation rationalism of "moderation" in matters public. That, at any rate, is the self-perception touted by occidental establishments, and rather stridently since the inception of the "War on Terror."

Quite different trajectories of civic and economic modernity provide the foundations for societies such as those of China, India, South Africa, South Korea and Turkey, as well as of Singapore and Malaysia. It is a trite observation that their historical experience of the nexus of Religion and State is radically removed from the institutional tussles of Church and Polity that are so central to occidental narratives. Even in Turkey, where the long Ottoman encounter with institutional Islam was a central feature of public life (and the aftermath of Kemalist secular republicanism has effectively kept religion in the public square), the tussle of faith and politics is akin less to Italy or France than to India and Malaysia. Durkheim's invocation of the receding sacred in the face of industrial modernity has as little purchase in Istanbul as it does in Orhan Pamuk's rural Kars (2005)—or in Mumbai, Ahmedabad or Kuala Lumpur.

Yet we are told in the wake of September 11 that what globalization alone cannot deliver through economic convergence, should be pursued for reasons of "security" through a "rational" public sphere, where governance is the business of a secular polity that eschews religious conflict and violence along with bureaucratic corruption. The "public reason" that undergirds this claim—to recall John Rawls (1993, 1999), Jürgen Habermas (1991, 1996) and William Galston (2004/5)—is attached to the conditions of citizen participation and wellbeing. "Reasonable" pluralism requires that only shared conceptions of the public good can support the political institutions of society: citizens may not appeal to the truths of a particular philosophy, religion or other comprehensive doctrine, but only to "plain truths, now widely accepted, or available, to citizens generally" (Rawls 1993). Otherwise, the very basis of our constitutional freedoms as expressed in the rule of law and human rights is unsustainable.

Rather inconveniently, however, liberal establishments themselves have been found seriously wanting in their esteem for the rule of law and human rights in the War on Terror and its fallout. Far from being merely episodic, this reflects a historic pattern in the officially-mandated curtailment of individual and group rights in the name of the public good, even if the "public" in question has less to do with the polity than with hegemonic segments thereof (Brown 2003, Dworkin 2002). Further, they seek to advance their cause through the apparatus of public law, in the name of safeguarding civic values (Ackerman 2006). At least 460 inmates of "terror camps" in Afghanistan, Iraq and elsewhere have died or been subjected to serious abuse according to a coalition of US academics and human rights monitors (DAA 2006). Aside from the fact that the figure is conservative because of the limited access to inmates for independent monitors (including the Red Cross)—despite the norms of the 1949 Geneva Conventions—there is the sheer arbitrariness of rounding up suspects on the basis of untested evidence.

Not surprisingly, this template of turning the rule *of* law into rule *by* law has also been seized upon by assorted polities, validated by the trump of "partnership" in upholding international security against the forces of evil, viz. al-Qaeda and its countless nameless adjuncts. Any connection to political Islam, no matter how tenuous or contrived, will serve. In India, for example, the pattern of human rights violations associated with Kashmir were subsumed into arbitrary arrests, torture and potentially grave miscarriages of justice with respect to alleged plotters in the December 13, 2001, attack on Parliament—quite literally in the shadow of the War on Terror (Roy 2006). Again, the Lebanese-Shi'a movement, Hezballah, has been equated with al-Qaeda amid rationalizations of Israel's ravaging of Lebanon in July–August 2006, in flagrant disregard of the most basic norms of international humanitarian law (Norton 2006, AI 2006, HRW 2006). True, Hezballah itself is not innocent of uncivil conduct. Yet it is the movement's "religiously-inspired" conduct that seems to merit the concern of the political establishment in the West, over Israeli brutality in the name of "secular-rational" security (Laor 2006). The pedigree of that strategy includes Abu Ghraib, Guantanamo Bay, and erudite defences of the use of torture for the collective good (Lewinson 2004, HRW 2006).

II

Now there are many problems with a Rawlsian view of public reason as a pathway to fostering an overlapping consensus among societal groups, to form and sustain "reasonably just democratic constitutional societies" (Rawls 1999: 6). Not the least of these, as Bryan Turner observes in his chapter, is a lack of attention to the reality of the "overlapping social bonds" of civil society, which require cooperation from oft-contending groups with comprehensive doctrines of the good life. It is one thing to postulate an ethic of reciprocity as a primary norm in the solidarity of civic culture. It is another to account, empirically, for the capacity of this norm to perform the political and social task—not just the ethical one—of eliciting more than a *modus vivendi* in the public sphere. The dynamics of group life in plural societies, Turner cogently argues, militate against the civic congruence that Rawls wants to elicit through reciprocity.

We have a prior hurdle, though, to overcome in that picture of "reasonably just democratic constitutional societies"—which was the point of my excursus into the post-September 11 landscape of the state of civil liberties. One cannot escape the sense, even in reading the revised edition of *A Theory of Justice* (Rawls 1999a), that it was essentially about a New England universe of contending Protestants, Catholics and Jews, salted by the revivalism of fundamentalist Christian movements. In vain does one look in this American universe for a hint of Buddhists, Hindus, Muslims, even Native Americans. Rawls embraces a politics of privatized religion, in keeping with the Durkheimian-Weberian premise of modernity, against the tide of the postmodern return of religion to the naked public square (Heclo & McClay 2003). He does so without acknowledging the presence, much less the analytical implications, of large segments of his society that partake in lifeworlds of those other, supposedly non-Western traditions. One is reminded of Samuel Huntington's claim in *The Clash of Civilizations* that, "A multicivilizational US will not be the US; it will be the UN ... When Americans look to their cultural roots, they find them in Europe." (Huntington 1996: 306–7)

To paraphrase Max Weber (on civil society in the Orient), this "cluster of absences" allows a leap, post-September 11, from the interests of privileged segments of the population to that of the public at large. We are back, then, with the problem of "discourses of power, ideological fictions—mind-forg'd manacles— ... too easily made, applied and guarded." Yes, that is Edward Said's voice on the upshot of orientalism (1979). Except that the implications of invisibility in our context here extend to minorities as well as quiescent majorities in the East and South. From Indonesia after the 2002 Bali bombings, to Malaysia, Singapore and Thailand in the past decade, and post-Soviet Tajikistan, Uzbekistan and Kyrgyzstan, Muslim societies are rapidly being reduced by scholars and policy analysts to the clamor of forces seen to dominate public religion in the postmodern West. These are fundamentalism and cosmopolitan spirituality, both tied to globalism and its information network (Ruthven 2004, Taylor 2002).

What is missing in this perspective is the middle ground between the text/rule-centric drive of fundamentalism, and the relaxed, relativistic impulses of urban spiritualism. This hybrid-middle has been explored with regard to the wider Middle East in the work of Dale Eickelman (2002/3), among others, and shown to involve a dense "reintellectualization" of Islamic discourses through new global media. Among the key features of the terrain are neo-*ijtihad* in a pluralist entwining of particularist and universalist readings of texts, gender and minority inclusion, and a renewed commitment to ethics beyond traditional rule-bound understandings. Khun Eng Kuah-Pearce's chapter suggests that contemporary Buddhist welfarism in Singapore also finds expression in this public space—while Eiko Ikegami has explored penetratingly the role of religion in the emergence of Japanese civic bonding (Ikegami 2005). Not surprisingly, diasporic communities of Muslims in North America and Western Europe are heavily engaged in the reintellectualization of traditional legal-ethical precepts, despite the conspicuous attention accorded to "isolationist" clusters; civic citizenship trumps separatism (Saeed 2005).

A nuanced appreciation of this terrain has the merit of avoiding the slippage that the fundamentalism-versus-cosmopolitan spirituality reduction can lead to. For if the main challenge is seen as the intrusion of institutionalized religion via fundamentalism, and the "irrational" (or "non-rational") worldview of spirituality against the "public reason" of the civitas, then why shouldn't we privatize religion as reasonable public policy? Welcome back, Rawls. But if the middle ground is recognized as a substantial and promising habitus, drawing on traditional bonds of faith as well as modern communicative action in creating social capital (Dasgupta & Sergeldin 2000), then there is a different ethos that public policy must contend with. Pluralist religious actors and institutions engage mutually and with secular counterparts in defiance of the wall of separation whose limits Thio Li-Ann has shown in her chapter. Exit Rawls?

Not if Bryan Turner is right in warning here that the habitus (Bourdieu 1977, 1990) of a religious ethos is fraught with "rituals of intimacy" that are exclusionary in their reinforcing of sectarian identities—and of patriarchal dominance. Certainly, when it comes to fundamentalist drives for a restoration of orthodoxy, notably through tighter compliance with shari'a-centric codes, then pluralist public space is compromised. In this case, the closer we hew to a constitutional separation of Religion and State, the greater the promise of at least a *modus vivendi*, perhaps even an overlapping Rawlsian consensus. But there is far too much evidence of a "middle habitus" to bear out the case for fundamentalist dominance. Indeed, can we assume that all fundamentalisms are static in their appetite for anti-pluralist codes? If so, how do we account for sharp swings of the pendulum between rigid and milder forms of Buddhist, Catholic, Hindu, Jewish and Protestant fundamentalisms in the past century? (Armstrong 2000, Ruthven 2004).

III

The ethical lifeworld of religion, like any secular lifeworld, is a complex habitus in which the rituals of intimacy are both inclusive *and* exclusive. Wearing the *tudung* in a specific style, reciting the Qur'an in a favored tonal-style, and discouraging intermarriage appear to be exclusionary. Yet in the dietary prohibition of pork and alcohol, the performance of the *hajj*, and the rendering of *zakat*, the primacy of the global *umma* prevails over the particularism of the local. Or consider the institution of *waqfs* for socio-religious welfare, which defies a neat public/private or local/global division. Likewise, in a diverse marketplace, *halal* beef in a downtown Singapore foodcourt, *kosher* lamb in a Paris supermarket, or vegan burgers in a Vancouver restaurant, no longer cater to tidy cliques of Muslims, Jews, or health-food trendies. *Halal* beef in Singapore is also marketed as "Malay cuisine." Muslims famously shop for *kosher* meat as a favored choice where the available *halal* options are limited. "Mad cow" disease and the "avian-flu" virus have turned many of us into vegans … in keeping with strict Hindu dietary preferences.

We inhabit a global bazaar, even if we shop in local stalls. What happens in one stall, no matter how clamorous, does not necessarily reflect the entire habitus of the bazaar. Take the case of apostasy (*ridda*), about which the world heard so much when an Afghan convert to Christianity of many years, Abdul Rahman, was suddenly caught in a post-Taliban powerplay in early 2006. Apostasy, like blasphemy, has long been more of a political than a theological issue (Safi 2006, Sachedina 1988). The disposition of Rahim's fate was not determined by his fundamentalist persecutors, but rather by the more tolerant Muslim public actors in Kabul who arranged for his freedom. A ritual of exclusion was configured by a convergence of local and global—in an overlap of ethical, religious and human rights concerns.

Attending to the outward form of rituals alone leaves out the ethos and context. It is to observe the habitus without the benefit of the "social imaginary" that accompanies it (about which more below). In the same vein, to perceive ethics in Islamic contexts as no more than a shari'a-centric code, attached to *jihad* as identity-purification, is to privilege the narrowest of interpretations. It fails to do justice to the historical and contemporary contours of pluralist lifeworlds of Muslim praxis (Sajoo 2004, Azzam 2006). Militant Wahhabism or the Taliban may cast the shari'a as an austere code—much like some Protestant revivalists favour reading of the Old Testament as a blueprint for the militancy of United States foreign policy in the Middle East. But these literalist approaches are a far cry from emerging consumerist brands of popular religiosity (Tammam and Haenni 2003). Literalism is also the target of sustained attack by activist Muslim intellectuals whose pluralist appeals have solid historical antecedents (Safi 2004, Ahmed 2003, El Fadl 2001/3).

Ibn al-'Arabi of Andalus (1165–1240), as Bryan Turner sagely notes in his chapter, was among those antecedents, his influence extending to Damascus and the Arabian Peninsula. It is true that his native Andalusia provided a cosmopolitan habitus for the flowering of al-'Arabi's thought. But his ability to envision the legitimacy of diverse faith revelations was coupled with a firm conviction about the "unity of being" (*wahdat-al-wujud*). In this, he followed the *sufi* gnosis and intellectualism of the Persian Ibn Sina (980–1037), and the Central Asian al-Farabi (879–950). There was also al-'Arabi's even more adventurous contemporary, Ibn Rushd (1126–89), whose reflections on reason and revelation in his commentaries on Aristotle and Plato not only challenged orthodoxy at home, but were to shape the European Renaissance (Fakhry 1999). This line of cosmopolitan thought, and the praxis that it inspired, attest to pluralist commitments that are bound-up with Muslim ethics (Sajoo 2004). If we are to pit al-'Arabi against Rawls, the habitus must be understood in all its complexity of *din wa duniya* (sacred and secular).

There are prominent contemporary bearers of that cosmopolitan religiosity in Southeast Asia, including Nurcolish Madjid, Ahmad Saefuddin, Chandra Muzzafar, Zainah Anwar and, of course Abdurrahman Wahid (Federspiel 2006, Fealy & Hooker 2006, Johns & Saeed 2004, Sajoo 1994). And there are public institutions such as Muis (the Islamic Religious Council of Singapore), whose statutory mandate since the 1968 Administration of Muslim Law Act reflects a commitment to expressing faith-inspired public ethics in concrete welfarist terms, including the administration of *zakat*, *waqf*, *madrassas*, certification of *halal* foods, outreach and organizational development, and poor relief. As with ICMI (the Islamic Intellectuals Association of Indonesia), a 1990 creation of the Suharto government, the formal association of Religion and State might be perceived by Western analysts as problematic from the standpoint of civil society. Yet formal autonomy can also make civic actors, individual and institutional, irrelevant—while upholding the norm of being "extrapolitical" (Taylor 1995); it is the effective generation of social capital that is the weightier issue.

I will return to the role of Muslim public intellectuals in fostering pluralist politics in the next section. The argument at this juncture is that without a discourse of public ethics where religion plays a dynamic role, vital commitments to civic life are in fact jeopardized. These include social citizenship and democratic accountability (Isin & Turner 2002), as well as nonviolent discourse. I locate ethics within civil society, girded by human rights (2002, 2004)—away from the poles of secular and religious fundamentalism. The admixture of overlap and divergence in how societies encounter modernity leads me to propose that the trajectories which undergird public religion are optimally explored through the underlying "social imaginary." As elucidated by Charles Taylor (2004, 2001), the social imaginary is a background repository of images and narratives that shape how citizens envision their shared spaces *as a moral order*—"making possible common practices and a widely accepted sense of legitimacy."

Like Cornelius Castoriadis who invoked this concept with a view to challenging the determinism of Marxist theories of social change (1987), Taylor locates the social imaginary between the embodied practices of the habitus, on the one hand, and formal doctrines or theories, on the other. Castoriadis and Taylor stress the *agency* of ordinary men and women who shape a social imaginary and its moral order. This allows a symbolic idiom (of democracy, for instance)—and social capital—to emerge from the habitus of practices. At the same time, it keeps the imaginary grounded in the ordinary, rather than belonging to elites who create theory and doctrine. Varied imaginaries yield "multiple modernities" rather than that of the West alone; their locus in secular time is not about the absence of religion but its centrality to personal identities, making it a defining component of political identities (Taylor 2004).

IV

What does a social imaginary in which public ethics plays a vital role in the exercise of pluralist citizenship look like? A growing number of Muslim intellectuals within the Islamic world and its diaspora have averred that civil society shorn of public religion and ethics falls short of the ideals of civility embodied in their heritages (Nasr 1975, Rahman 1982, Noor 2002, Abu-Rabi 2006). They follow in the wake of colonial-era engagement with a hegemonial European modernity by the likes of Shah Walliullah, Namik Kemal Bey, Ali Abd'al Raziq, and Muhammad Iqbal. In this vein, leading voices in our time include Fazlur Rahman, Abdolkarim Soroush, Abdulaziz Sachedina, Abdullahi An-Na'im, Tariq Ramadan, Ebrahim Moosa, Amina Wadud, and Nobel laureate Shirin Ebadi—in addition to those cited in the previous section. What Nilüfer Göle has called the "forbidden modern," in reference to the challenge that head scarf-wearing, highly educated, profes-sional Muslim women pose to secularist assumptions is about a clash of imaginaries within Muslim public spheres (Göle 1997 2002).

For Indonesia's Nurcolish Madjid, liberal political toleration is not far removed from that of Muslim religiosity; indeed, it is rooted in his reading of the Qur'an and *sunna*, albeit in historical context (Johns & Saeed 2004, Fealy & Hooker 2006). Madjid has successfully straddled the turbulent divides of state and politics in the Suharto era and its aftermath, as a mem-ber of ICMI and the legislature, as well as the founder of a private foun-dation committed to interfaith welfarism. Like Göle's critique of Kemalist republicanism in Turkey (old and new), his insistence on a public ethics of interfaith accommodation and welfare as well as gender makes room for a nonexclusive religiosity. Amid recent interethnic and interreligious violence in Ambon and Sulawesi, Madjid's voice has been heard as consistently as it was during the Suharto era; and he was not alone in this invocation of what might be called "confessional reason" against the anti-pluralism of the Majlis Ulama Indonesia (Fealy and Hooker 2006). This recourse, it would seem, is more likely than a separationist stance to engender the dialogue necessary for an overlapping consensus of social actors.

For naysayers who join the occidental critique, *a fortiori* post-September 11, theocracies such as Taliban-led Afghanistan and Iran, or the hard-line orthodoxy of Saudi Arabia, are easily disposed of. Their "modernity" is con-tested robustly enough by large sectors of their own populations. Rather, it is the very presence of "political Islam" in civil society that is problematic, as articulated in the works of Amin Maalouf, Azar Nafisi, Orhan Pamuk, among others. The conjoining of religion and civic identity is, for them, a recipe for a Hobbesian universe of conflict and violence. Or as Mohammed Arkoun casts it, into religious imaginaries trapped in a "closed official corpus" (1994, 2002). Yet pathologies of political violence are a salient facet of the secular habitus, in liberal and authoritarian settings. Pluralism is not a default mode of occidental civic culture (Sajoo 2006).

All pluralist social imaginaries, religious *and* secular, must navigate their impulses of univocal, exclusive and often violent modes of public discourse in fostering civil society. The limits of secular human rights as a redoubt against incursive officialdom, manifest in the post-September 11 period, suggest that public ethics have a critical role in civic space, and that religion, suitably framed in relation to public reason, is more likely than its absence to support that role. This imaginary entails cultural as well as political expressions, from education, architecture, the arts and journals of opinion, to institutions of governance, religion and indeed, of the sciences (Lewontin 1991). Only then can citizenship and the rule of law attract a widely accepted democratic legitimacy.

A vital feature of this legitimacy is the capacity of a society to accommodate the "competing affiliations" of cultural and political identity (Sen 2006)—in which individuals and communities are not reduced to single ethnic, religious, sexual, ideological or other social markers. Multiple and overlapping affiliations allow for recognition of civic sharing and empathy that finds expression in common citizenship. Singular/exclusive affiliations involving Buddhists, Christians, Hindus, Jews or Muslims simply lapse into tribal discourses and practices in the "clash of civilizations" mode. True, individual and communal choices of identities are not unlimited: we are significantly predisposed to particular affiliations by dint of genetic, cultural, economic and social heritages and habitus. Yet the degree to which public space allows us to choose our priorities among alternative affiliations is vital. So is the capacity to retain the integrity of particular ethical commitments, without which pluralism erodes into relativism. The scope for the freedom to choose is, in our time, felt to be the domain of human rights law in an appropriate constitutional framework. But again there are limits to what human rights norms can do in fostering an ethos that privileges pluralist identities.

Like M-R Menocal in her study of cosmopolitan civility in Muslim Spain (Menocal 2002), Amartya Sen draws upon Mughal India in the 16th and 17th centuries to illustrate the mediation of multiple ethno-religious affiliations (Sen 2006). The mediation turned out to be successful to a degree that demolishes the myth of occidental, secular modernity as uniquely tolerant, or of Islamdom as reflexively intolerant. Like Abbasid Baghdad and Fatimid Cairo, Cordoba under the Umayyad rule of Abd-al-

Rahman III (r. 912–961) revelled in trading networks of Christians, Jews and Muslims, enormous multilingual libraries, innovative science, and graceful public architecture, in short a universe "where piety and observance were not seen as inimical to an intellectual and 'secular' life and society." (Menocal: 87). Civil ecumenism in Mughal India under Akbar (r. 1556–1605) engaged Hindus, Jains, Sikhs, Catholics, Muslims and even atheists in *rahi 'aql* or "the path of reason." Indeed, Akbar drew doctrinal inspiration from the Andalusian Ibn al-'Arabi's encompassing *wahdat-al-wujud*. Early in his reign he abolished the *jizya* or poll tax on non-Muslims (long before the liberalizing Ottomans); a proclamation from Agra in the 1590s held that "anyone is to be allowed to go over to a religion that pleases him;" and translations of Hindu epic texts were commissioned for Akbar's own edification. It should be noted that a preexisting milieu of socio-religious pluralism under the Mughals allowed Akbar's ecumenism to thrive (Richards 1993)—and that this was not novel either. More than a millennium earlier, edicts of the Mauryan emperor Ashoka (r. 273–232 BC) affirmed, not only reverence for all sects, but also engagement among them that extended to marginalized peoples.

Faith commitments, then, may be folded into a civic imaginary that engenders a more rather than less inclusive ethos. But attempting to fold religious commitments into narrow ideological agendas of the state is a different matter. While both these approaches involve the engineering of public policy, the former engages with civil society as a democratic actor in advancing a shared interest; the latter approach curtails the autonomy of civil society, often straying into authoritarianism. Failing to appreciate the distinction has serious implications for our post-September 11 age:

> The basic recognition of the multiplicity of identities would militate against trying to see people in exclusively religious terms, no matter how religious they are … What religious extremism has done to demote and downgrade the responsible political action of citizens has been, to some extent, reinforced rather than eradicated by the attempt to fight terrorism by trying to recruit the religious establishment on 'the right side." In the downplaying of political and social identities as opposed to religious identity, it is civil society that has been the loser, precisely at a time when there is a great need to strengthen it. (Sen 2006: 83)

V

Even where public policy engages with civil society as an autonomous actor in a pluralist setting, striking a balance between collective and individual as well as secular and religious identities is a key challenge for modern citizenship. A practical illustration is provided by a recent episode concerning the Muslim diasporic community in Canada. Civic issues ranging from access to justice and expressive religious autonomy to gender and minority rights came to the fore when the province of Ontario was faced with the use of its Arbitration Act by a community of Muslims. In essence, the idea was to apply processes of alternative dispute resolution (ADR) in matters of inheritance, matrimonial and other family disputes by using the personal law norms of the Shari'a. This would occur under the aegis of the Islamic Institute of Civil Justice (IICJ), established by a retired lawyer, Syed Mumtaz Ali, in late 2003 (Korteweg 2006, Boyd 2004). A stormy public debate ensued, pitting the proponents of the IICJ against those who saw the Shari'a as inherently problematic for the rights of women—though all rulings would be subject to human rights law under the Canadian Charter of Rights and Freedoms.

In a public review of how Ontario's Arbitration Act would square with the notion of religiously-based arbitration, and particularly the IICJ (with which the provincial government had no connection), strong representations were made about the perils of such recourse. While Christians, Jews and the Ismaili Muslim community already had ADR processes under the province's Arbitration Act, the new Institute was cast as different; this was because of its more "exclusive" aspirations in relation to secular law, and the perceived nature of the Shari'a as rigid and insensitive to gender equity (Boyd 2004). The public review, conducted by a former Ontario attorney-general with marked feminist leanings, was thorough and incisive. Meanwhile, the debate had become national, then Euro-Canadian; its focus was not on the merits of religious-based arbitration in relation to norms of human rights and social justice (including on gender and access to justice), but rather on the Shari'a as an Islamic code of ethics and law (Korteweg 2006). It attests to the acuity of the public review that it was able to sift through the barrage of submissions—and public demonstrations—that painted the IICJ initiative as akin to a beachhead for the Taliban.

Subject to carefully drawn legislative and practical safeguards, the review recommended that the "Arbitration Act should continue to allow disputes to be arbitrated using religious law" (Boyd 2004: 133); in effect, that the IICJ should receive equal treatment with other faith-based arbitral initiatives. Such was the negative response from those opposed to the initiative, who successfully lobbied the women's caucus in the province's ruling party, that the government backed away from the outcome of its own review. On February 14, 2006, amendments to the Arbitration Act outlawed all forms of religious arbitration, allowing only the use of provincial or national law in family-related ADR, whose impact was also borne by the Jewish community (Korteweg 2006). An opportunity to test innovative ways in which faith-based arbitral processes could serve communal as well as societal expectations of equity and justice became a casualty of a "secular absolutism." This stance, in the tradition associated with France, holds that separation of Church and State entails an exclusive role for the State in matters "regulated elsewhere by state law" (Sachar 2001: 73). The rationale is that secular law is neutral and treats all citizens equally, even if some have far closer ties to the mainstream ethos.

Yet fidelity to democratic values surely requires recognition of religious as well as secular identities—in their fragmented complexity—that "intersect" in the individual citizen (Boyd 2004: 91–92). To insist that this complexity can be captured by a fixed boundary between "public" and "private" is surely untenable. The implications are far-reaching. Evidently, the Ontario Muslims who wished to deploy the Arbitration Act—and national human rights laws—as enabling instruments for ADR sought to engage with the state in furthering their objectives. Judicial oversight of the Institute's rulings guaranteed an institutionalized overlap, not only of process and systems, but also ultimately of religious and civic identities. In obstructing this avenue, the state must bear its share of responsibility for any resulting "enclaving" of society, instead of fostering (with appropriate safeguards) a pluralist engagement toward effective citizenship. The cost of that failure may well be the highest for vulnerable members of religious communities who lose the benefit of state-supported human rights protections in an integrated arbitral system; from domestic violence to single parenthood in poverty, those vulnerabilities are no small matter in diasporic Ontario (Korteweg 2006, Boyd 2004). Ironically, it was in the name of such disadvantaged women that much of the vocal opposition to the IICJ was purportedly launched.

The lesson that secular absolutism is no less capable than its religious counterpart of pitting itself against the overlapping collective and individual identities of citizens is hard-earned in modern democracies of various stripes. Consider the results of two recent surveys of religiosity in Turkey and Britain; both involved extensive and independent polling, and received prominent media coverage. In Turkey, 45 per cent identified themselves as "Muslim first," while 19 per cent said that they were "Turkish first" (Akyol 2006); the figures having changed from 36 and 21 per cent respectively in 1999. Only 25 per cent favoured political parties that are religious, however, down from 41 per cent in 1999; and just 9 per cent favour the idea of a Shari'a-based constitution, down from 21 per cent. In Britain, two-thirds said they were not religious, with 43 per cent never attending religious services; 82 per cent actually deemed religion a divisive force in society (Glover and Topping 2006).

Not surprisingly, for a country whose French-style constitutional secularism has defined itself in direct opposition to Islam, the Turkish survey's findings were taken as evidence of the success of Mustapha Kemal's modernist legacy (Akyol 2006). The western press weighed in reassuringly on this Europeanizing trend (Saunders 2006), also holding that "pious Islam and political Islam are not the same thing" (*Economist* 2006). While noting that "paradox," the *New York Times* cautioned that "increased religiosity, or at least identification with religion, could eventually present a serious problem for Turkish society." None saw fit to remark that the survey pushed a reductive choice between being Muslim and being Turkish, as if the identities could have no parity. Nor did the seriousness of a declining identification with Turkish identity as a mark of shared citizenship elicit comment (though the *New York Times* reported that a robust economy had "eased the integration of religious Turks into the country's secular society"). The prime concern was the familiar contest of "Muslim" and "secular" identities, and how closely this mirrored the western experience of modernity. Of special interest was the fact that only 11 per cent of women favor the headscarf, down from 16 per cent in 1999; most "secular" Turks had thought the opposite was true, in their apprehension of political Islam.

Again, there was no dearth of reductive analysis about the British survey. Under the headline "Beyond Belief," a *Guardian* editorial saw the poll as "an important corrective to the impression that religion increasingly colors our sense of identity" (*Guardian* 2006). Insofar as the target was politicians for whom "religion can be a flag of convenience, a way of categorizing people that avoids more difficult issues of race and class," the editorial rightly noted the complexity of British identity. But it also claimed that "people regard language, law and institutions, not religion, as the defining aspects of their Britishness," and "politicians create the climate that elevates religion's significance." The assumption: left to its own devices, religion will fade not only from the public domain and civil society, but also from the private sphere, judging by the declining attendance at services, and of self-identification as "religious." Still, two-thirds identified themselves as Christian, a marker whose significance cannot but be contextualized in the wake of September 11, 2001, the history of IRA bombings, and the London transport attacks of July 7, 2005 (Devichand 2006). Amid a staple of news reports that blithely link religion to violence, how willingly may the average citizen confess to religious conviction?

On a civic landscape where personal "expressive" modes of religiosity vie with institutional creeds and affiliations that are ever more fragmented, the meaning of what it is to be religious is deeply contested (Taylor 2002: 63–107). The expressivism ranges from liberal or "air-conditioned" modes (Tammam and Haenni 2003) to highly conservative ones (Azzam 2006). This landscape is more variegated and pluralist than the "civil religion" sketched by Robert Bellah with regard to the United States (Bellah 1970); nor is it confined to liberal democracies. It extends to societies ranging from Turkey and India to Malaysia, Indonesia, ex-Soviet Central Asia, and parts of the Middle East. The received modernity of the Occident overlaps with the vernaculars to engender alternative modernities and practices of citizenship (Sajoo 2007). Reductive definitions of religiosity of the kind thrown up by the opinion surveys noted above fail to enlighten on where we are, and the new imaginaries of civic identity in our globalized age. In the aftermath of September 11, such reductive definitions also feed into a reflexive equation of religiosity and political violence that sheds more heat than light on the emerging civic landscape.

VI

Let me propose some policy-relevant conclusions that flow from the foregoing.

+ Whether in the context of growing ethno-religious plurality or post-September 11 security, public policy must contend with the growing national and transnational role of civil society. An exclusively top-down approach *ipso facto* fails the test of democratic legitimacy, quite apart from the issue of effective governance. A purely adversarial view of state–civil society actors fails the test of a purposive commitment to enhancing social capital. A variegated public is more likely than a homogenous one to bolster civil society—and hence provide legitimate partnership in governance. Ethno-political conflicts in post-Cold War contexts where authoritarian or totalitarian control gave the impression of successful policy management—as in ex-Yugoslavia, Central Asia—attest to the need for mediatory civil society in good governance.

Claims on behalf of "secular" public space as the appropriate canvas for modern governance can no longer retreat into assumptions about the "irrationality" of non-religious public discourse as the primary choice for "liberal neutrality." Occidental civic cultures have been compelled to revisit the contours of Church–State separation as constituted through 20th-century constitutional accords. Non-western societies neither can, nor should, adopt discredited templates of rigid institutional separation. Formulaic strategies in building democratic societies have foundered in post-Cold War Afghanistan, Chechnya, Haiti, Rwanda, and Somalia, to name but a few instances—having struggled also in Northern Ireland. The record in Iraq is hardly reassuring on the export of neoconservative models.

+ Pluralist legitimacy requires attention to markers of citizen identity, participation and dignity in the midst of multiple/inclusive identities. Public religions with sound ethical commitments can serve these objectives of citizenship—where public trust and solidarity trump the perils of fragmentation and incivility. These ethical commitments cannot be reduced, in the case of Islam, to *shari'a* codes or *fiqh* rulings; certainly Muslim history does not support such a reading. Mediatory avenues of moral reasoning come into play, aided by the institutions of civil society as a central tenet of democratic culture. This is not to suggest that civil society, *ipso facto*, guarantees public accountability. Appropriate civic institutions and norms are required, and their *renewal* is always a matter of concern, as attested in the aftermath of the "War on Terror."

+ Political violence, whether secular or religious, is an embedded feature of the habitus and social imaginary of modern societies. Hence the permanent need for safeguards of the rule of law and human rights. Religious ethics can be mobilized to enhance the legitimacy of those constraints on uncivil conduct. Only then will the abjuring of uncivil means of seeking change be grounded in an enduring consensus—rather than a purely tactical *modus vivendi*. At the same time, the persistent failure of the international community to attend to issues of social and distributive justice, as well as political self-determination (as in Palestine, Chechnya, Kashmir), will exacerbate the tendency to feed single/exclusionary identities at the expense of civic ones.

+ Democratic governance requires a commitment to pluralism that in most societies cannot tidily be divorced from public religion. The success of this nexus is tied to public ethics as a source of civic solidarity/citizenship (and as constraining uncivil/violent conduct), through avenues that are not merely political but also socio-cultural. These encompass a broad spectrum of instruments of education, socialization and engagement for the general welfare—which also serve to countervail the more exclusive rituals of denominational membership. Within and across geo-cultural boundaries, a hegemonial modernity that is exclusively technocentric, individualist and secular is untenable. Modes of governance must come to terms with accountabilities to this new landscape.

+ Transnational migration enhanced by globalization has spurred citizen diasporas that test the fidelity of host polities to democratic values, while challenging old assumptions about constitutional norms of governance. In areas such as personal law, dispute resolution and religious expression, creative approaches to the nexus of public and private are required. If the contemporary record on access to justice, distributive equity, expressive freedoms, and gender/minority rights is to be improved, civil society and the state must shun the pitfalls of both secular and religious absolutism that ultimately subvert citizenship.

References

Abou El Fadl, Khaled (2001) *Speaking in God's Name: Islamic Law, Authority and Women.* Oxford: Oneworld.

—— (2002) *The Place of Tolerance in Islam.* Khaled Abou El Fadl, ed. Boston: Beacon Press.

Abu-Rabi', Ibrahim (2006) *Contemporary Islamic Intellectual History: A Theoretical Perspective.* Singapore: Muis Occasional Paper Series, #2.

Ackerman, Bruce (2006) *Before the Next Attack: Preserving Civil Liberties in an Age of Terrorism.* New Haven: Yale University Press.

Ahmed, Akbar S. (2003) *Islam Under Siege: Living Dangerously in a Post-Honor World.* Cambridge & Oxford: Polity Press.

Akyol, Mustafa (2006) "No real threat to secularism, says TESEV," *Turkish Daily News,* November 22, 2006: http://www.turkishweekly.net/news.php?id=41217.

Amnesty International (AI 2006) "Deliberate destruction or 'collateral damage'? Israeli attacks against civilian infrastructure," Report of Aug.. 23, 2006 (Ref: MDE 18/007/2006); http://web.amnesty.org.library/index/engmde18007. 2006.

Anderson, Benedict (2006) *Imagined Communities: Reflections on the Origin and Spread of Nationalism*. Revised ed. New York: Verso.

Arkoun, Mohammed (2002) *The Unthought in Contemporary Islamic Thought*. London: Saqi Books.

—— (1994) *Rethinking Islam*, Boulder: Westview Press.

Armstrong, Karen (2000) *The Battle for God*. New York: Alfred Knopf, 2000.

Azzam, Maha (2006) "Islamism revisited," *International Affairs* (London), 82(6): 1119–1132.

Bellah, Robert (1970) *Beyond Belief: Essays on Religion in a Post-Traditional World*. New York: HarperCollins, Chapter 9.

Brown, Cynthia, ed. (2003) *Lost Liberties: Ashcroft and the Assault on Personal Freedom*. New York: The New Press.

Bourdieu, Pierre (1977) *Outline of a Theory of Practice*. Cambridge: Cambridge University Press.

Bourdieu, Pierre (1990) *The Logic of Practice*. Palo Alto, CA: Stanford University Press.

Boyd, Marion (2004) "Dispute resolution in family law: protecting choice, promoting inclusion." Report to the Attorney General and Minister Responsible for Women's Issues, Ontario (Canada), December 20, 2004: http://www.attorneygeneral.jus.gov.on.ca/english/about/pubs/boyd/.

Casanova, José (1994) *Public Religions in the Modern World*. Chicago: University of Chicago Press.

Castoriadis, Cornelius (1987) *The Imaginary Institution of Society*, trans. Kathleen Blamey. Cambridge, MA: MIT Press.

Dasgupta, Partha and Sergeldin, Ismail, ed. (2000) *Social Capital: A Multifaceted Perspective*. Washington: World Bank.

Detainee Abuse and Accountability Project (DAA 2006) *By the Numbers: Findings*. New York, April 2006: http://hrw.org/reports/2006/ct0406/index.htm.

Devichand, Mukuk (2006) "Telling Muslim tales," *Open Democracy* (London), 29 Dec. 2006: http://www.opendemocracy.net/conflict-terrorism/muslim_tales_4219.jsp.

Dworkin, Ronald (2002) "The threat to patriotism", 273–284, in *Understanding September 11*, Craig Calhoun *et al* eds. New York: Social Science Research Council.

Economist (2006) "A chance to get friendlier: The pope's controversial trip to Turkey." *The Economist*, Nov 27.

Eickelman, Dale (2002) "Islam and ethical pluralism," 115–34, in *Islamic Political Ethics*, ed. Sohail Hashmi. Princeton, NJ: Princeton University Press.

Eickelman, Dale and Anderson, Jon (2003) *New Media in the Muslim World: The Emerging Public Sphere*. 2nd ed. Bloomington & Indianapolis: University of Indiana Press.

Etzioni, Amitai (1995) *New Communitarian Thinking: Persons, Virtues, Institutions, and Communities*. Charlottesville, VA: University of Virginia Press.

Fakhry, Majid (1999) "Philosophy and theology," 268–303, in *The Oxford History of Islam*, ed. John L. Esposito. Oxford & New York: Oxford University Press.

Fealy,Greg and Hooker, Virginia (eds) (2006) *Voices of Islam in Southeast Asia: A Contemporary Source Book*, Singapore: Institute of Southeast Asian Studies.

Federspiel, Howard M. (2006) *Indonesian Muslim Intellectuals of the 20th Century*. Singapore: Institute of Southeast Asian Studies (ISEAS).

Galston, William (2005) *The Practice of Value Pluralism*. Cambridge: Cambridge University Press.

—— (2004) "Religious pluralism and the limits of public reason." *How Naked a Public Square? Reconsidering the Place of Religion in American Public Life*. Princeton University

Conference, Oct. 22–23, 2004: http://web.princeton.edu/sites/jmadison/events/conferences/religion/religion.htm.

Gellner, Ernest (1994) *Conditions of Liberty: Civil Society and Its Rivals*. London & New York: Penguin.

Göle, Nilüfer (1997) *The Forbidden Modern: Civilization and Veiling*. Ann Arbor, MI: University of Michigan Press.

Göle, Nilüfer (2002) "Islam in public: new visibilities and new imaginaries," *Public Culture*, 14(1): 173–190.

Habermas, Jürgen (1991) *The Structural Transformation of the Public Sphere*, Cambridge, MA: MIT Press.

Habermas, Jürgen (1996) *Between Facts and Norms: Contributions to a Discourse Theory of Law and Democracy*. Cambridge, MA: MIT Press.

Heater, Derek (2004) *Citizenship: The Civic Ideal in World History, Politics and Education*. Manchester & New York.

Heclo, Hugh and Wilfred McClay, eds. (2003) *Religion Returns to the Public Square*. Washington & Baltimore: Wilson Centre & Johns Hopkins University Press.

Human Rights Watch (HRW 2006) *Fatal Strikes*, Report, August 3, 2006. New York. http://hrw.org/reports/2006/lebanon0806/.

Human Rights Watch (2004) *The Road to Abu Ghraib*, Report, June 9, 2004. New York. http://hrw.org/reports/2004/usa0604/.

Huntington, Samuel (1996) *The Clash of Civilizations and the Remaking of World Order*. New York: Simon & Schuster.

Janoski, Thomas (1998) *Citizenship and Civil Society*. Cambridge & Melbourne: Cambridge University Press.

Johns, Anthony H. and Abdullah Saeed (2004) "Nurcolish Madjid and the interpretation of the Qur'an: religious pluralism and tolerance," 67–96, in *Modern Muslim Intellectuals and the Qur'an*, Suha Taji-Faruki ed. Oxford & New York: Oxford University Press.

Ikegami, Eiko (2005) *Bonds of Civility: Aesthetic Networks and the Political Origins of Japanese Culture*. Cambridge & New York: Cambridge University Press.

Isin, Engin and Bryan S. Turner (2002) *Handbook of Citizenship Studies*. London: Sage.

Korteweg, Anna C. (2006) "The Sharia debate in Ontario." *ISIM Review* (International Institute for the Study of Islam in the Modern World, Leiden, Netherlands), #18 (Autumn 2006), pp. 50–51: http://www.isim.nl/files/Review_18/Review_18-50.pdf.

Laor, Yitzhak. "You are terrorists, and we are virtuous." *London Review of Books*, 28: 16 (17 August 2006): http://www.lrb.co.uk/v28/n16/laor01_.html.

Lewinson, Sanford (2004) ed. *Torture: A Collection*. Oxford & New York: Oxford University Press.

Lewontin, R.C. (1991) *Biology as Ideology: The Doctrine of DNA*. Toronto: Anansi.

Lister, Ruth (1997) *Citizenship: Feminist Perspectives*. London: Macmillan.

Maalouf, Amin (2001) *In the Name of Identity: Violence and the Need to Belong*. New York: Arcade.

Menocal, Maria-Rosa (2002) *Ornament of the World: How Muslims, Jews and Christians Created a Culture of Tolerance in Medieval Spain*. Boston & London: Little, Brown.

Nafisi, Azar (2003) *Reading Lolita in Tehran: A Memoir in Books*. New York: Random House.

Nasr, Seyyid Hossein (1975) *Islam and the Plight of Modern Man*. London & New York: Longmans.

Noor, Farish (2002) *New Voices of Islam*. Leiden, Netherlands: Institute for the Study of Islam in the Modern World (ISIM).

Norton, Augustus Richard. "Hizballah through the fog of the Lebanon War," *Journal of Palestine Studies*, XXXVI(1): 54–70.

Pamuk, Orhan (2004) *Snow: a novel*, trans. Maureen Freely. New York: Alfred Knopf.

Rahman, Fazlur (1982) *Islam and Modernity: Transformation of an Intellectual Tradition*. Chicago: University of Chicago Press.

Rawls, John (1993) *Political Liberalism*. New York: Columbia University Press.

—— (1999) *The Law of Peoples*. Cambridge, MA: Harvard University Press.

—— (1999a) *A Theory of Justice* (revised). Oxford & New York: Oxford University Press.

Richards, John F. (1993) *The Mughal Empire*. Cambridge & New York: Cambridge University Press.

Roy, Arundhati (2006) "India's shame," *Guardian*, 15 Dec. 2006. Extended text in her introduction, *13 December-A Reader: The Strange Case of the Attack on the Indian Parliament*. New Delhi: Penguin.

Ruthven, Malise (2004) *Fundamentalism: The Search for Meaning*. Oxford & New York: Oxford University Press.

Sachedina, Abdulaziz (1988) "Freedom of conscience and religion in the Qur'an," 53–90, in *Human Rights and the Conflict of Cultures*, David Little, *et al* eds. Columbia, SC: University of South Carolina Press.

Saeed, Abdullah (2005) *Muslims in Secular States: Between Isolationists and Participants in the West*. Singapore: Muis Occasional Paper Series, #1.

Said, Edward (1979) *Orientalism*. New York: Vintage.

Safi, Louay (2006) "Apostasy and religious freedom," *Center for the Study of Islam and Democracy Bulletin* (Washington, DC), April 12, 2006.

Sajoo, Amyn B. (2002) "Ethics in the civitas," 214–46, in *Civil Society in the Muslim World: Contemporary Perspectives*, Amyn B. Sajoo, ed. London & New York: I.B. Tauris.

—— (2004) *Muslim Ethics: Emerging Vistas*. London & New York: I.B. Tauris.

—— (1994) *Pluralism in "Old Societies and New States."* Singapore: Institute of Southeast Asian Studies (ISEAS).

—— (2006) "A shared quest." *The Vancouver Sun*, November 17, 2006, p. A15.

—— (2007) *Muslim Modernities: Expressions of the Civil Imagination*, Amyn B. Sajoo, ed. London & New York, I.B. Tauris, forthcoming.

Saunders, Doug (2006) "Papal visit underlines Turkish take on faith," *The Globe and Mail* (Canada), November 30.

Sen, Amartya (2006) *Identity and Violence: The Illusion of Destiny*. New York & London: Norton.

Shachar, Ayelet (2001) *Multicultural Jurisdictions: Cultural Differences and Women's Rights*. Cambridge & New York: Cambridge University Press.

Tammam, H. and P. Haenni (2003) "Egypt's air-conditioned Islam," *Le Monde diplomatique*, Sept. 2003, trans. Wendy Kristianasen: http://mondediplo.com/2003/09/03egyptislam.

Tavernise, Sabrina (2006) "Allure of Islam signals a shift within Turkey," *The New York Times*, Nov. 28.

Taylor, Charles (1993) "To follow a rule …" 45–60, in *Bourdieu, Critical Perspectives*, Craig Calhoun, *et al* ed. Cambridge & Oxford: Polity Press.

———— (2001) "Two theories of modernity," 172–196, in *Alternative Modernities*, D.P. Gaonkar, ed. Durham, NC: Duke University Press.

———— (2004) *Modern Social Imaginaries*. Durham, NC: Duke University Press.

———— (2002) *Varieties of Religion Today: William James Revisited*. Cambridge, MA: Harvard University Press.

———— (2005) "Liberal politics and the public sphere," 257–87, in *Philosophical Arguments*. Cambridge, MA: Harvard University Press.

3 | Religious Diversity and the Liberal Consensus

Bryan S. Turner

Introduction: The Idea of a Liberal Consensus

In classical social and political theory, "industrial society" was defined as a progressive stage in the development of human societies because it challenged the rigid status hierarchies of feudal society, or patrimonialism, or a caste system. However, industrialization also produced new divisions between social classes. By contrast, the divisions of "post-industrial society" appear to hinge more on ethnicity, culture and religious identity. Class politics has been replaced by identity politics, namely struggles to define an individual's place in society typically by reference to some imputed ethnic membership. This is one source of the contemporary idea of a "clash of civilizations" (Huntington 1993). Why have religious divisions emerged with such force in these late modern, post-industrial societies? Philosophical attempts to solve problems about multiculturalism have been dominated by the work of liberal political theorists such as John Rawls in his study of justice, and I use his ideas, partly as a foil, to examine the conditions that might sustain religious harmony in plural society.

Given the growth of various forms of religious fundamentalism and evangelism, there are important political questions about how plural societies can survive, about the role of urban cosmopolitan cultures, and about the possibility of a normative commitment to cultural diversity. What policies might support a commitment to ensuring civil harmony in societies that are necessarily more complex and heterogeneous as a consequence of international migration and involvement in the global economy? One argument from *The Laws of Peoples* (Rawls 1999) has been to suggest that what Rawls calls a "decent liberal society" will require "an overlapping consensus" in which social stability must be rooted in a reasonable political conception of right and justice affirmed by an overlapping consensus of comprehensive doctrines.

Rawls, in attempting to provide the classical liberal defence of freedom of speech and conscience, struggles with the problem that some religious fundamentalists may simply not accept the liberal version of a plural society. Rawls provides no convincing practical solution to the problem. Historically, liberalism solved religious conflict by making religion a matter of private belief, separating Church and State, excluding religious instruction from schools, and making "hate speech" a criminal activity. By and large, many religious groups outside liberal Protestantism have not accepted this Westphalian framework.

Rawls offers various legal and political solutions, such as the rule of law, norms of compromise, reasonableness, and protection of individual rights. For sociologists an overlapping consensus of comprehensive doctrines requires overlapping social groups, but inter-group reciprocity appears to be in decline in modern societies. The current prospects of civil harmony often look bleak. In addition, cultural co-operation and consensus have been bedevilled by the problem of cultural relativism. Universalists deny it; particularists celebrate it. Recent political philosophy has sought to develop notions of cosmopolitanism that might counter-act the slide towards cultural relativism. In my *Vulnerability and Human Rights* (Turner 2006a) I outlined a critical recognition theory. Liberal multiculturalists have embraced "recognition theory" as an ethical platform for inter-cultural co-operation and mutual respect, but it does not pay sufficient attention to cross cultural disagreement and mutual criticism. What happens in plural societies where "men of good will" simply disagree? One possible response is to discover elements in other cultures where the prospects for recognition and agreement are promising, and hence such a response keeps open the possibility of a conversation even where there are large areas of disagreement. If there is to be a dialogue between western secular liberals and religious leaders outside the West, we need some common ground. In this discussion, Ibn al-'Arabi's commentary on the diversity of religions is offered as one such starting point, making possible an ongoing conversation about the conditions for social harmony.

Bryan S. Turner

The Rise of Post-industrial Society

The notion of "industrial society" became important in the sociological debates in the early part of the nineteenth century in the work of French sociologists Auguste Comte and Claude H. Saint Simon. Their view of industrial society was essentially optimistic. It spelled the end of the hierarchical and military societies of feudal Europe and it would give rise to new social classes—the urban working class and the industrial bourgeoisie—which promised to bring a new dynamism to society. The French Revolution and the industrial revolution spelled the end of land-owning aristocracies and rural peasantry. Comte and Saint Simon also thought that these revolutions signalled the end of the hegemony of the Catholic Church, and a new religion would sweep through the developed world in the shape of secular humanism. Industrial society could now be planned in terms of rational models under the guidance of a science of society that they called "social physics" or "positivism" or "sociology". This stage in the development of sociology coined the notion of "ideology"; the social sciences promised to give governments precise knowledge of society rather than an ideology.

A more conflict-ridden picture of industrial society emerged in the sociology of Karl Marx. According to Marxist theory, the clash between working class and industrial capitalist class resulted in periodic crises of capitalist production that would lead eventually to a classless society, the end of private property, the disappearance of the state as an instrument of class rule and the erosion of the influence of religious belief and practice. Marx's analysis of society failed, according to his critics, simply because its basic predictions did not materialize. In fact, the best explanation of the limitations of Marxist sociology can be associated with the growth of social citizenship in the late nineteenth century which moderated the force of class divisions and provided sufficient social glue to offset the corrosive impact of class interest. The sociological theories of T. H. Marshall provided an explanation of how the growth of social welfare institutions in the twentieth century gave citizens an investment in society, thereby offsetting the negative effects of a market society (Turner 1986). In Britain, Marshallian citizenship was combined with the economic theories of John M. Keynes and in the period of post-war reconstruction the business cycle was increasingly controlled by state intervention through the stimulation of demand by investment in utilities such as roads, airports or cargo terminals. Having said that, there were significant differences between the Scandinavian model of welfare, the authoritarian systems of Germany, the Hapsburg Empire and Catholic Europe, the laissez-faire model of the United States, and the Asian models that emerged eventually in China, South Korea and Japan.

The assumption behind these models also entailed secularization, because it was assumed that industrial society would become a secular system in which public institutions were relatively free from religious control. Religion would become a matter of private conscience, the state would be separated from religion, and religious leaders (ministers and priests in western societies) should not be civil servants. Here again there were differences between northern European societies where secularization was a dominant feature of industrialism, the United States where religion played an important role in the formation of civil society in the absence of a welfare state, and in communist societies where religious groups were driven underground by a political system dogmatically committed to secularity.

One endemic issue in industrial society was the ever-present threat of social disruption from the clash of social classes either through relatively peaceful means (industrial disputes such as strikes and lock-outs) or more violent confrontations (general strikes, industrial espionage or armed class conflict). There are many explanations given about the failure of class confrontation to disrupt or dissolve capitalism, such as the existence of a dominant ideology (Abercrombie, Hill and Turner 1980). Other explanations involve the institutionalization of industrial conflict through legislation, the growth of citizenship and the rising prosperity of the working class.

The two last important sociological accounts of industrial society were Raymond Aron's *Eighteen Lectures on Industrial Society* (1967) and Ralph Dahrendorf's *Class and Class Conflict in Industrial Society* (1959). By the 1970s it was more common for sociologists to talk about "post-industrial society" as in Daniel Bell's *The Coming of Post-Industrial Society* (1974). Post-industrialism meant the dominance of the service sector over manufacturing industry, the rise of a new middle class (of managers), the centrality of the university and research centres to industrial production, the rise of leisure, consumerism and hire purchase, and the computerization of knowledge.

Class as a primary feature of identity disappears as gender and ethnicity become increasingly important. Religious identity reappears as a major issue but in post-industrial or post-modern society these religious identities themselves become commercialized as an aspect of "life style". Youth movements often embrace religious life styles but these are often post-institutional and post-denominational, and hence synthetic and hybrid.

Traditional religious leaders have to struggle to attract Internet audiences, and traditional forms of text-based authority have to compete with or employ new methods of communication.

Many sociologists have identified contemporary global movements that involve a "desecularization" of the world (Berger 1999). These religious revivals are often associated with fundamentalism (especially in evangelical Christianity and Islamic revivalism), but they can also involve the global spread of popular religions or new forms of hybrid spirituality. Sociologists have referred to modern societies as "spiritual marketplaces" in which religious groups compete for a "market share" alongside other movements selling spiritual life styles.

The Conditions for Multiculturalism

If industrial society was a class society, then post-industrial society is characterized by the dominance of ethnic membership in social stratification and by ethnic identity in politics. Furthermore, identity politics, multiculturalism, the politics of ethnic difference and post-nationalism appear to be dominant themes in contemporary social movements. In such societies where ethnic tensions are endemic, what are the conditions of successful social harmony? An examination of multiculturalism in North America, northern Europe (especially Sweden), Australia and New Zealand suggests that they have been, until recently at least, relatively successful societies in managing cultural and religious differences. Similar claims could be made for Singapore and Malaysia. I have argued elsewhere (Turner 2006b), that insofar as these societies have been relatively successful multicultural societies, the conditions of success appear to include:

+ a high and sustained rate of economic growth;
+ a safety-net welfare state and some redistribution of wealth through a progressive tax system;
+ the absence of a marginalized underclass defined by ethnicity;
+ a neutral state that does not take sides in overtly promoting the interests of a dominant ethnic group;
+ a significant rate of intermarriage between different social groups and limited prohibitions on interfaith marriage;
+ equal educational opportunity for women permitting their easy entry into the formal labour market;

- a common state educational system that, in principle, provides all children with opportunity and common cultural experiences;
- a range of explicit government policies that encourage awareness and respect for cultural diversity that I shall call "cosmopolitan virtue";
- effective and enforceable legislation to criminalize ethnic stereotyping, hate speech and racism;
- common experiences of social membership such as national sporting activities, transcending ethnic divisions;
- a patriotic ideology to counteract regional and ethnic loyalties, and educational provision for training in a common public language;
- relatively modest criteria of naturalization and open access to citizenship, including the possibility of dual citizenship;
- the rule of law and judicial guarantees of procedural fairness;
- and as a result relatively high levels of social capital resulting from civic engagement and involvement in voluntary associations;
- religious membership functions to create social solidarity not division and exclusion.

This model implies that successful social harmony in religiously diverse societies is based on the notion that migrants can achieve social mobility (at least in the second generation), that their culture receives some public endorsement from governments, that there is an ideology of patriotic inclusion, and that the rule of law guarantees personal security and fairness. The model indicates that in ethnically complex societies there must be a countervailing set of beliefs and sentiments. I have described these as patriotic rather than nationalist, since patriotism, or pride in the place where one lives, does not, unlike nationalism, suggest any racial exclusion. It is important to create conditions where migrants can become patriotic citizens without losing their ethnic identity. Whereas patriotism can be inclusive; nationalism is invariably exclusive (Viroli 1995).

These hypothetical conditions are an attempt to provide a sociological underpinning to Rawls's abstract liberal model of overlapping consensus. Liberal philosophers who are sympathetic to Rawls have sought to elaborate the notion of reasonableness in the Rawlsian position. For example, Lucas Swaine (2006) has argued that liberty of conscience involves freedom to reject doctrines, freedom to assent to a belief and freedom to distinguish between good and bad doctrines. Such an arrangement would allow for freedom of conscience, but the third principle also allows for debate and disagreement between members of different religions. While these philosophical ideas are useful, they fail to recognize the social implications and costs of doctrinal disagreements and disputes. My argument is simply that an overlapping consensus can only be sustained where there are overlapping social groups, and therefore some degree of overlapping loyalties, commitments and identities.

These favorable conditions are complex, numerous, and difficult to achieve. They are also controversial in the sense that they do not emphasize a policy of promoting cultural differences, but instead they support the idea that multiculturalism and religious diversity can only flourish peacefully where there are some common or compensating factors that bind people together. The immediate and possibly mundane policy implication that flows from this long list is that social harmony is unlikely to emerge on the basis of political indifference on the part of governments. Because a social consensus is unlikely in modern differentiated societies to be spontaneous, bubbling up from civil society, governments have to have multicultural policies and have to defend strategies that are designed to create social peace. The paradox here is that classical liberalism as the source of the idea of tolerance does not support state intervention over matters of conscience, and yet it appears that modern heterogeneous societies require state support, for example in condemning racial stereotypes in public life. The current problems facing Great Britain in terms of its faltering multiculturalism are the consequence of decades of indifference, where the tradition of liberalism itself was assumed to be sufficient to embrace waves of migrants from the old Commonwealth and beyond (Kristianasen 2006). It would be equally wrong to assume that government policies can create social harmony, as it were, out of thin air, because building up social capital and trust—that is investments in society through membership of civil society groups and participation in social institutions—is a long and arduous process (Knight 2001).

The conditions that undermine multiculturalism are equally numerous, but they include as a minimum political situations where a government is seen openly to take sides in ethnic conflict, and appears to promote the interests of one group over another. Communal hostilities are then fuelled by distrust, because the rule of law is overtly flaunted. Ethnic conflict creates conditions for the development of civil strife and civil strife can lead ultimately to civil conflict escalating ultimately to ethnic violence and "news wars" (Munkler 2005). Civil distrust is sustained by the social isolation of individuals and the social distance that builds up between groups, resulting in prejudice.

One aspect of social distance is the lack of intermarriage, and the prohibition on intermarriage is typically sustained by religious prescriptions on eligible marriage partners. Finally, there are important economic circumstances that contribute to conflict, especially high levels of unemployment, low wages and exploitative working conditions. These circumstances make it difficult for young people to benefit from secular citizenship, and these circumstances in turn make militant alternatives look attractive. These forms of social and cultural alienation are the breeding ground of terrorism.

The Problem of Liberal Tolerance

Cosmopolitanism, deliberative democracy and multiculturalism have become standard policy responses to the strains created by social and cultural diversity. However, these political debates have often taken place at a macro-sociological level in terms of "the clash of civilizations", "the law of peoples" or the Westphalian "privatization of religion" (Turner 2003). *The Law of Peoples* provides a classic example of such generalizations in arguing that the existence of a reasonable pluralism in a liberal democracy requires tolerance between religious groups, in which no one group imposes its hegemonic beliefs on any other group.

These very general assertions about the separation of religion and politics, the secularization of the public sphere and political tolerance tell us very little about how people in religiously diverse societies, within which there may be significant religious renewal and revivalism, actually go about the task of managing their everyday lives. What are the daily practices by which people can be recognized as "good Muslims" or "good Christians"?

In societies that are being transformed by global migration and the emergence of large diasporic communities, people in their everyday lives find that they may be increasingly forced to interact with strangers, that is people with very different religious commitments, customs and life styles. How do ordinary people manage the complexity of this everyday world in terms of maintaining a special diet, selecting friends, choosing restaurants, managing domestic servants or sending their children to school? How does the global transformation of religious identities work out at the everyday level of managing situations which may be perceived as embarrassing, contaminating or even dangerous? To take a mundane example from Singapore, the government supports racial harmony through such events as "Racial Harmony Month", but this official project can be limited by the informal compartmentalization of daily life around racial groups or CMIO (Chinese, Malay, Indian and Others). At a daily level, tensions often emerge around the impact of customary practices (Chin and Vasu 2006). While Chinese middle class housewives like to keep dogs as pets, devout Muslim neighbors may embrace customary Muslim norms, thereby regarding dogs as religiously polluting. How does one behave towards neighbors when faced with the threat of religious pollution? There are of course many studies of similar situations in the West where migrants have to accommodate their practices to a secular environment (Spellman 2004). How does the private domestic world interact and interconnect with broad changes in global religious identities, especially where these emerging religious cultures have such significant consequences? Islamic fundamentalism, Christian evangelism, Hindu revivalism and Jewish ultra-orthodoxy are, in socially and religiously diverse societies, posing the question: how do I behave as a "good Muslim" or "good Christian" or "good Hindu" and so forth? Traditional standards of religious behavior are being both redefined and intensified by such processes, and these changes often make the achievement of liberal tolerance, cosmopolitan virtue and multiculturalism deeply problematic.

There has been a significant world-wide growth of religious fundamentalism (Armstrong 2001, Berger 1999, Vasquez and Marquardt 2003). It may be more accurate to regard these changes as examples of increasing commitment to norms of piety involving diet, dress codes, marriage practices, and devotional activities. The unintended consequences of "pietization" often results in practices and beliefs that have the effect of producing social exclusions. There are consequently important political questions about how plural societies can survive, and about the role of urban cosmopolitanism, and the possibility of a normative commitment to pluralism in a context of significant pietization (Turner 2002). What policies might support a commitment to ensuring civil harmony in societies that are necessarily more complex and heterogeneous because of international migration and involvement in the global economy? What policies might be relevant in societies with religious groups that are being transformed by fundamentalism, conservative orthodoxy and revivalism? As we have seen, Rawls argues that what he calls a "decent liberal society" will require "an overlapping consensus". He (1999: 16) argues that

> [b]ecause, philosophical or moral unity is neither possible nor necessary for social unity, if social stability is not merely a *modus vivendi*, it must be

rooted in a reasonable political conception of right and justice affirmed by an overlapping consensus of comprehensive doctrines.

Rawls, in providing the classical liberal defence of freedom of speech and individual conscience, struggles with the problem that religious fundamentalists do not necessarily accept the liberal version of a decent society. Their "comprehensive doctrines" often appear to rule out any easy tolerance of difference, and they do not wholly welcome people leaving the group, for example as a result of marriage into another religious tradition or by converting as a result of evangelism to some other comprehensive doctrine. Rawls provides no real practical solution to these problems. Historically liberalism had attempted to manage religious conflict by making religion a matter of private belief, separating Church and State, excluding religious instruction from schools, and making "hate speech" a criminal offence. By and large, many religious groups outside liberal Protestantism do not fit into, and consequently have not accepted, this Westphalian framework (Spinner-Halev 2005).

Rawls is acutely aware that his liberal model is problematic in the face of determined exclusionary "comprehensive doctrines" such as those emerging from the belief systems of evangelical movements or fundamentalism. Recognizing that "differences between citizens arising from their comprehensive doctrines" may turn out to be "irreconcilable" (Rawls 1999: 136), his solution is to propose a criterion of "reasonableness" or reciprocity in which citizens are "prepared to offer one another fair terms of cooperation of political justice" and according to which they will accept each other even at the cost of their own interests. He defines this criterion of reciprocity by appeal to a classical notion of Greek political philosophy namely "civic friendship" (Rawls 1999: 137). Aristotle paid little attention to eros, but two books were devoted to friendship, being a relationship that was regarded as good in its own right and not for some utilitarian purpose (Huby 1967). Because "friendship" has, in the modern world, lost its political, if not its ethical, significance. Rawls's argument might be lost on a modern audience. In classical Greece, friendship (*philotes/philia*) designated a set of obligations, on the part of the head of a household (*oiko-despotes*) towards strangers involving reverence or respect. In the *Nichomachean Ethics*, Aristotle claimed that friendship was a universal emotion forming the basis of the *polis*, because the citizen was always the "fellow-citizen" of the *civis* (Benveniste, 1973).

Rawls's ideas are laudable and indeed it is difficult to see how any civil society could function without the rule of law, tolerance and mutual respect. Civil society needs the social solidarity that is associated with fellow feeling or friendship. While these ideas are ethically important, they are not sociologically convincing. Does merely the promise of reciprocity solve the problem of mutually exclusive belief systems? On the basis of changes in the nature of everyday norms and customs in religiously plural societies, Rawls's criteria for "a realistic utopia" that is for "reasonably just constitutional democratic societies" look unpromising (Rawls 1999: 6). Even allowing for the plausibility of such utopian principles, these criteria of functional democracies are seriously challenged by contemporary religious movements.

The principal weakness of Rawls's argument is sociological, that is, a consensus of overlapping comprehensive doctrines can only provide the basis for a workable consensus if there are overlapping social networks creating mutual bonds and interpersonal trust. A multicultural society with diverse comprehensive doctrines—the product of diverse fundamentalist religions—can only function without serious social conflict if there exist overlapping social groups. The existence of overlapping social groups is only possible where there are high rates of inter-marriage, state schools catering to ethnically distinct communities, sports teams that recruit from various ethnic groups, neighborhoods that are not zoned by separate housing arrangements, restaurants serving a variety of cuisines, and government policies that promote multicultural participation across the society. In view of the growth of personal piety in new religious movements, such overlapping social bonds are not easily created or sustained because the implication of competing religious movements (such as Catholic and Protestant missions, charismatic movements, Pentecostalism, the globalization of various Buddhist groups and Islamic revivalism) is the creation of a social mosaic of separate and sequestered communities.

If we consider the most basic and traditional sociological perspectives on the social group, then we would have to conclude that the dynamics of group life tend, in plural societies, to work against Rawlsian reciprocity (Shibutani 1961). Sustaining group loyalty through revivalism and exclusionary religious norms is important for maintaining group cohesion, but it is not compatible with the idea of cosmopolitan societies emerging with social pluralism. In particular, marriage homogamy ("like marries like") has long been recognized by sociologists as a fundamental feature of courtship and marriage. The trend towards marital homogamy in Southeast Asia has increased with religious norms prescribing intra-faith marriage as a religious duty. A series of *fatwas* from the Indonesian Council of Ulemas (MUI) in July 2005 proclaimed that inter-faith marriages were against *Shari'a* law, and condemned ecumenical activities between different faiths. These pronouncements are not automatically underwritten by the state but they significantly impact on daily practice. For example, Indonesians of Chinese descent and Indonesians whose religion falls outside the official list of recognized religions have difficulty getting their marriages registered, and very few officials will participate in weddings of couples from different religions. In Malaysia PAS (Parti Islam Se-Malaysia) has advocated the creation of a strong Islamic state that would enforce customary *hudud* penalties on women requiring severe limitations on their rights to divorce, and permitting men to have numerous wives (Anwar 2001).

The emphasis on conversion and the dangers of apostasy make the achievement of social harmony within culturally diverse societies highly problematic. Several cases have recently appeared in the international media. The most spectacular was the attempt by Muslim clerics to put to death Mr Abdul Rahman an Afghan man in March 2006 who had converted to Christianity. According to some interpretations, the apostasy rule goes back to the foundations of Islam when tribal leaders joined in a social contract with the Prophet that came to be the Constitution of Medina, creating the original Muslim *umma*. When the Prophet died, some of these tribes attempted to leave the community resulting in the War of the *Ridda* or Apostasy War. Subsequently the apostasy rule is that any Muslim, on leaving the *umma*, who maligns the good name of the community, shall be severely punished. The apostasy rule has been criticized by some Muslims including the former Indonesian president who pointed out in the *Washington Post* that the teaching of the *Qur'an* states "Let there be no compulsion in religion" (Wahid 2006). Nevertheless there is considerable customary pressure for Muslims not to quit the community. The same censure against people leaving the community also operates in Christianity and Judaism. These apostasy norms are somewhat similar to the generic hostility towards "whistle blowing" that occurs in all social groups.

Revivalism and an emphasis on strong religious identities mean in practice that women, or more specifically mothers, are very important in the construction of religious identities because women are responsible for domestic arrangements such as managing the children's religious education, making choices about food and diet, and organizing private space. For example,

Al-Kaysi's *Morals and Manners in Islam* (1986) warns of the need to Islamize customary behavior and ensure that children are raised according to correct norms. Group cohesion is enhanced by in-marriage, by ensuring the effective transmission of culture across generations, and punishing all attempts to exit the group. Group cohesion requires the domestic and public regulation of women, and hence patriarchal norms are typically invoked when social groups are under threat, or perceived to be under threat. In Aceh, newly enforced religious rules prevent local women from serving alcohol to western visitors and in May 2006 Syarifah Binti Jauhari was sentenced to ten months in jail for breaking this rule. Similarly, attempts to impose rules against pornography in Indonesia will prevent women having bare arms in public spaces (Tedjasukama and Cangkring 2006). Muslim militant groups or vigilantes are now common in some cities in Indonesia since the fall of Suharto in 1998 to enforce restrictive sexual norms, typically against single women in public.

The Rituals of Intimacy

These group norms emphasizing solidarity are more likely to be invoked when a community is a displaced minority or where the majority feels it is under threat by a minority which, for example, is economically dominant. These everyday mores that are important for defining religious differences, sustaining group identities and maintaining the continuity of the group may be called "rituals of intimacy". This notion is useful in expressing sociological ideas about social contexts, intimacy and the expressions of self. These norms and practices are part of the drama of representing the religious self in contexts that may be ambiguous, contradictory or dangerous. They are guides to good action such as whether it is appropriate for a good Muslim to serve alcohol to strangers. These rituals or codes of conduct provide a series of solutions to questions about how to behave towards strangers who are not co-religionists and how to maintain religious purity in societies that are secular.

Norms regulating correct everyday behavior have been present in all traditional religious systems. These behavioral guides were often fashioned in traditional societies along social class lines, in which what applied to court administrators would not apply to peasants. In volume one of his *The Venture of Islam*, Marshall Hodgson (1974) spoke of two normative poles of behavior that emerged during the "civilization of the high caliphate". One pole emphasized the importance of moral relationships between people and another pole—the *adab* culture of the court—emphasized the importance of learning and arts. The moral code was the work of the *ulema* scholars, while the aesthetic code of the *adab* culture was cultivated by the court bureaucrats, and was the high culture of the wealthy merchants. There was consequently an important tension between the piety of the religious scholars and the worldly ethic of the court.

What then is new in the contemporary situation? One can argue that Islamic norms were originally constructed for the guidance of behavior in societies which were wholly or predominantly Muslim. With the growth of the world-wide Muslim diaspora, there is a new need to define correct behavior and to expunge "foreign elements" whether these are western or indigenous folk components. The second issue is that with fundamentalism there is, as it were, an inflationary pressure to increase the scope and depth of these norms. As Muslim *imams* compete for lay followers, there is a tendency to increase the strictness of norms that are seen to be required by *Shari'h*. One interesting example is that, while *halal* food such as the prohibition of pork is well known, in an inflationary religious setting these norms also come to include the ideal of *halal* water. Similarly the pornography bill before the Indonesian Parliament will inflate the range of activities and circumstances that can be defined as pornographic from kissing in the street to revealing "sensual" body parts. Thirdly, the growth of the Internet has greatly increased this sense of the global *umma*, and the importance of strict adherence to norms (Mandeville 2001). Finally there are a series of contingent circumstances that have enhanced the perceived need to defend Islamic practice. In particular, 9/11, the clash of civilizations and the War on Terror have all conspired to enhance the norms of group identity and group separateness (Roy 1994 and 2004).

These rituals of intimacy define what Pierre Bourdieu (1977) has called "the habitus". Bourdieu's notion of habitus has become popular in contemporary sociology to describe the dispositions of individuals that define their taste. These daily practices include preferences for food and dress, the selection of intimate friends, the organization of courtship and marriage. How do women in different social classes manage the everyday life of immediate intimate contacts? How do they sustain separate and pure religious practices? Where do they get advice about proper conduct? Are these rituals changing over time to become more exclusive? The concept of habitus is useful in defining the religious dispositions of individuals and how their taste for a range of religious services and commodities (such as *halal* food) is shaped. However, this modern usage often obscures the fact that the notion is actually derived from the tradition of so-called "virtue ethics" in the philosophical tradition of Aristotle. In this tradition, habitus contributes to the shaping of ethical practices that in turn create particular types of character. The religious habitus is designed to create a particular character, namely the good Muslim or the good Christian. We can treat these norms of religious behavior as the emergence of the "politics of piety" (Mahmood 2005) which aims to create a new subjectivity, especially among women. These pious practices have been embraced by women who operate outside the sphere of state activity, creating a sphere of activity in civil society that enhances their freedom of action and cultivates their own subjectivity.

However, the unintended consequences of rituals of intimacy are likely to be exclusionary. If a ritual or norm defines a person as my friend or peer or co-religionist, it automatically defines some other person or group as not my friend, peer or co-believer. Intimacy is an exclusionary practice that must inevitably create a circle of intimates and outsiders. The stronger the codes of intimacy, the more intense the web of exclusion. These rituals are partly a creation of modern times (through religious inflation), where religious identities are becoming more critical and challenging. At the same time these rituals quarantine the everyday world, making future inter-group conflicts more likely by reducing the conditions for Rawlsian reciprocity.

Cosmopolitan Civil Harmony

These micro-practices of the everyday world make the achievement of macro-social harmony far more problematic insofar as the everyday world diverges significantly from the liberal ideal of a tolerant, integrated and plural society. In many western societies, the liberal world of secular multicultur-alism is under attack (Joppke 2004). Of course this view of heterogeneity in modern times is constantly challenged by the historical imagination—is ethnic diversity a consequence of modernity or were such questions of cul-tural difference always present in pre-colonial Southeast Asia, or in Islamic Spain or in the Ottoman Empire? There is an argument that appears fre-quently in the multicultural literature that promotes the idea that Islamic Spain and the Ottoman lands were socially tolerant. Will Kymlicka (1995: 156) in his *Multicultural Citizenship* notes that the millet system in the Ottoman Empire allowed minorities (essentially Jews and Christians) to enforce their own legal traditions and religious practices, but were not allowed to proselytize or erect religious buildings without a licence. It was a remarkably tolerant system, he argues, even if it did not fully respect individual rights. Referring to Rawls's view that common citizenship is necessary if compromise and reasonableness are to be achieved between social groups, Kymlicka (1995: 183) nevertheless insists that any attempt to impose common citizenship on minorities is likely to be counterproductive. This dilemma brings us back to the fundamental problem for liberalism, namely how to respond to intolerance. What happens when a minority itself attempts to impose its own standards on others, for example by attempting to suppress popular or folk religion?

The argument about the growing disjunction between the state and the public realm on the one hand, and the everyday world on the other, can be rendered more valuable from an analytical perspective by drawing a distinction between popular religion, official or institutional religion, and spirituality. The dichotomy between the great and the little tradition or between official and popular religion has been a fundamental idea of both anthropology and sociology (Spiro 1970, Turner 1998, Weber 1996). Indeed this distinction was fundamental to the whole legacy of Kantian philosophy that shaped the sociology of religion of Durkheim and Weber (Kant 1960). The presence of popular forms of religion has in part expressed this cultural gap between the everyday world of peasants and the official culture of the literate, urban classes. The development of modern fundamentalism can be seen as yet another attempt to control, to cleanse or to eradicate popular religion by inculcating norms that essentially rationalize everyday life in the name of a stricter ethical code.

This development is close to the original meaning of *jihad* as an ethical struggle to purify religious practice. In modern Islam there is a widespread "peaceful *jihad*" involving a negotiation of identity against a background of secular modernity (Lukens-Bull 2005). There are good reasons therefore to regard fundamentalism as a global version of Weber's Protestant Ethic that brings everyday behavior under the control of religious discipline, which attacks magical or mystical practices, and which promotes literacy through the study of sacred texts and discourses (Weber 2002). Fundamentalism is simply the modern version of reformist responses to popular religion that has been underway, for example in Islam, since at least the rise of Wahhabism in the late eighteenth century. But the difference is that these fundamentalist reforms are genuinely global, and they are no longer contained within specific regions, religious groups or communities.

We can however argue that the globalization of religion takes three forms (Cox 2003). There is, as we have seen, a global fundamentalism that is based typically on some notion of institutionalized religion (whether it is a church, a mosque, a temple or a monastery) and an orthodox set of beliefs that are imposed authoritatively. Secondly, there is the continuity of various forms of popular or traditional religion which is practised predominantly by the poorly educated that seek healing and conform from such traditional religious practices. Examples of these traditional practices are numerous— one can point for example to the importance of healing and sacrifice in contemporary Morocco (Combs-Schilling 1989) which has been explored in North Africa since the beginning of anthropological research (Gellner 1981). Finally there is also the spread of syncretism in urban, commercialized religiosity. These religious developments are no longer local popular cults, but burgeoning global popular religions carried by the Internet, movies, rock music, popular TV shows and "pulp fiction". These forms of spirituality can be transmitted by films such as *Crouching Tiger, Hidden Dragon*, and *House of Flying Daggers*. This development is one aspect of "a new techno-mysticism most spectacularly presented to us in the use of special effects in blockbuster films" (Warde 2006: 18). To these films, one can also note the popularity of such books as *The Da Vinci Code*. These phenomena have been regarded as aspects of "new religious movements" (Beckford 2003) that are manifest in "spiritual market places" (Roof 1993). Such forms of religion tend to be highly individualistic, they are unorthodox in the sense that they follow no official creed, they are characterized by their syncretism, and they have little or no connection with institutions such as churches, mosques or temples. They are post-institutional and in this sense they can be legitimately called "post-modern" religions. If global fundamentalism involves modernization, the global post-institutional religions are typical of "post-modernization".

In order to describe these new developments, some sociologists have usefully called them new forms of spirituality in contrast to religion and religiosity. Globalization thus involves the spread of personal spirituality, on the one hand, and fundamentalist religion, on the other. Spiritualities typically provide, not so much guidance in the everyday world, but subjective, personalized meaning. Such religious phenomena are often combined with therapeutic or healing services, or the promise of personal enhancement through meditation (Hunt 2005). Fundamentalist norms of personal discipline appeal most to social groups that are upwardly socially mobile, such as the lower-middle-class, newly-educated couples. Spirituality is more closely associated with middle-class singles who have been thoroughly influenced by western consumer values.

Religion, folk religiosity and spirituality can be seen to be in a state of mutual conflict and antagonism. The spiritual individualism of the upwardly mobile, cosmopolitan, middle-class world is incompatible with the ascetic norms of fundamentalism. We can assume that this explains the intellectual hostility of fundamentalist religious leaders to the consumerist individualism of the new spirituality. Although there is conflict and competition between these expressions of religion in post-industrial society, all three forms are also involved to some degree in the processes of religious commodification. There is a world-wide market for Muslim cassettes for preachers and recitations from the Qur'an, just as there is a global market for Sufi music and dance. There is another global market for the sale of traditional Buddhist amulets. While there is much criticism in religious circles of western capitalism or the dominance of Hollywood in global popular culture, religion, both formal and popular, has become an aspect of a new commercial culture in which religious groups promote specific lifestyles.

Normative Cosmopolitanism

Multiculturalism and tolerance of others can only be sustained where there exist some overlapping associational supports for social harmony and where there is sufficient countervailing social bonding to counteract political tensions arising from cultural (in this case religious) diversity. These conditions for social harmony are various: economic, cultural and educational, and political and juridical.

Recent sociological criticism of multicultural policies claim that governments that have emphasized difference and identity politics have, perhaps consciously, obscured the importance of economic equality. What has been referred to as "critical multiculturalism" requires mutual recognition but also requires some redistribution of national economic resources to create some degree of equality of objective condition between host and migrant communities (Hamilton 1996). However, greater economic equality will never in itself be sufficient. In this respect, the multicultural record of social democratic societies which enjoy considerable economic, or at least income, equality such as Denmark, the Netherlands and Sweden is not entirely encouraging. There must be direct governmental confrontation with racism and racist ideologies alongside the creation of effective social policies with respect to education, employment and welfare. The move in both Britain and the Netherlands to ban the *hijab* in public places because, in obscuring the face of women and limiting their visibility, it undermines trust in social interaction, will only exacerbate tensions between the Muslim minority and the dominant majority.

In fact the foundation for tolerance and successful multiculturalism in Rawlsian-type democracies must be the presence of overlapping social and cultural ties creating social bonds between diverse social groups. A critical issue in cultural recognition and the forging of consensus is the question of gender, and the issue of inter-faith marriage. In this discussion, I have drawn attention to the low level of interfaith marriages in many societies experiencing religious revivalism. There is little prospect of an easy policy solution to this issue, since many religious groups encourage or indeed require intra-faith marriages. In addition, there may be rigid expectations that children of inter-faith marriages should acquire the religion of the husband. The politics of gender (such as gender equality, absence of polygamous marriages, equality in terms of divorce laws, female education, freedom to reject the veil and seclusion, the prohibition of cliterectomy and circumcision, the proscription of honour killings, and acceptance of homosexuality) remain the most troublesome aspect of multicultural society.

Conclusion: Ibn al-Arabi and Religious Diversity

Rawls's liberal philosophy of civil peace is an attractive framework for multiculturalism. However, I have explored the limitations of Rawls's approach with respect to fundamentalism and what I call "rituals of intimacy". An additional problem with Rawls is the unabashed focus on western political philosophy. If we are to obtain overlapping consensus between comprehensive doctrines and if we are to promote cosmopolitan virtue, then western commentators need to take other philosophies more seriously.

We might, in response to Rawls's western presuppositions, simply note that religious diversity is hardly a modern issue. The question of "other religions" has been an important aspect of theological debate in the three major prophetic, monotheistic religions (Judaism, Christianity and Islam) since their foundation. In fact, we can argue that the issue of religious diversity becomes an acute problem primarily in monotheistic religious cultures. Because the notions of cosmopolitanism and cosmopolitan virtue are closely associated with western or Christian culture from the time of the Stoics, it is important to identify other frameworks of religious tolerance and recognition of diversity if we are to promote religious dialogue. In Islam the issue of religious diversity was addressed famously by Muhammad Ibn al-'Arabi, also known as Muhyi al-Din (the "Revivifier of Religion") or al-Shayk al-Akbar (the Greatest Master). Ibn al-'Arabi is particularly pertinent to the modern debate about diversity, partly because his contribution has been recognized by contemporary political philosophers.

Born in Murcia in south-eastern Spain, he lived from 1165 to 1240. Ibn al-'Arabi has been defined as a Sufi teacher who embraced the idea of the "Unity of Religions" (Sharif 1963). Over-simplified interpretations of his philosophy have been questioned by recent scholarship (Chittick 1994) and his philosophy has enjoyed something of a revival in the West where his neo-platonism was explored by political philosophers like Leo Strauss (1997). Because Ibn al-'Arabi was particularly concerned about the issue of religious diversity, the importance of his writing on the diversity of religions has been recognized by social scientists in recent analyses of the problems of multiculturalism (Hartman and Gerteis 2005, Parens 1994). Ibn al-'Arabi's philosophical and theological account of religious differences is directly relevant to the search for a theory of religious pluralism.

Following Quranic teaching closely, Ibn al-'Arabi recognized the existence of multiple prophets in different lands and traditions, but did not deny their validity. These different religious revelations were all reflections of a divine presence and deserved respect. Ibn al-'Arabi provides an alternative to both Kantian Enlightenment universalism, on the one hand, and post-modern cultural relativism, on the other. He rejected the ambition of revealed religion to aspire to universal rule, recognizing that diverse communities are best served by their own diverse laws and customs. He recognized that, from the point of view of political psychology, different communities need to believe that their laws and political structures are not simply arbitrary. Theology and law function to make people feel that their communities are just and legitimate, and worth defending. The possibility of some absolute or universal inclusion of people under a universal law is properly an aspect of philosophical metaphysics. For Ibn al-'Arabi, the proper role of politics is to recognize that a sense of belonging to a particular place (and therefore some degree of exclusion) is an inevitable fact of political psychology (in Plato's *Laws*). Arabi's interpretation of Plato forces us to moderate any claim that *our* moral vision (such as an interpretation of human rights) is the best framework for all societies. However, by separating knowledge from power, he argued that our understanding of the world is not merely partisan, not merely relative.

The relevance of Arabi to modern multiculturalism needs further exploration but in conclusion we might note two important lessons. Fundamentalism appears to be able to harness the emotional commitment of individuals to social movements in a manner that contrasts with liberal cosmopolitanism. Any framework for secular multiculturalism needs to pay attention to the social psychology of group membership. Secondly and more optimistically, perhaps the real importance of "western" interest in Arabi is that the contrast between West and East is itself erroneous. Arabi as a follower of Plato demonstrated the importance of an overlapping consensus between Greek philosophy and the Abrahamic religions, between reason and revelation.

References

Abercrombie, Nicholas, Hill, Stephen and Turner, Bryan S. (1980) *The Dominant Ideology Thesis*, London :Allen & Unwin.

Al-Kaysi, Marwan Ibrahim (1989) *Morals and Manners in Islam. A Guide to Islamic Adab*, Leicester: The Islamic Foundation.

Anwar, Zainah (2001) "What Islam, whose Islam? Sisters in Islam and the struggle for women's rights" in *The Politics of Multiculturalism. Pluralism and Citizenship in Malaysia, Singapore and Indonesia*, Robert W. Hefner, ed. Honolulu: University of Hawai'i Press, pp. 227–252.

Aron, Raymond (1967) *Eighteen Lectures on Industrial Society*.

Armstrong, Karen (2001) *The Battle for God. Fundamentalism in Judaism, Christianity and Islam* London: HarperCollins.

Beckford, James (2003) *Social Theory and Religion*, Cambridge: Cambridge University Press.

Bell, Daniel (1974) *The Coming of Post-Industrial Society*.

Berger, Peter L., ed. (1999) *The Desecularization of the World*, Michigan: William B. Eerdmans Publishing Co.

Beyer, Peter (1994) *Religion and Globalization*, London: Sage.

Bourdieu, Pierre (1977) *Outline of a Theory of Practice* Cambridge: Cambridge University Press.

Chin, Y. and Vasu, N. 2006) "Rethinking racial harmony in Singapore", Singapore: IDSS Commentaries: 1–3.

Chittick, William C. (1994) *Imaginal Worlds. Ibn al-Arabi and the Problem of Religious Diversity* New York: State University of New York Press.

Dahrendorf, Ralf (1959) *Class and Class Conflict in Industrial Society*. London: Routledge and Kegan Paul.

Derrida, Jacques (2001) *On Cosmopolitanism and Forgiveness*. London: Routledge.

Hamilton, C. (1996) "Multiculturalism as a political strategy" in *Mapping Multiculturalism*, A. Gordon and C. Newfield, eds. Minneapolis: University of Minnesota Press, pp. 167–176.

Harman, Douglas and Gerteis, Joseph (2005) "Dealing with diversity: mapping multiculturalism in sociological terms," *Sociological Theory* 23(2): 218–240.

Hirschman, Albert O. (1970) *Exit Voice and Loyalty. Responses to Decline in Firms, Organizations, and States*. Cambridge, Mass.: Harvard University Press.

Hodgson, Marshall G. S. (1974) *The Venture of Islam*. Chicago: University of Chicago Press.

Hunt, Stephen (2005) *Religion and Everyday Life. The new sociology*, London: Routledge.

Huby, Pamela H. (1967) *Greek Ethics* London: Macmillan.

Huntington, Samuel P. (1993) "The clash of civilizations," *Foreign Affairs* 72(3): 22–48.

Ignatieff, Michael (2001) *Human Rights as Politics and Idolatry* Princeton: Princeton University Press.

Joppke, Christian (2004) "The retreat of multiculturalism in the liberal state: theory and policy" *British Journal of Sociology* 55(2): 237–257.

Kant, Immanuel (1960) *Religion within the Limits of Pure Reason*, New York: Harper & Row.

Knight, Jack (2001) "Social norms and the rule of law: fostering trust in a socially diverse society" in *Trust in Society*, Karen S. Cook, ed. New York: Russell Sage Foundation, pp. 354–373.

Kristianasen, Wendy (2006) "Britain's multiculturalism falters," *Le Monde diplomatique* November ,pp.1–3.

Levy, Daniel and Sznaider, Natan (2006) "Forgive and not forget: reconciliation between forgiveness and resentment" in *Taking Wrongs Seriously: Apologies and Reconciliation*, E. Barkan and A. Karn, eds. Stanford, California: Stanford University Press, pp. 83–100.

Lukens-Bull, Ronald (2005) *A Peaceful Jihad. Negotiating Identity and Modernity in Muslim Java* New York: Palgrave Macmillan.

Mandaville, Peter (2001) *Transnational Muslim Politics*. London and New York: Routledge.

Parens, Joshua (1994) "Multiculturalism and the problem of particularism," *American Political Science Review* 88(1): 169–181.

Rawls, John (1999) *The Law of Peoples*. Cambridge, Mass.: Harvard University Press.

Roof, Wade Clark (1993) *A Generation of Seekers: The Spiritual Journeys of the Baby Boom Generation*. San Francisco: Harper.

Roy, Olivier (1994) *The Failure of Political Islam*. Cambridge, Mass: Harvard University Press.

——— (2004) *Globalised Islam. The Search for the New Ummah*. London: Hurst and Co.

Sharif, M. M. (1963) *A History of Muslim Philosophy*. Wiesbaden: Otto Harrassowitz.

Shibutani, Tamotsu (1961) *Society and Personality*. Englewood Cliffs, NJ: Prentice-Hall.

Smart, Ninian (1989) *The World's Religions. Old Traditions and Modern Transformations*. Cambridge: Cambridge University Press.

Spellman, Kathryn (2004) *Religion and Nation. Iranian Local and Transnational Networks in Britain*. New York: Berghahn Books.

Spinner-Halev, Jeff (2005) "Hinduism, Christianity, and liberal religious tolerance," *Political Theory* 33(1): 28–57.

Spiro, Melford E. (1970) *Buddhism and Society. A Great Tradition and its Burmese Vicissitudes.* Berkeley: University of California Press.

Strauss, Leo (1997) "Quelques remarques sur la science politique de Maimonide et de Farabi," *Gesammelte Schriften.* Stuttgart: J. B. Metzler, pp. 125–158.

Swaine, Lucas (2006) *The Liberal Conscience. Politics and Principle in a World of Religious Pluralism.* New York: Columbia University Press.

Tedjasukmana, Jason and Cangkring, Tegal (2006) "Indonesia's skin wars," *Time Magazine* April 10.

Turner, Bryan S. (1986) *Citizenship and Capitalism: The Debate Over Reformism.* London: Allen & Unwin.

—— (1998) *Weber and Islam.* London and New York: Routledge.

—— (2002) "Cosmopolitan virtue, globalization and patriotism," *Theory Culture & Society* 19(1–2): 45–63.

—— (2003) "Historical sociology of religion: politics and modernity" in *Handbook of Historical Sociology,* G. Delanty and E. F. Isin, eds. London Sage: 349–363.

—— (2006a) *Vulnerability and Rights,* PA: Penn State University Press.

—— (2006b) "Citizenship and the crisis of multiculturalism," *Citizenship Studies* 10(5): 607–618.

Turner, Bryan S. and Rojek, Chris (2001) *Society and Culture. Principles of Scarcity and Solidarity.* London : Sage.

Vasquez, Manuel A. and Marquardt F. (2003) *Globalizing the Sacred. Religion across the Americas.* New Brunswick: Rutgers University Press.

Viroli, Maurizio (1995) *For Love of Country. An Essay on Patriotism and Nationalism.* Oxford: Clarendon Press.

Ven, Johannes A. van der, Dreyer, Jaco S. and Pieterse, Hendrik J. C. (2004) *Is there a God of Human Rights? The Complex Relationship Between Human Rights and Religion.* Leiden: Brill.

Wahid, A. (2006) "Extremism isn't in Islamic law" *Washington Post,* May 23.

Weber, Max (1966) *Sociology of Religion,* London: Methuen.

—— (2002) *The Protestant Ethic and the Spirit of Capitalism.* London : Penguin.

Young, Lawrence A., ed. (1997) *Rational Choice Theory and Religion.* New York: Routledge.

4 | Religion in the Public Sphere of Singapore: Wall of Division or Public Square?

Li-ann Thio

I. Quasi-secular State, Religious Society

Ambivalence: Religion, War and Peace

The word "religion" is derived from the Latin terms *re* (to bind) and *legare* (what is broken), connoting healing, which reins in humanity's baser nature. Religion is not a monolithic category but an umbrella term covering a wide range of mutually exclusive beliefs. It addresses matters of ultimate concern which cut to the heart of our existence, relating to life, death and the conduct of life. Religion inspires the deepest loyalties and fiercest resentment and unsurprisingly, may polarize societies divided along ethno-religious lines.

History testifies to the potent force religion exerts in human affairs in bringing both harm and healing. Both religion and anti-theistic ideologies are equally guilty of inspiring hatred, violence and war. (Ignatieff 2001: 86) While religious groups have contributed to societal welfare in fields like education and charity, frictions between and within religious communities, and between religious and non-religious communities can unravel the social fabric. This explains an ambivalence towards religion, a central concern of contemporary statecraft in an era of identity politics, particularly in Singapore where the government consciously manages the problems posed by a multi-confessional society, aspiring towards a model of religious pluralism which appropriately reconciles religious liberty and social harmony. A *laissez-faire* approach towards religion is not embraced without qualification, as the government conscientiously reminds religionists of their community responsibilities and urges religious leaders to practice their faith in a manner beneficial to the public good (Ling 1989: 692).

Official Attitudes Towards Religion

Sustaining religious harmony and preserving religious freedom is of enduring concern in Singapore where maintaining racial and religious harmony is one of five government-declared shared values (Shared Values white paper 1999); this is closely associated with a "thin" conception of the rule of law characterized primarily as preserving law and order, considered integral to the continuing economic development imperative (Thio 2002a). Fears of social disharmony date back to Singapore's colonial and early post-independence history where racial-religious riots took place.

Despite rising levels of urbanization and industrialization associated with religion's decline, Clammer noted that Singapore manifested unconventional trends towards growing levels of religious piety where "the great majority of Singaporeans profess religious belief, [and] the level of religious activity is high and ... increasing" (Clammer 1990: 180). Today, all major world religions are represented among Singapore's population which numbers around 4.2 million, with some 86% of Singaporeans professing a religious faith (*Straits Times* 16 July 2005). Singapore may rightly be termed a religious society even if the state is "secular", itself an elusive term warranting further exploration (Finnis 1998, Benson 2000). The religious breakdown of the population has been reported as: Buddhists and Taoists (51%); Muslims (15%); Christians (15%); Hindus (4%); No religion (13%) and other religions (2%) (Chan 2003).

Within the multi-confessional Singapore polity, religion is correctly recognized and valued as a "constructive social force" (Shared Values white paper, para 45) which enriches the common good and individual spirituality. Paragraph 6 of the Maintenance of Religious Harmony Act (Cap 167A) ("MRHA") white paper states that the government "views religion as a positive factor in Singapore society," acknowledging the "major contribution" of religious groups to the nation as the "various faiths" provided a source of "spiritual strength and moral guidance" to Singaporeans. It noted the potential for greater "future contributions" of religious groups, particularly concerning their engagement "in educational, community and social work, running schools, helping the aged and the handicapped, and operating crèches for children."

However, this statement also reflects government ambivalence and suspicion towards religion, by confining the legitimate ambit of religion to matters of social welfare, preventing its entry into the realm of political causes (Winslow 1990, Tamney 1996, Sinha 2005, Thio 2006). This stems from understandings that religion can be a destabilizing factor in precipitating conflict within a plural state. Indeed, the MRHA authorizes the issuance of non-justiciable executive restraining orders against religious leaders, or those who instigate religious leaders, who incite inter-group religious hatred, promote political causes, undertake subversive activities or excite disaffection against the government under the guise of propagating or practicing any religious belief. This legislation was rapidly enacted after the so-called "Marxist conspiracy" where a group of some 20 Singaporeans in 1987, some of whom were affiliated with the Catholic church, were accused of entering into activities to subvert the state and were preventively detained under the Internal Security Act (Cap 43). These activities included campaigning for the rights of maids, workers, press freedom and other social justice issues (Hill 1999), which threatened to weaken a semi-authoritarian state (Thio (a) 2004). Furthermore, the government has expressed concern regarding over-zealous proselytizing which can ignite inter-religious sensitivities and insecurities (Kuo *et al* 1988).

Furthermore, the state opposes religious practices it considers to threaten state-defined interests. For example, the refusal of male Jehovah's Witnesses to perform compulsory national military service is not viewed as an exercise of the right to conscientious objection, but criminal conduct (Singapore Permanent Representative 2002). Indeed, the Singapore High Court has consistently deferred to the government's view of state interests in this respect. In *Colin Chan v Public Prosecutor* (Chan 1994: 688E–G, Thio 1995), then Chief Justice Yong, while stating that constitutional liberties like religious beliefs warranted "proper protection," declared that actions pursuant to them must "conform with the general law relating to public order and social protection." He declared: "the sovereignty, integrity and unity of Singapore" to be the "paramount" constitutional mandate such that "anything, including religious beliefs and practices, which tend to run counter to these objectives must be restrained." Thus, the Jehovah Witnesses' religious beliefs were subordinated to the statutory regime of national service which Yong

CJ declared a "fundamental tenet" such that "anything which detracts from this should not and cannot be upheld" (Chan 1994: 678B).

Further threats to religious harmony can be triggered by ethnic hatred and suspicion as the identity of certain groups is shaped by a conflation of religious and ethnic identity (Ling 1989). In the post 9/11 political landscape which has witnessed some demonization in equating Islamic fundamentalism with terrorism, the "*tudung* controversy" in Singapore (where four schoolgirls violated school uniforms policies by wearing *tudungs* or Muslim head scarfs) and the discovery of the Jemaah Islamiyah bomb plot, a group with Al Qaeda links, caused ethnic relations to plummet to a post-Independence low (Thio 2002b). The government-initiated response was to involve mainstream religious leaders in drafting the Declaration on Religious Harmony (Thio 2004b), a set of non-binding principles designed to guide mutual interaction within a multi-religious setting. While the Declaration's impact may be minimal, this exercise indicated that the government was not indifferent to potential ethnic-religious tensions.

The Constitutional and Legal Framework for State–Religion Relations

Any discussion about whether religious perspectives have a legitimate role in public policy debate and formulation must be anchored within the constitutional foundations and historical background informing state–religion relations in Singapore.

Religious liberty is the pre-eminent civil liberty and a fundamental human right (Tahzib 1996) going to the heart of personal autonomy: the enjoyment of a free conscience on matters of divine or ultimate concern is predicated on the ability to make fully informed decisions without intimidation from public or private actors. Article 15(1) of the Singapore Constitution declares the right of everyone "to profess and practice his religion and to propagate it." The liberty applies to citizen and non-citizen alike and cannot be curtailed even during emergencies where necessity temporarily suspends the enjoyment of certain freedoms. Thus, the Constitution recognizes the importance of religion as a source of identity, and appreciates that it embodies the principle of free conscience which sustains a free society.

The freedom *of* religion (exercising religious rights) and the freedom *from* religion (freedom from religious compulsion) must be preserved and this necessitates a delicate equilibrium between individual and group rights to religious freedom, and the state's interests in preserving a stable framework where disparate religious groups can peacefully co-exist. Thus, religious practices are not absolute and may not be exercised in a manner detrimental to public order, health or morality.

(i) Qualified Secularism

While governance and government in Singapore is a primarily pragmatic affair, Singapore adopted a principled basis for constructing a model of religious liberty and pluralism. As Lee Kuan Yew noted, "[a]ll that separation had done was to divide one society into two—in altogether dissimilar parts," and "Whereas before we would have sought one solution for the whole, now there are two experiments being carried out in two places." (*Straits Times* 15 Dec. 1965) He further observed in 1965: "Alone in Southeast Asia, we are a state without an established church" (*Straits Times*, 5 Jan. 1967). While there is no constitutional principle explicitly embracing secularity this is apparent from the 1966 Wee Constitutional Commission report (Tan and Thio 1997: 1025), which describes Singapore as a "multi-racial secular society" and a "democratic secular state".

That the Singapore Constitution did not list an official religion was a radical departure from the state-religion model practiced in the Malaysian Federation from which it seceded on 9 August 1965. Article 3 of the 1957 Federal Constitution of Malaysia confesses that Islam is the religion of the Federation, although the inclusion of this "innocuous" (Tan and Thio 1997: 982) clause was not meant to alter the secular nature of the Malayan polity (Fernando 2006: 249). However, Islam is privileged insofar as Article 12(2) authorizes government expenditure to establish Islamic institutions and to fund Islamic instruction, and Article 11(4) enables state legislatures to enact anti-propagation laws restricting the propagation of other faiths to Muslims, although assimilationist state policies through attempted conversions of indigenous peoples to Islam take place (Nicholas 2000). In contrast, Singapore refused to adopt an anti-propagation clause as "singling out a particular religion for special treatment" would be "inappropriate" and "inconsistent" in the Singapore context, as noted by the Wee Commission, whose mandate was to recommend constitutional safeguards for the "rights of racial, linguistic and religious minorities" (Tan and Thio 1997: 1020).

However, while the government declares a policy of strict neutrality in treating different religious groups, Article 152 obliges it to protect religious and racial minorities and to safeguard the "special position of Malays" as indigenous people and to promote, *inter alia*, their religious interests.

Most Malays are Muslims and may apply their personal, customary law in matters relating to religious office, matrimonial and divorce proceedings and testamentary disposition, administered through separate religious or *Shariah* courts established under the Administration of Muslim Law Act (Cap 3). This limited degree of legal pluralism is effectuated by dint of Article 153 which empowers Parliament to enact laws to regulate Muslim religious affairs and to constitute the Majlis Ugama Islam Singapura (Muis) (Islamic Religious Council of Singapore) to advise the President on Muslim religion-related matters. People's Action Party MPs have asserted that Muis's role demonstrates that "Singapore is not anti-religion" as religion is "allowed to play its role in forging a harmonious and cohesive society". Thus, this is another strand of Singapore's "unique" brand of "secularism with a soul" (Rasheed 2002: col. 2220). Critics, however, consider that Muis, as a statutory board under the care and budget of the Ministry of Community Development, primarily serves the state (Kadir 2005).

When Singapore acceded to the UN Convention for the Elimination of All Forms of Discrimination against Women (CEDAW) in 1995 (Thio 1997), it attached reservations to Articles 2 and 6 (modification or abolition of laws and customs that discriminate against women) "where compliance with these provisions would be contrary to their religious or personal laws." This significantly limits CEDAW's potential reach in eliminating gender-biased stereotypes in allowing the continued operation of gender-biased *sharia*-derived rules (*e.g.*, Islamic inheritance law stipulates that a male should receive double the share of a female (Fyzee 1974)) in the name of religious communal autonomy.

Further, the Muslim community is given special consideration through policies such as the government facilitated "one mosque per town" (Othman 1977) programme and access to government machinery to facilitate the collection of donations towards the Mosque Building Fund (Mattar 1982), a facility denied the Hindu community. These linkages between state and religious institutions are not precluded by an "establishment" clause, as Yong CJ in *Colin Chan v PP* noted: "the Singapore Constitution does not prohibit the 'establishment' of any religion", which relates to providing financial or non-pecuniary support for a religion, as the Singapore government does so in relation to Islam (Chan 1994: 681G).

The freedom from state interference with respect to religion is also safeguarded by Article 15(3) which guarantees the autonomy of religious institutions in managing their own affairs, establishing religious or charitable institutions and holding property.

(ii) The Principle of Individual Choice

The Singapore Constitution in matters of conscience adopts a more liberal, expansive definition of religious liberty than Malaysia does. Paragraph 18(c) of the MRHA white paper recognizes that religious affiliation rests on personal choice, as Singaporeans should "respect the right of each individual to hold his own beliefs, and to accept or not to accept any religion."

In contrast, the current understandings of the article 11 Malaysian right to religious freedom apparently excludes the free conscience principle as Malay Muslims have no right to renounce their religion [*Mamat* 2001], which constitutes major state interference with personal identity. A Malaysian High Court judge (Lina Joy 2004) declared that "A Malay under Art 160(2) remains in the Islamic faith until his or her dying days" (Thio 2006). In contrast, the Singapore Constitution does not conflate ethnic with religious identity, allowing for the possibility that Malay citizens might renounce Islam, without legal sanction. While a sensitive issue, the government has placed no formal barriers against the evangelism of Muslims, although Lee Kuan Yew urged missionary efforts to be directed towards non-Muslims (Prime Minister's Statement 1965). However, the underlying fundamental principle remains that the Singapore government recognizes its duty lies in ensuring that "every citizen is free to choose his own religion" (MRHA white paper, para 5). Consonant with this, Article 15(2) provides that one is not compelled to pay religious tax other than for one's own religion.

Notably, the Court of Appeal narrowly defined religion as "a citizen's faith in a personal God, sometimes described as a belief in a supernatural being," thereby excluding philosophical beliefs from the ambit of religious freedom guarantees, such as worship of the state through saluting flags (*Nappalli* 1999: 576H–I) as "... the State commands no supernatural existence in a citizen's personal belief system (*Nappalli* 1999: 576C–D)." If Singapore had adopted a broad view towards defining religion, as the American courts have in including secular humanism as a "sincere and meaningful belief" within its ambit (*Seeger* 1965), it might be accused of establishing or imposing the "religion" of Neo-Confucianism as declared in the Shared Values white paper (Englehart 2000) which the government characterized as a secular document.

Thus, Singapore adopts a more "laissez-faire" attitude towards religious choice and propagation than Malaysia's more protectionist approach in respect of Islam.

(iii) Quasi-Secularism, Singapore Style

Secularism is a protean term, encompassing connotations which range from a benevolent to malevolent attitude towards religion. A radical anti-theistic secularism seeks to banish religion entirely from the public square or culture, in the name of civil peace. However, confining religion to the private realm trivializes it as this implies that only politically impotent religious views unable to influence our common life are tolerated in public life. A more benevolent, co-operationist model of state–religion relations (Durham 1996: 12) does not draw rigid "bright lines" but recognizes the permeable nature of the spheres of religion and public life. Indeed, one might argue that the public–private divide is a false dichotomy as religion is both social and private. Certainly, Christianity, Judaism and Islam do not distinguish between the sacred and secular spheres of life: religion is holistic, implicating every facet of life and living. Nevertheless, some degree of compromise will be necessary in the context of a multi-confessional society, at least in our lifetimes, to ensure peace and order.

If "secular" is understood in its original sense of indicating a temporal–eternal jurisdictional divide, this still does not provide easy guidelines for determining how to render unto Caesar and God their due. Ultimately, the meaning accorded to the constitutional conception of "secular" affects the practice of law and politics.

What does secularism connote in the Singapore context? To elucidate the concept, its component parts may be parsed out. The model of secularism practiced defines the role of religious perspectives in public policy debates. Insofar as is possible or desirable, light needs to be shed in distinguishing the realms of "politics" and "religion".

1. "Accommodative Secularism". Singapore does not practice a strict, militant, anti-theistic secularism akin to that of communist states or laicist France and Turkey; neither does it follow the deeply contested American

approach towards Church and State (Beer 1991). Instead, Singapore practice is closer to the accommodative British approach, under which statutes allow public authorities, like schools, to exact collective acts of worship after a broadly Christian character, while allowing exemptions from this general rule. Article 16(3) of the Singapore Constitution protects people from being coerced into receiving instruction or partaking in religious acts of faiths "other than his own" in the educational context.

The Singapore model of religious pluralism seeks to maintain "a sense of equity among religious groups" (Thio 1995: 36). The Court of Appeal affirmed that "accommodative secularism" relates to religious freedom guarantees premised upon "removing restrictions to one's choice of religious belief" (*Nappalli* 1999: 576G). Individual religious choice acts in tandem with treating religious faiths equally under this model. Thus, religious tolerance and pluralism requires that the state be agnostic about the veracity of religious truth claims, and to confine its role to sustaining a legal framework facilitating the co-existence of distinct religious groups. "Secularism" connotes the equal treatment of all religions.

Furthermore, secularism in Singapore does not connote state hostility towards religion of the kind manifested by communist states (*Straits Times*, 16 Oct. 2002) or liberal fundamentalists (*Wall Street Journal* 16 May 2005). Rather, a respectful attitude towards religion is preserved; in 2005, for example, the government prosecuted bloggers posting incendiary insults about Islam on their websites under the Sedition Act (Cap 290) (*Koh* 2005). Further, "the Government should not be antagonistic to the religious beliefs of the population" (MHRA white paper, para 5). Secularity does not connote anti-theism as "Singapore's government is secular, but it is certainly not atheistic. It is neutral." (*Straits Times*, 8 Oct. 1992). State neutrality entails that the government should neither prefer nor disadvantage theistic or anti-theistic views.

Thus, "secularism" is pragmatic, rather than dogmatic or doctrinaire, and religious liberty is enjoyed, subject to statist imperatives. A secular basis for the state was embraced "precisely because Singaporeans belong to varied and strongly-held religious faiths" (Jayakumar 1989). This sensible approach is evident in that when it comes to official national meetings such as commemorating national disasters like the 1997 Silkair airplane crash in Sumatra (*Straits Times* 31 Dec. 1997) or the December 2004 Tsunami disaster (*Straits Times* 31 Jan. 2005), religious and political leaders stand shoulder to shoulder. This might be contrasted with the Canadian government's decision to eliminate all mention of faith and holy words at a national service for 9/11 victims (religioustolerance.org, 3 Jan. 2001), which would be considered an exemplar of religious intolerance in Singapore. Notably, the Swiss Federal Court, affirmed by the European Court of Human Rights, considered that "neutrality" does not entail "that all religious or metaphysical aspects" be excluded from state activities, underscoring that an irreligious or anti-religious attitude "does not qualify as neutral." (*Dahlab* 2001) Instead, neutrality seeks to ensure that unbiased consideration is given "all conceptions existing in a plural society," with state officials obliged to refrain from religious considerations that might jeopardize citizen freedom in a pluralistic society. This is distinct from the exclusionist French secular "neutrality" or "radical laicism" (Campenhausen 2004: 696) where the laïcist statehood ideal requires official distance from religious matters.

2. Secularism as Source of Legitimating Power. The Singapore polity is secular insofar as the Constitution and legal framework provides that legitimacy to govern derives from democratic elections as "ultimate political authority" rather than "any divine or ecclesiastical sanction" (*MRHA white paper*, para 5). This is reflected in the refusal of Singapore courts to entertain "divine law" arguments as a basis for invalidating secular laws requiring mandatory military service (*Chai* 1998).

3. Secularism as Part of the Peace Architecture. Given the mutual exclusivity of religious beliefs, Minister Lee Hsien Loong in 1990 noted: "We have to find some way to compromise practically what is impossible to reconcile theologically." (*Straits Times*, 31 Jan. 1990, quoted in Sinha 2005: 28)

Notably, the government stated that the reason for separating religion from politics is not to determine the validity of any belief system which may have socio-political implications; rather it is "to establish working rules by which many faiths can accept fundamental differences between them and co-exist peacefully in Singapore" (MRHA white paper, para 27). Muslims in Singapore (*Straits Times*, 2 Oct. 2004) who do not accept a sacred/secular divide comprehend secularism in practical terms as a form of "non-partisan (neutral) government that does not take the side of any religion in order to ensure inter-racial harmony" (*Straits Times*, 11 Oct. 2004). That is, limits on religious freedom are instrumental to overriding state objectives which prioritize social order and religious harmony.

4. Not Mixing Religion and Politics: Political Party vs. Personal. Both formal and informal norms attempt to delineate the non self-evident provinces of "religion" and "politics" in Singapore. However, dichotomous thinking is too stark as there are clear overlaps over matters both religion and politics are concurrently concerned with—the issue really is: when do secular considerations "trump" the sacred?

The courts have indirectly defined "politics" broadly as "the multitude of issues concerning how Singapore should be governed in the interest and for the welfare of its people", including political and social-economic government policies (*Dow Jones* 1989). The problem is, as the government has acknowledged, certain religions espouse comprehensive worldviews which reject a strict separation between the public (secular) and private (sacred) (MHRA white paper, para 25). Indeed, the government in paragraph 26 of the MHRA white paper singled out three examples involving a clash between political and religious views: abortion and Christianity, national military service and the Jehovah's Witnesses and the treatment by certain sects of radical social action as integral to their faith. Abortion, for example, is characterized as a "privatized" choice, although on such issues "religious groups may and do properly take positions and preach to their followers." (MRHA white paper, para 26(a)). However, as the other two examples are viewed as public order threats, by constituting criminal conduct and potentially causing politico-religious tensions, these are subject to legal regulation. Inevitably, "turf wars" will take place between government policy and religions with holistic visions of life, though the secular trumps the religious as the government monopolizes coercive power.

II. Differentiating between Politics, Political Power, Public Culture and Participatory Rights

To better navigate the religion/politics divide, it is imperative to distinguish the types of malign and benign "mixing" of religion and politics.

A. Politics and Political Powers: Cordoning Off Religion

(i) Political Power, Group Politics and Social Cohesion

Paragraph 19 of the MRHA white paper warns that if religious groups venture into politics or if political parties exploit religious sentiments, the social fabric will be imperilled by an intensification of group politics advocating policies favouring one religion or another. Religious groups may wield considerable political influence through the votes of a readily mobilized constituency. Indeed, local commentators have mused that Singapore religious groups may one day wield the kind of political clout which influenced the re-election of US President George Bush (*Straits Times*, 5 Nov. 2004). In Singapore, the fear is conflict may be sparked if religious groups were "to oppose the Government or perhaps to influence it" (MRHA white paper, para 19).

The government seeks to steer religion away from the realm of politics and political accountability, relating to elections, political campaigning and formal legal power; a clear example of religion's power to topple authoritarianism is the Catholic Church's role in galvanizing people power, leading to the ousting of Philippines dictator, Marcos from office. Paragraph 21 of the MRHA white paper notes:

> The Government does not claim that it is always right in its policies or that it is always deserving of support. But in Singapore, the safeguards for political rights and democratic values must be secular, not religious institutions. If political leaders become corrupt, or the government of the day acts contrary to the interests of the people, the remedy must be sought through checks and balances in the political system, for example by public meetings, publicity in the media, debates and motions of no confidence in Parliament, actions in the Courts and finally by campaigning to oust a government in a general election, It is the duty of the opposition political parties and the electorate, not of any religious group, to overthrow a government which has lost the mandate of the people ...

This presupposes the existence of a functioning political system with a viable alternative government, free press and supporting civil liberties able to effectuate popular will (Thio 2002, Hood 1998).

(ii) On Religion and Democracy

The desire to keep religious groups away from political power is motivated by the realization that religious loyalties can supersede national loyalty, placing state and religious authority in competition. Religion can play a "subversive" role by providing the adherent a transcendent reason to question state power; hence, the self-preservationist attempts of the state to domesticate religion, which can be an emancipatory force. Freedom of religion is the freedom to dissent against orthodoxies imposed by state or religious authority, in vindicating the principle of free conscience which assigns to the individual the freedom and duty "to render the Creator such homage and such only, as he believes to be acceptable to him. This duty is precedent both in order of time and degree of obligation, to the claims of Civil Society. Before any man can be considered as a member of Civil Society, he must be considered as a subject of the Government of the Universe." (Madison 1785) This rightly limits the province of civil government.

Religion and democracy are symbiotically linked. In the American context, Alexis de Tocqueville argued that democracy was inherently weak and that secular materialist premises did not sustain it as democracy's "inherent tendencies" was to "lower tastes and passions, to devolve into materialistic preoccupations, and to undercut its own principles by a morally indifferent relativism". Thus, de Tocqueville noted that:

> Religion regards civil liberty as a noble exercise of men's faculties, the world of politics being a sphere intended by the Creator for the free play of intelligence. Religion, being free and powerful within its own sphere and content with the position reserved for it, realized that its sway is all the better established because it relies only on its own powers and rules men's hearts without external support. Freedom sees religion as the companion of its struggles and triumphs, the cradle of its infancy, and the divine source of its rights. Religion is considered as the guardian of mores, and mores are regarded as the guarantee of the laws and pledge for the maintenance of freedom itself. (Novak 2002)

Prior to the advent of Judeo-Christian values, which brought about a moral revolution in emphasizing the intrinsic worth of the individual created *imago dei* (Friedrich 1974: 12–13), pagan philosophy considered that most men were by nature slaves. It is this moral basis in the *dignity* of individuals, the belief in their *equality* before God (which Kant secularized through advocating that autonomous and rational man be treated as the end and never the means) ,and the centrality of human *liberty* to God's purposes in creating the cosmos, which tempers democracy's baser impulses. Certainly religion is a spur to moral progress, whereas democracy "induces a taste for physical pleasures and tends to lower tastes, and thus weakens most people in their commitment to the high and difficult principles on which democratic life depends" (Novak 2002); a democracy cannot exist in the absence of the moderating effect of ethics and civic virtue, to which religious faith is a primary contributor. Indeed, humanist historian Will Durant, who wrote the magisterial ten volume study on the *Story of Civilisation*, noted that: "Even the sceptical historian develops a humble respect for religion, since he sees it functioning and seemingly indispensable, in every land and age." He concluded that there was "no significant example in history, before our time, of a society successfully maintaining moral life without the aid of religion." In *The Lessons of History*, Durant quotes the agnostic Renan who said in 1866: "If Rationalism wishes to govern the world without regard to the religious needs of the soul, the experience of the French Revolution is there to teach us the consequences of such a blunder" (Durant 1968: 50–51).

Where religious freedom is diminished, the state's impulse towards totalitarianism spurs attempts to control more areas of the common life, including the autonomy of religious institutions. The autonomous existence of religious communities and their inclusion in the political process is indispensable to a democratic society.

(iii) The Personal and the Political

Religionists are urged not to endorse political parties, given religion's mobilizing power, although members of religious groups have the inalienable political right to "participate in the democratic political process as individual citizens" (MHRA white paper, para 22). The government's chief concern is not so much participation in politics but the manner of this. The views of isolated individuals are less daunting than the force of cumulative views, explaining the urge to "disaggregate" the collective influence of the religiously like-minded.

B. Religion, Politics and Public Culture: Participation and Public Policy

The idea of "public life" must be broadly understood to encompass not only religious, economic and social life but the political dimension, involving electoral rights and holding public office. A distinction should be maintained between "politics", in the sense of relating to political power and legitimacy, and "public culture." It is with respect to the former that the MRHA seeks to separate religion and politics. The specific danger to be contained is to prevent religious-ethnic entrepreneurs from abusing religious ideology to promote subversive political causes or disrupt social harmony; abusing religion to justify violence or coerce belief within a plural democracy cannot be condoned.

The public culture relates to the shared values which shape the civic identity of distinct groups within a plural society; in a democracy, this stems from democratic processes and ideas communicated by the political values of public reason, rather than any one version of metaphysics.

The question about the legitimate role of religious perspectives in shaping public policy was highlighted by the US Presidential elections where some attributed the successful re-election of George W. Bush to his successful "moral values" campaign, aided by the evangelical Christian vote. There is evidence in particular societies of an increasing intolerance towards expressions of religious faith in public culture, "the curious rise of anti-religious hysteria" (Fuderi 2006) in Anglo-American culture. There have been instances of such anti-religious bigotry spilling over into the context of Singapore public debate. For example, the view that government should be "neutral" and not co-operate with religiously affiliated voluntary welfare organizations regarding sex education programmes as this would be imposing religious views (*Straits Times*, 6 Dec. 2003). However, such views are disingenuous as they seek to impose a particularistic morality in the guise of false neutrality (*Straits Times*, 11 Dec. 2003).

(i) The Case for Excluding Religious Perspectives from Public Culture and Policy

The Singapore constitution does not demand a strict separation of religion and state after the American model; however, radical secularists or exclusionists insist religion has no place in public life and debate, sounding threats of a "creeping theocracy" (May 2004). Stemming from their contempt for religion which they consider unscientific and irrational, religious values are not "tolerated" but demonized as archaic, irrelevant, even noxious and inaccessible to the non-adherent (*Straits Times* 14 Feb. 2005, 22 Feb. 2005). To them, religion should be confined to the private realm. Essentially, the argument is that public policy should have an objective and reasonable basis; as religion is caricatured as subjective and irrational, it should be excluded from public discourse and otherwise rendered impotent in the public field.

This paean to objective rationality and neutrality flows from assumptions underlying the post-Enlightenment binary conception of religion and law, which are both distinct systems of social regulation. Religion is not viewed as part of the secular legal order but as law's prelude and "other", belonging to an "extralegal field" in being "natural, irrational, incontestable and imposed." (Sunder 2003: 1402). Rather than blending into law and serving as a source of legal justification, religion "tends to supplant or retreat" (Becker 1988: 238) from law to which it poses a "special kind of problem" (Smith 1998: 212–213). Thus, while reason operates in the public sphere, religion is reduced from a political force to a private, often falsely homogenized belief (Sunder 2003: 1423–1424). The dualism between the physical and spiritual translates into rendering unto Caesar the body, and rendering unto God the conscience or soul.

This dichotomous treatment of the public–private, secular–sacred divide is problematical, not only in its trivialization of religion but the difficulty involved in demarcating religion–state boundaries without objective criteria or an impartial method of delineation.

(ii) Critique of the Exclusionist Case

1. Maintaining an Objective and Reasonable Basis for Public Policy? Exclusionists consider religion to be based on prejudice rather than reason, a harmful ideology that needs monitoring. This last point undermines the idea of a liberal state in sending signals about the inferiority of a view. Religion is characterized as an attempt to legislatively impose subjective religious morality on the collective or alternatively, to exclude religious and non-religious minorities.

These arguments all rest on flawed premises, manifesting a hubristic, aggressive secularism. The goal of the anti-religious exclusionary crusade is to assert that only secular voices which claim to be rational, logical and "neutral" may speak to public policy, being devoid of religious prejudices (secular prejudices are fine). It seeks to privatize religion by insisting that preachers should sermonize only their flock and not throw stones against those holding contrary views on moral-political hot potatoes like euthanasia and who may enter civil marriage.

(a) *Epistemological Snobbery/Impasse*. Firstly, it is epistemological snobbery and over-simplistic to characterize religion as irrational, mystical and to consider revelation an inferior form of reasoning compared to scientific materialism. It is hard to avoid the patronizing implication that religion is the opiate of the masses, the province of the simple, as religion has its own logic—faith does not ignore, but transcends critical reasoning and exposes its limitations. Indeed, reason itself is a matter of faith resting on the belief that one's thoughts bear any relation to reality.

As religion operates in the realm of the transcendent, it is argued that since this is beyond the ken of non-adherents as a privileged, inaccessible insight, resort should not be had to a source of values only open to some. However, secular liberal values which support a separationist church–state model are themselves based on a privileged insight and comprehensive worldview and can be irrational, just as religious claims can be rational and widely apprehended. Ultimately, all perspectives derive from some comprehensive or "religious" (in the sense of being based on an *a priori* assumption) worldview, in claiming to be based on a universal justification, but resting on non-accessible comprehensive convictions or religious judgments: "Is it not true that all persons ultimately rely on forms of insights which are inaccessible to others?" (Idleman 1993: 446). Even those basing a decision on non-religious grounds must rely on one or more personal bases of decisions such as perception, intuition and deference to the opinions of others. The liberal state rests on the privileged insight that a state must be neutral amongst competing conceptions of the good but the ideal of neutrality is assumed as it cannot be justified on its own terms; it "rests on untestable faith." (Idleman 1993: 446) Advocates of neutrality cannot answer the question of "Why be neutral?" without commitment to some substantive vision or social good (Budziszewski 1993). If all religious or moral insight based on privileged insight was excluded from public discourse, discourse would become a sterile dialogue, severely limited to a small range of data on which all citizens could agree.

It is not always possible to separate religious from non-religious insights. What in fact, is a religious value? "Thou shalt not kill" clearly resonates with our instincts for self-preservation and valuation of life. At best, the line between religion and non-religion is imprecise.

The assumption that religious values cannot be communicated to citizens outside the faith community is also false, as it is possible to express religiously motivated viewpoints on public issues in reasonable terms within an appeal to divine sanction. Indeed, values from secular and religious sources can overlap; both religionists and non-religionists may unite in opposing pornography which degrades women, for example. All citizens are concerned with public issues with moral implications like the AIDS epidemic, and whether policies might intensify the problem by encouraging promiscuity, undermining the common good. For example, Muis as a religious body expressed its opposition to having a casino in both religious and social terms (*Straits Times*, 11 Feb. 2005). The high social costs of gambling's "negative implications", particularly among youth and lower-income groups, is easily comprehended. Neither is there anything particularly obscure with the religious view expressed by Muis: "In Islam, we totally reject the idea of gambling as it can bring harm to society", as one should make a living through honest work and not luck. This resonates with the Protestant work ethic as well as the "Asian values" which emphasizes discipline, strong families, hard work and savings as key to economic growth. Thus, non-Muslims can easily stand in solidarity with these views, providing the government reliable feedback of the views of a religious minority it is constitutionally enjoined to care for.

This is the best way towards building genuine consensus. Otherwise, religious people would have to forsake a crucial part of their identity if precluded from expressing their deepest convictions, which the hearer may or may not find persuasive. Indeed, the observation in paragraph 24 of the MRHA white paper that: "it is neither possible nor desirable to compartmentalize completely the minds of voters into secular and religious halves" ensuring "only the secular mind influences ... voting behavior", equally applies to the citizen, with religious convictions engaging in public policy debate.

(b) Imposition of Religious Values? Secondly, to argue that religion be excluded from public policy debates to avoid imposing religious values on non-believers is problematical and misleading, resting on the false assertion that secular belief systems are "rational" and therefore "neutral"; that the opposite of neutrality is religion. However, such radical secularism is riddled with dangerous ideological bias; secular fundamentalism seeks to impose as public dogma its own anti-theistic, relative and personally determined morality. Indeed, secular neutrality is a misnomer as it is itself a value-laden worldview whose holder is not neutral towards metaphysical claims. A March 2004 *Wall Street Journal* editorial noted that secular absolutism was "a potent religious force" in the US where the secular left pursuant to their "liberal jihad" (O'Reilly 2006) sought to impose their irreligious views and agenda on all under the guise of a "false tolerance". Indeed the "pluralism" espoused by liberal neu-

trality is a guise for hegemony and the credo that the intolerant must not be tolerated.

This is associated with the weak argument that the state should not legislate (religious) morality. In fact, all public policy has a moral basis so the relevant question is: which morality should be legislated? As such, any adopted policy, which will embody a moral stance, will constitute an "imposition" on parties with dissenting views. In this exercise of ordering our public life, the central question is "what serves the common good?" To exclude religious voices from discussing the common weal represents nothing more than an attempt to privilege secular humanism, an ideology which posits that we live in a godless universe, which has not been shown to be superior. Religion provides ethical guidance for many, being an important source of morality beyond human invention, as it appeals to God or a transcendent authority. To rubbish this as a poor source of guidance is to purport to judge this form of religious guidance by a superior standard. To exclude religious values from public debate unfairly prefers the views of anti-theists. Hostility to religion is hardly "neutral". Religious and secular ideologies assume distinct moral stances. Hence, to avoid double standards, both must be subject to scrutiny and critique rather than unquestioning acceptance.

(c) Excluding Views one Dislikes in the Name of False Neutrality and Tolerance is Censorship By Any Other Name. Thirdly, excluding religious voices from public debate essentially boils down to an attempt to exclude substantive views one does not like, by reference to their origin. However, a Talmudic proverb urges we should "examine the contents, not the bottle" if rigorous debate is the goal in a democracy. This is censorship by any other name, an attempt to render a disliked ideology or ethos stillborn by preventing its articulation in the public square. Further, to the argument that those espousing religious values are not open-minded, contrary to the liberal tenet that participants in a public forum must be amenable to reason, it may be noted that non-religious persons also manifest rigidity when pursuing their legal and political agendas and are not somehow less susceptible to this than the religiously devout.

Where religious views were once considered "old-fashioned and gauche", this scorn has "turned into bigotry and hatred." (Furedi 2006) This intolerance is often accompanied by the technique of "argument by insult." This seeks to exclude opposing views through stigmatization and intimidation by character assassination, which precludes authentic debate by halting conversation, preventing a close examination of substantive merits. Preferred terms of rhetorical abuse include "fundamentalist", "intolerant", "prejudiced", "dogmatic", "exclusive", "extremist", "irrational", or "right-wing". (Neuchterlein 1996, Prager 2003). This form of argument is rhetorical rather than rational and extremely divisive, a shouting match rather than a civil conversation and does not advance public discussion. For example, the response to those who oppose same-sex "marriage" on the basis of the moral belief that a family is based on the fundamental norm of a married man and woman, is to declare them "homophobic" (Prager 2005).

Furthermore, radical secularists are apt to claim the mantle of being tolerant when they in fact manifest intolerance, animosity and indeed, "sacraphobia" (Moore 2003). This is evident in relegating religion to the private life and the ready ridiculing of religion, *e.g.* by the media. Religion and its old taboos, particularly its disapproval of things like homosexuality or abortion, impede progression towards a secular humanist utopia where the only absolute acknowledged in a godless culture is "indiscriminate tolerance" and the imperative to "be nice" (i.e. permissive). Everyone must be permitted to feel good about themselves, no matter what they do, and to enjoy a positive self-image, free of traditional moral restrictions and immune from criticism" (Moore 2003). The supreme value is non-judgementalism and a virtue is made of moral indeterminacy. Uncompromising religious perspectives with their moral claims are not to be borne, in this utopia whose vision of "inclusivity" permits the denigration of citizens who confess a religious faith—a "bad faith worrying about real faith" (Moore 2003). Indeed, sexual ethics has become a battleground for religious and humanist voices because, as the acclaimed journalist Malcolm Muggeridge observed, "Sex is the mysticism of the materialists" (Woodard 2001: B3). Further, there are values we should be intolerant about because they are wrong, harmful or evil. Not everyone accepts we are "beyond good and evil" or that society lacks a moral dimension; society needs a sense of moral purpose based on a morality which bears resonance to life. Religion speaks to this, indeed to all of human existence. Furthermore, a moral conservatism buttressed by religious tenets may serve as a beneficial bulwark against dangerous social experiments with wide-ranging repercussions, such as attempts to redefine the institution of marriage to allow for unisex marriage, under the guise of "equality" or "liberty" claims.

Even more disingenuously, radical secularists claim to be both tolerant *and* neutral in matters of morality, after the liberal tenet of neutrality which considers that the state should not make judgements on the "good life" but provide the framework wherein individuals can make their own decisions autonomously (Budziszewski 1993). Public morality is considered "intolerant" and neutrality requires confining morality to the private domain (George 2000). It is misleading to assert the state is being neutral in leaving these decisions to the citizens; not to take a stand, is to take a stand. Indeed the liberal model may be suitable to a society of autonomous individuals or disparate collection of distinct societies, but in the real world, a call to "live and let live" may be a call to indifference, not community.

2. Practice: What Secularism in Singapore Does Not Require. Secularism as a constitutional principle in the Singapore context connotes the co-existence of religious and non-religious communities, and their even-handed treatment by the government. It does not require what radical secularists demand—the religious cleansing of the public square.

This position, which effectively imposes a religious apartheid in attempting to de-legitimate and silence religious voices, is misconceived: there is a critical difference between a healthy separation of religion and state and an absolutist radical secularism that intolerantly seeks to deny all public manifestation of religion. This should be firmly resisted as secularism does not connote state-sanctioned atheism. Indeed, the state should be agnostic and affirm that all citizens may as a matter of democratic right engage in public debate, whether drawing from religious or irreligious convictions.

(iii) The Case for Inclusion

"Inclusionists" insist on free and open democratic debate, welcoming both religious and secular arguments. This is true pluralism and tolerance, rightly understood and a good prescription to follow. So conceived, religion has a legitimate and proper role in public life and debate, although religious perspectives are neither definitive nor immune from external and internal critique (Ong 1998, Neo 2003: 61–64). To have persuasive force, religious views and values will need to appeal to the public reason (Rawls 1999, Greenawalt 1988, Berman 1974), otherwise, they will be just another voice crying in the political wilderness.

1. The Argument from Democracy and Equality. A blanket exclusion of religious values from public debate is undemocratic, risking the erosion of constitutional guarantees of religious liberty, and would censor the speech

of up to 86% of Singaporeans professing a religious faith. A chief aspect of the right of political participation is the ability of all citizens to engage in public affairs regardless of religious affiliation. By definition, public policy determines how we order our common lives. Historically, religious convictions have grounded important social reforms, like the anti-slavery and child labour protection work of British parliamentarians William Wilberforce and Lord Shaftsbury. While it can and has been exploited in the past, religion can and has had a humanizing influence on civilization.

Former PM Goh displayed this enlightened attitude. In his last National Day rally speech he clarified that despite the June 2003 announcement that subject to disclosure, the government had relaxed its policy of hiring homosexuals in key civil service positions, he did not "encourage or endorse a gay lifestyle". This announcement had sparked public concern that a further liberalization of the homosexual agenda would harm public morality and health and undermine social institutions. PM Goh approvingly noted that both "conservative Singaporeans and religious leaders" had articulated their views "clearly but responsibly," warning that the "conservative mainstream" would resist homosexual activism for more public space (Goh 2003). In trying to stir up a participatory ethos, then DPM Lee Hsien Loong in his 2004 Harvard Club Speech said: "People should debate issues with reason, passion and conviction, and not be passive bystanders in their own fate. Disagreement does not necessarily imply rebellion, nor should unity of purpose and vision mean sameness in views and ideas" (Lee 2004).

In seeking to persuade others in democratic deliberative discourse, members of the faith community should primarily appeal to the public reason rather than divine authority, speaking in accessible terms with reference to what serves the common good and individual welfare. For example, with respect to the homosexual agenda, in addition to issues of public morality which are partially informed by religious values, a shared and legitimate public concern is that of public health issues and the AIDs epidemic. To say that an argument is accessible, of course, is not to suggest that all its hearers will accept it. A value that is not shared does not mean it cannot be relied upon in making political arguments in an attempt to persuade.

2. The Argument from Free Speech and Freedom of Religion. Free speech requires protecting the speech we dislike. In a democracy, the thinking individual must be able to consider all views to facilitate informed decisions about the common good. The false notion that "secular" equals neutrality

and that "religion" connotes ignorance or prejudice must be quashed. A belief in morality means we all make moral judgments; there is no morally neutral ground. Kant considered that the logic of any moral argument is its capacity to be universalized. Within a democratic society, contesting perspectives will help shape informed views.

All Singaporeans, of religious or non-religious persuasion, have the right to speak about and influence public policy; religious values cannot be excluded from public issues as the state cannot determine which convictions and moral judgements may enter public deliberation, which would discriminate between citizens as bearers of opinion. Thoughtful debate over how to shape our life as a community is precluded if religious voices are gagged as "Religion in public is but the public opinion of those citizens who are religious" (Neuhaus 1992). This would disenfranchise people of religious faith, be undemocratic in denying them equal access to the public square. Furthermore, religion is a valuable source of morality, unlike the substantively "thin" moral content of liberalism. The utility of secularism is in providing a framework for the peaceful co-existence of distinct religious groups; however, as a form of moral minimalism, it lends no guidance to how we should live together as the liberal state is "deprived of divine revelation" (Ackerman 1980: 127). As a vendor of comfort, hope, values and guardian of social order, religion helps provide moral gravitas or depth, which informs the conception of common morality; it helps maintain a shared language of right or wrong, without which we lose our moral compass and risk descent into the abyss of moral relativism.

Every political conflict entails a choice between competing moral codes. In the context of the universality of human rights law, Singapore foreign minister Wong Kan Seng observed:

> Most rights are still essentially contested concepts. There may be a general consensus ... coupled with continuing ... conflicts of interpretation. Singaporeans, and people in many other parts of the world do not agree, for instance, that pornography is an acceptable manifestation of free expression or that homosexual relationships is just a matter of lifestyle choice. Most of us will also maintain that the right to marry is confined to those of the opposite gender. (Wong 1993)

Notably this culture war or conflict between values is not a West versus Rest debate but is internal to states. Such morally contentious disputes are unlikely to be resolved legally, much less morally, in this lifetime, with advocates on opposing sides adopting the self-righteous mantle of crusaders who see their way as that of enlightenment, whether arguing from the epistemology of faith or "reason." Thus, in a post-modern world, there is no one conception of the common good and we may be left with an overlapping consensus to some extent; dialogue is key to negotiating and finding, in this lifetime, some kind of compromise, if Paradise cannot be regained.

A function of constitutional democracy is to channel potential disputes off the streets and to steer this towards deliberate democratic discourse and the politics of persuasion. Crucial to this is access to this process. In this regard, to shut out a perspective informed by religious values, to demonize the agenda as less legitimate than other agendas, is to privilege one perspective over the other. To support a cause is to oppose another. Secular humanism is fundamentally at odds as an ideology with other ideologies, particularly those which do not subscribe to a godless universe. We have different views of what is progressive and regressive because we have different worldviews. Furthermore, alienating religious communities and denuding participatory democracy will have costly de-legitimizing effects. National values can only be developed if these take root through broad-based acceptance (Chan 2000: 25).

Religious freedom entails more than just attending church or mosque or temple; it extends to debate in the public square in the process of consensus-seeking; precluding this constitutes illiberal censorship and promotes atheism as the unofficial state religion. It deprives the prophetic voice of religious communities on fundamental issues pertaining to good and evil and moral culture. There are more things in heaven and earth than are dreamt of in our philosophy; we should not shut off the transcendent by fiat (nor impose religious tenets by fiat) as this would diminish us. Every political actor has an interest in persuading endorsement of her position but it is wrong and demagogic to question the right of religious people to participate in politics; this is not to advocate neutrality, but to silence a viewpoint.

The listener has a right to hear and judge such perspectives; the speaker, to articulate them; and the government, an interest in accurate feedback which promotes good governance. If a sizeable percentage of the faith community opposes a policy, this is a factor a representative government may well want to take into account. This concern with having an accurate barometer of popular feeling is reflected in the consideration in paragraph 18 of the Shared Values white paper that any proposal which "conflicts with the teachings of Islam, Christianity, Hinduism, Taoism or Buddhism is unlikely to gain general acceptance." Ultimately, any view advanced in the public square not resonating broadly with most Singaporeans' reason and conscience will be unpersuasive.

III. Conclusion: Wall of Division or Public Square?

In an age of modernity and globalization, the persistence of religious ideas, practices and institutions remains a key feature of local and global politics. Whether religion has a legitimate role in public policy will continue to be a pressing matter, as issues of social morality continue to emerge, giving rise to tensions between religious organizations and their members who want their views to count, and those with competing agendas. One could not say that either group is progressive or regressive because, as GK Chesterton observed, "progressive is a comparative of which we have not settled the superlative" (Chesterton 1905). How then are we going to find the superlative in terms of moral views in relation to public policy in this post-modern age? To build a community, the emphasis has to be placed squarely on participation in our shared life, rather than the things that divide us.

In a society with distinct ethno-cultural groups, there is a division between the separate domain and the common space. However, the "common space" does not mean that one has to be shorn of his individual values such as religious identity—it was wrong to think of this in terms of a "zero sum game", as Muslim Minister Yaacob Ibrahim has noted (Ibrahim 2003, *Straits Times* 25 Oct. 2002). He considered the common space "reflects what makes us uniquely Singaporean, while embracing the diverse cultures and faiths that we come from." Expanding the common space rests largely on "how the different communities see the value in preserving a uniquely Singaporean identity" (Ibrahim 2003, col. 1786) such as having shared beliefs in "nurturing strong families, meritocracy, multi-racialism and a corrupt-free government" (Ibrahim 2003, col. 1787). This rejection of viewing common and private space as compartmentalized, distinct areas of life stands in contradistinction with other views that religious practice should be limited to personal space. To be sure, some degree of pragmatic compromise will be called for, where religious values and public policy are, or appear, incompatible. Islam bans gambling and in response to the disappointing decision to have a casino in Singapore, Minister Yaacob Ibrahim asked Muslims to be pragmatic and to respect the difference between public and private morality; the values which the community considered "good and right for society" should be shared graciously and respectfully "through dialogue and education, without imposing on others" (*Straits Times* 19 April 2005).

At heart, the chief issue is how the state should relate to religion, whether the sacred and secular should exist in exclusive jurisdictions divided by a "wall of separation," or whether a post-modern architectural metaphor like the "public square" is more apt, as this connotes the public spaces in national life. As Treitel notes, the metaphor of a wall "expresses a dualism which asks: "What is included? What is excluded?" This is "determined by the various communities which situate themselves on either side of the wall" (Treitel 1993) and reflects contemporary understandings of "secularism" as being in opposition to religion. However, one should recall that when George Holyoake coined the term "secularism" in 1846, this was described as "a form of opinion which concerns itself only with questions, the issues of which can be tested by the experience of this life, that is, a materialistic philosophy and a disinterest in the spiritual. It did not connote an opposition to religion per se" (Holyoake 1897: 63).

State neutrality is mythical, as neither law nor public institutions can be value-free. In the interests of democracy, religious freedom and free expression in Singapore, religious perspectives should be welcomed in the public sphere, alongside views arising from exclusively secular convictions, insofar as these are identifiable, in delineating the *civitas terrena* and *civitas dei* within a religiously plural state.

The "wall of separation" metaphor is giving way to the more fitting metaphor of the public square, which represents a shift towards "architecture with a narrative. It is a move toward representation. Unlike a wall's simple two-sidedness, a square circumscribes an area. In architecture, a public square defines a common area, one with the potential for shared use by the community" (Treitel 1993: 102–103). It is within the public square that public dialogue may be advanced, through a commitment to deliberative civil discourse. Even though there is a realm of privacy which prudence dictates the state should not intrude into, no man is an island entire of itself and private choices are not hermetically sealed off from having public consequences.

While thorny issues may never be resolved, the advantage of thinking in terms of a public square is that it directs our attention to our shared spaces and common lives where we seek to translate ideals into social realities. Engagement is part of the process of maintaining peace, while alienation of religious communities from public life is divisive and undermines the nurturing of a shared citizenship (Bowden 2004).

Hearing all sides relevant to a public policy issue in civil debate, encompassing religious and non-religious views and accepting both as equipollent in relation to public behavior, empowers us to make informed choices about our lives and community welfare; this notion of deliberative secularism requires the state to be transparent in its justifications for public policy, facilitating public scrutiny; it socializes citizens to the needs of the larger community and facilitates the give-and-take which sustains our pacific co-existence. Lastly, it aids the apprehension that politics is the art of the possible, not perfect, which is, as some believe, a hope to be realized in an age to come, where faith becomes sight.

References

Ackerman, Bruce (1980) *Social Justice in the Liberal State.* Yale University Press.

Becker, Larry Cata, (1988) "Religion as object and the grammar of law," *Marquette. Law Review* 81: 229.

Beer, Lawrence Ward, (1991) "The influence of American constitutionalism in Asia" in *American Constitutionalism Abroad: Selected Essays in Comparative Constitutional History*, George Athan Billias ed. Greenwood Press, 113–121.

Benson, Iain T (2000) "Notes towards a (re)definition of the 'secular'," *University of British Columbia Law Review* 33: 519.

Berman, Harold J. (1974) *The Interaction of Law and Religion.* Nashville: Abingdon Press.

Bowden, John (2004) "Secular values and the process of secularisation" 29 Jan. 2004, archived at http://www.islamonline.net/english/Contemporary/2004/01/Article03.shtml [accessed 20 Dec. 2006].

Budziszewski, J. (1993) "The illusion of moral neutrality," *First Things* 35: 32–37 at http://www.firstthings.com/ftissues/ft9308/articles/budziszewski.html [accessed 20 Dec. 2006].

Campenhausen, Axel von (2004) "The German headscarf debate," *Brigham Young University Law Review* 2004(2): 665.

Chai Tshun Chieh v Chief Military Prosecutor [1998] Singapore Military Court of Appeal (SGMCA) 3.

Chan, David (2003) *Attitude on Race and Religion in Singapore.* (Ministry of Community Development, 2003, at http://www.mcds.gov.sg/MCDSFiles/download/SAS02RR.pdf. [Accessed 20 Dec. 2006].

Chan Hiang Leng, Colin v Public Prosecutor [1994] *Singapore Law Reports* 3: 662.

Chan, Sek Keong (2000) "Cultural issues and crime", *Singapore Academy of Law Journal* 12(1).

Chesterton, G.K. (1905) Chapter II, "On the negative spirit" in *Heretics*, New York: John Lane Company.

Clammer, John (1990) "Religion and society in Singapore: ethnicity, identity and social change" in *Society, Culture and Patterns of Behaviour*, Seyschab, Sievers and Szynkiewicz eds. Germany: Horleman Verlag Unkel/Rhein und Bad Honnef, 157–182.

Dahlab v Switzerland Application No.42393/98, ECHR 2001-V, judgment of 15 February 2001, translation available at www.strasbourgconference.org/ caselaw/DahlabvSwissDecision.pdf.

Daud bin Mamat v Majlis Agama Islam [2001] 2 *Malayan Law Journal* (*MLJ*) 390.

Dow Jones Publishing v AG [1989] *Malayan Law Journal* (*MLJ*) 2: 385.

Durant, Will and Ariel (1968) *The Lessons of History*. New York: MJF Books.

Durham, Cole (1996) "Perspectives on religious liberty: a comparative framework" in *Religious Human Rights in Global Perspective*, van der Vyver and Witte, eds, 1st ed. Martinus Nijhoff.

Englehart, Neil A. (2000) "Rights and culture in the Asian values argument: the rise and fall of Confucian ethics in Singapore" *Human Rights Quarterly* 22(2): 548–568.

Fernando, Joseph (2006) "The position of Islam in the constitution of Malaysia" *Journal of Southeast Asian Studies* 37: 249–266.

Finnis, John (1998) "On the practical meaning of secularism" *Notre Dame Law Review* 73: 491.

Friedrich, Carl J. (1974) *Limited Government: A Comparison*, New Jersey: Prentice Hall.

Fuderi, Frank (2006) "The curious rise of anti-religious hysteria: it is the Anglo-American cultural elites' insecurity about their own values that encourages their frenzied attacks on religion" Spiked essays, 23 Jan. 2006, at http://www.spiked-online.com/Articles/0000000CAF37.htm [accessed 20 Dec. 2006].

Fyzee, Asaf (1974) *Outlines of Muhammadan Law*, 4th ed. Delhi: Oxford University Press.

George, Robert P. (2000) "The concept of public morality," *American Journal of Jurisprudence* 45: 17.

Goh, Chok Tong (2003) "From the valley to the highlands", 2003 National Day Rally Speech, full text available at http://www.gov.sg/nd/ND03.htm [accessed 20 Dec. 2006].

Greenawalt, Kent (1988) *Religious Convictions and Political Choice*. Oxford University Press.

Hill, Michael (1999) "Conversion and Subversion: Religion and the Management of Moral Panics in Singapore" Asia Studies Institute, available at http://www.vuw.ac.nz/asianstudies/publications/working/conversion.html 22 March 1999 [accessed 20 Dec. 2006].

Holyoake, George (1877) *English Secularism: A Confession of Belief*. Chicago: Open Court Publishing Company.

Hood, Steven J. (1998) "The myth of Asian-style democracy," *Asian Survey* 38(9): 853–866.

Idleman, Scott (1993) "The role of religious values in decision making" *Indiana Law Journal* 68: 433.

Ignatieff, Michael (2001) *Human Rights as Politics and Idolatry*, Amy Guttman ed. Princeton and Oxford: Princeton University Press.

Kadir, Suzaina (2005) "The role of education in ethnic/religious conflict management: the Singapore case," *International Center for Islam and Pluralism Journal* 2(1): 1.

PP v Koh Song Huat Benjamin [2005] Singapore District Court (SGDC) 272.

Kuo, Eddie CY, Quah, Jon ST and Tong, Chee Kiong (1988) National University of Singapore, *Religion and Religious Revivalism in Singapore*, Report prepared for the Ministry of Community Development (Oct. 1988).

Lee, Hsien Loong (2004) Speech, Harvard Club of Singapore's 35th Anniversary Dinner, 6 Jan. 2004, at http://app.feedback.gov.sg/asp/new/new0001.asp?id=501 [accessed 20 Dec. 2006].

Lee, Kuan Yew (1965) Transcript of the Prime Minister's statement to religious representatives and members of the Inter-Religious Council, 30th September 1965.

Lina Joy v Majlis Agama Wilayah [2004] *Malayan Law Journal* 2: 119.

Ling, Trevor (1989) "Religion" in *Management of Success: The Moulding of Modern Singapore*, KS Sandhu and Paul Wheatley eds. Singapore: Institute of Southeast Asian Studies, 692–709.

Madison, James, *Memorial and Remonstrance Against Religious Assessments* (1785) at http://religiousfreedom.lib.virginia.edu/sacred/madison_m&r_1785.html (accessed 20 Dec. 2006).

Maintenance of Religious Harmony Act (MRHA) white paper, (1989) (Singapore Parliament: Cmd 21 of 1989).

May, Todd (2004) "Religion, the election, and the politics of fear", Countercurrents.org, 19 Nov. 2004 at http://www.countercurrents.org/us-may191104.htm.

Moens, Gabriël A (2004) "The menace of neutrality in religion," *Brigham Young University Law Review* 2004(2): 535.

Moore, Charles W. (2003) "An unholy hatred: Author and journalist Joe Campbell coined the word 'sacraphobia' to describe the modern world's fear and loathing of the sacred", Op-Ed, *The Gazette* (Montreal, Quebec), July 20 2003 at A13.

Nappalli Peter Williams v Institute of Technical Education [1999] *Singapore Law Reports* 2: 569.

Neuchterlein, James (1996) "When insults no longer insult" *First Things* 65(August/September): 13–14, archived at http://www.catholiceducation.org/articles/homosexuality/ho0032.html.

Neuhas, Richard John (1992) "A new order of religious freedom" *First Things* 20: 13–17, at http://www.firstthings.com/ftissues/ft9202/articles/neuhaus.html.

Nicholas, Colin (2000) "Islamisation and assimilation" in The Orang Asli and the Contest for Resources, International Work Group for Indigenous Affairs: Copenhagen 2000, 98–102.

Novak, Michael (2002) "Democracy and religion in America: Tocqueville's surprising linkage" *National Review Online* 2 Oct. 2002 at http://www.nationalreview.com/novak/novak100202.asp.

Ong, Aihwa (1998) "Sisterly solidarity in the Malaysian public sphere" in *Religion, Ethnicity and Modernity in Southeast Asia*, Oh Myung-Seok and Kim Hyung-Jun, eds. Seoul National University Press, 54–67.

Neo, Jaclyn Ling-Chien (2003) "'Anti-God, anti-Islam and anti-Quran': expanding the range of participants and parameters in discourse over women's rights and Islam in Malaysia," *UCLA Pacific Basin Law Journal* 21: 29.

O'Reilly, Bill, Liberal Jihad: http://www.townhall.com/Columnists/BillOReilly/2006/08/05/liberal_jihad.

Prager, Dennis (2003) "Homosexuality—an attempt at clarity", townhall.com. 29 April 2003 at http://www.townhall.com/columnists/DennisPrager/2003/04/29/homosexuality_an_attempt_at_clarity [accessed 20 Dec. 2006].

Prager, Dennis (2005) "The difficulty of intellectually engaging the Left", townhall.com 25 Oct 2005 at http://www.townhall.com/opinion/column/dennisprager/2005/10/25/172686.html [accessed 20 Dec. 2006].

Religioustolerance.org News (2001): "Canada: Anglican primate concerned about role of religion". 3 Jan. 2001 at http://www.religioustolerance.org/news_02jan.htm [accessed 20 Dec. 2006].

Rawls, John (1999) "The idea of public reason revisited" in *The Law of Peoples*. Harvard University Press.

Shared Values white paper (1991) (Singapore Parliament, cmd 1 of 1991.).

Singapore Permanent Representative (2002) Letter to the UN Commission on Human Rights Chair (24 April 2002) UN Doc E/CN.4/2002/188.

Sinha, Vineeta (2005) "Theorising 'talk' about 'religious pluralism' and 'religious harmony' in Singapore," *Journal of Contemporary Religion* 20(1): 25–40.

Singapore Parliamentary debates.

Othman bin Wok (1977) 37 *Singapore Parliament Reports* vol. 37, 29 June 1977, (Mosque Building Fund Scheme), col. 62–63.

Ahmad Mattar (1982) *Singapore Parliament Report*, vol. 42, 3 Dec 1982 (Contributions from Hindus for Temples etc and Monies from Muslims for Mosques etc) col. 309–311.

S. Jayakumar (1989) *Singapore Parliament Reports*, vol. 54, 6 Oct 1989, col 637.

Zainul Abidin Rasheed (2002) *Singapore Parliament Reports* vol. 74, 23 May 2002, col. 2220.

Yaacob Ibrahim (2003) *Singapore Parliament Reports*, vol. 76, 20 March 2003. 1788.

Smith, Steven D. (1998) "Legal discourse and the de facto disestablishment," *Marquette Law Review* 21: 203.

Straits Times (Singapore).

"Lee hopes for 'new quid pro quo' relationship", *Straits Times*, 15 Dec. 1965.

"No dominance by religious group over others—Lee" *Straits Times*, Jan. 1967 at 6.

Government is secular: not atheistic: BG Yeo" *The Straits Times*, 8 Oct 1992 at 2.

Zuraidah Ibrahim, "The nation mourns", *Straits Times*, 31 Dec. 1997 at 1.

Canon James Wong, quoted in "Religious code goes beyond keeping peace", *Straits Times*, 16 Oct 2002 at H2.

"Let's redefine common space, says minister" *Straits Times* (25 Oct. 2002) (Lexis).

H. Neo "Does this group deserving funding" *Straits Times*, Forum, 6 Dec. 2003.

L. Thio, "State, Religion and the Public Square" *Straits Times*, Forum, 11 Dec. 2003.

Law that governs Muslims' lives dynamic and realistic", *Straits Times*, 1 Oct. 2004 at 14.

Mafoot Simon, "Soul-searching continues for Muslims in S'pore", *Straits Times*, 2 Oct. 2004 at 30.

Chua Mui Hoong, "Beware of mixing religion and politics", *Straits Times*, Insight, 5 Nov. 2004 at 33.

Tracy Sua and Sharlene Tan, "Thousands gather to pray for tsunami victims", *Straits Times*, 31 Jan. 2005 (available on LEXIS).

"Muis against having a casino", *Straits Times*, 11 Feb. 2005.

P. Tan, "How to judge if the Govt. is 'listening", *Straits Times*, Forum 14 Feb. 2005.

L. Thio, "In a democracy, all have a right to be heard" *Straits Times*, Forum, 22 Feb. 2005.

Azhar Ghani, "Muslims urged to view decision with pragmatism", *Straits Times*, 19 April 2005, available on LEXIS.

Lydia Lim and Aaron Lowe, "Nation of believers: modernisation and economic development have done little to dent Singaporeans' faith in God, according to a key finding of a recent Straits Times survey", *Straits Times*, 16 July 2005, Saturday Special Report (available on LEXIS).

Sunder, Madhavi (2003) "Piercing the veil" *Yale Law Journal* 12: 1399.

Tahzib, Bahiyyih G. (1996) *Freedom of Religion or Belief.* The Hague/Boston/London: Martinus Nijhoff Publishers.

Tamney, Joseph (1996) *The Struggle over Singapore's Soul: Western Modernisation and Asian Culture.* Berlin and New York: Walter de Gruyter.

Tan, Kevin Y.L. and Thio Li-ann (1997) Appendix D (1966 Constitutional Commission Report) *Constitutional Law in Malaysia and Singapore.* Asia: Butterworths.

§   Chapter I, Wee Constitutional Commission report, para 38,.

§   Paragraph 12, "Note of dissent by Mr Justice Abdul Hamid", in the 1956–1957 Constitutional Commission Report, reproduced in Tan and Thio, at 982.

§   Terms of Reference spelt out by Law Minister EW Barker, *Singapore Parliament Reports*, 22 Dec. 1965, Tan and Thio, 1020.

Teitel, Ruti G. (1993) "Postmodernist architectures in the law of religion," *Brigham Young Law Review* 2003(1) 97.

Thio, Li-ann (1993) "The Secular Trumps the Sacred: Constitutional Issues Arising out of *Colin Chan v PP*' (1995) *Singapore Law Review* 26.

——— (1997) "The impact of internationalisation on domestic governance: the transformative potential of CEDAW," *Singapore Journal of International and Comparative Law* 1: 248.

——— (2002a) "*Lex Rex or Rex Lex*: competing conceptions of the rule of law in Singapore," *UCLA Pacific Basin Law Journal* 20: 1.

——— (2002b) "Recent constitutional developments: of shadows and whips, race, rifts and rights, terror and tudungs, women and wrongs," *Singapore Journal of Legal Studies*: 328–373.

——— (2002c) "The right to political participation in Singapore: tailor-making a Westminster-modelled constitution to fit the imperatives of 'Asian' democracy," *Singapore Journal of International and Comparative Law* 6: 516–574.

——— (2004a) "Pragmatism and realism do not mean abdication: a critical inquiry into Singapore's engagement with international human rights law" *Singapore Yearbook of International Law* 8: 41–91.

——— (2004b) "constitutional 'soft' law and the management of religious liberty and order: the 2003 declaration on religious harmony," *Singapore Journal of Legal Studies*: 414–443.

——— (2005) "Control, co-optation and co-operating: managing religious harmony in Singapore's multi-ethnic, quasi-secular state," *Hastings Constitutional Law Quarterly* 33(2 & 3): 197–253.

——— (2006) "Apostasy and religious freedom: constitutional issues arising from the *Lina Joy* litigation," *Malayan Law Journal* 2: i.

US v Seeger 380 U.S. 163 (1965).

Wall Street Journal.

"Secular absolutism: the irreligious left tries to impose its religious views on everyone else". 14 March 2004 at http://www.opinionjournal.com/editorial/feature.html?id=110004819.

"Liberal fundamentalism: who are the intolerant extremists?" *Review and Outlook*: 16 May 2005 at http://www.opinionjournal.com/extra/?id=110006694.

Winslow, Valentine S (1990) "The separation of religion and politics: The Maintenance of Religious Harmony Act" *Malaya Law Review* 32: 327.

Wong, Kan Seng (1993) "The real world of human rights," *Singapore Journal Legal Stud.*: 605.

Woodard, Joe (2001) "Christian God in exile: Christianity is being banished from the public square in Canada" *The Gazette* (Montreal, Quebec), 12 Feb. 2001: B3

5 | State, Religion, and the Dynamics of Transition: Repertoire of Violence in Post-Suharto Indonesia

Noorhaidi Hasan

The collapse of the Suharto-led New Order authoritarian regime in May 1998 heralded the *Reformasi* that has had tremendous impact on the relationship between Islam and the Indonesian nation-state. Coupled with the weakening of state power, a far-reaching process of liberalization and democratization that followed its demise opened up a space that enabled a large number of people in Indonesian society to discuss and develop opinions on issues that affected their lives. A variety of groups, identities, and interests thus emerged, competing for the newly liberated public sphere. Reflecting a common outcome of economic and socio-political instability, ethnic and religious conflicts flared up in various regions of Indonesia, threatening a society apparently imbued with a culture of tolerance based on harmonious inter-ethnic and inter-faith relations. In the Moluccas a fight between two youths quickly devolved into the bloody communal violence between Christians and Muslims, which claimed thousands of lives and wounded many others. Likewise, in Central Sulawesi, West and Central Kalimantan, protracted bloody communal confrontations which involved different ethnic groups resulted in property destruction and the mass exodus of refugees.[1]

In a flurry of conflicts, a number of militant Muslim groups with names like the Laskar Pembela Islam (Defenders of Islam Force), the Laskar Jihad (Holy War Force), and the Laskar Mujahidin Indonesia (Indonesian Holy Warriors Force) came to the fore and achieved notoriety by taking to the streets to demand the comprehensive implementation of the *Shari'a* (Islamic law), raiding cafes, discotheques, casinos, brothels, and other reputed dens of iniquity, and, most importantly, calling for jihad in the Moluccas and other Indonesian trouble spots. While the Laskar Pembela Islam was primarily concerned with issues of morality, the Laskar Jihad preferred to launch a mission to fight jihad in the Moluccas. In fact, they were clearly distinguishable in terms of origin and institutional profile. Unlike the Laskar Jihad which might be considered the largest and most organized militant Muslim group uniting young men who call themselves Salafis, followers of the *Salaf al-Salih* (pious ancestors), the Laskar Pembela Islam is loosely organized with open membership mostly from the mosque youth associations scattered throughout Jakarta and a number of Islamic schools in the region. Another group, Laskar Mujahidin, emerged as the latest, but probably most deeply rooted, militant Muslim organization which championed the implementation of the *Shari'a* and spearheaded anti-American actions. It is a loose alliance of a number of minor Muslim paramilitary groups and hard-line organizations scattered across various cities in Indonesia, where the Darul Islam rebellions had their roots (Hasan 2002; Hasan 2005).[2]

These militant organizations have consistently viewed the existing system of government as illegitimate and rejected the idea of compromise and participation. They did not follow other Islamic groups' determination to use the opening of the political opportunity under Habibie's presidency to transform themselves into political parties. In fact, a dozen political parties which endorsed the *Shari'a* and other conservative positions came to the political arena of post-New Order Indonesia. Of these, seven, including the Partai Bulan Bintang (PBB, Crescent and Moon Party) and the Partai Keadilan (PK, Justice Party), explicitly declared Islam as their sole ideological basis and philosophy. The Partai Persatuan Pembangunan (PPP, United Development Party), the only existing Islamic party under the party fusion system introduced by Suharto in 1973 and had accepted the Pancasila, ideology of the state, as its sole ideological foundation, lost no time in returning to Islam and its old symbol, *Ka'ba*, a large cuboidal building in Mecca which has become the direction Muslims face during prayer. All these parties took part in the general elections in June 1999 and, by so doing, became engaged in the on-going process of democratic political system.

The atmosphere of *Reformasi* brought about by Suharto's departure has facilitated the attempts made by the parties to propose the introduction of the *Shari'a* into the Indonesian Constitution, thus giving the *Shari'a* a constitutional status. The Partai Persatuan Pembangunan and the Partai Bulan Bintang were at the forefront of reviving debate on seven words *"dengan kewajiban menjalankan syariat bagi pemeluknya,"* which had been removed from the Preamble to the Indonesian Constitution only a day after Independence.[3] Known as the *Piagam Jakarta* (Jakarta Charter), the words stipulate the obligation for adherents of Islam to follow the *Shari'a*. Later, the debates shifted from the idea of Islam becoming the foundation of the state (*Dasar Negara*) to the amendment of Article 29 of the Constitution, which declares that "The State shall be based upon the belief in the One and Only God" so that it includes a constitutional obligation on Muslims to practice the *Shari'a* (Hosen 2005). Although these attempts ended in failure, the demands for the implementation of the *Shari'a* have resonated across the country and to some extent materialized with the enactment of Regional Regulations (*Perda*) on different aspects of the *Shari'a*, which has to do with the introduction of regional autonomy packages and direct elections of regional administrators (*pilkada*).

No doubt, the mounting demands for the *Shari'a* constitute the strongest signs of the expansion of political Islam in the political landscape of post-New Order Indonesia.[4] The term "political Islam" can be applied to the discourses and activist projects that conceive of Islam, not merely as a religion, but also as a political ideology, whereby an Islamic state, or at least an Islamic society characterized by a high respect for and obedience to the *Shari'a*, is established. It is a religio-political project that attempts to enable Islam not only to be represented in the state but also to be established as a comprehensive system that regulates all aspects of life. Islam is underscored as a complete system governing all religious, social, political, cultural and economic orders and encompassing all things material, spiritual, societal, individual, and personal. Battles over dress, morality, marriage, celebrations, entertainment, sexuality, and faith as well as conflicts over governance and law are thus at the centre of the project (See Ayubi 1991, cf. Lawrence 1995 and Moussalli 1998). In fact, by demanding its inclusion into the Indonesian Constitution, both implicitly and explicitly, the advocates of the *Shari'a* sounded an alarm challenging the legitimacy of the secular system adopted by the Indonesian State, perceived as an extension of the western hegemony responsible for the on-going politico-economic crisis.

State's Control over Religion

The rising tide of political Islam in the aftermath of the collapse of the New Order regime coincided with the weakening control of the state over religion. Since its establishment in 1967 the New Order has sought to establish hegemony over society and expand its power and control. Being aware of Sukarno's failure might have been caused by his focus on ideological and political affairs that resulted in never-ending tension between religion and the state, Suharto decided to focus on a strategy of development and modernization. Consequently, religious expressions were marginalized in the political process, in spite of the considerable role that was played by Muslims in bringing the New Order into existence. The quest for the revitalization of Muslim politics was rejected by Suharto, under the shadow of his two primary advisers, Ali Murtopo and Sujono Humardani. Rather, a policy of the regimentation of political Islam was advanced. Masyumi, the first largest banned Islamic political party that had placed second in the 1955 general election, did not obtain a green light to be resuscitated. Rather, a new party, Parmusi, was designed to accommodate Muslim modernists minus leadership of former Masyumi figures. As a result of the regime's intervention in the party's internal affairs, the new party failed to draw votes in the 1971 general election. Other Islamic parties were likewise ineffective in challenging the Golongan Karya (Golkar, Functionalist Group), the new political machine created by Suharto's regime which gained 62.8 percent of total votes.

After the 1971 general election that gave an absolute victory to the Golongan Karya, Suharto explicitly intensified the marginalization of political Islam by implementing the "parties fusion" policy, as indicated before. This policy obliged all Muslim parties to be fused into one, the Partai Persatuan Pembangunan, just as the nationalist and Christian parties were fused into the Partai Demokrasi Indonesia (PDI, Indonesian Democratic Party). To shore up his policy, Suharto popularized development jargon and imposed the Pancasila as the state's governing doctrine. Any aspirations that challenged the Pancasila could be easily labelled either "left extreme" or "right extreme"; the Anti-Subversive Act inherited from Sukarno was used by the state to justify its methods (Thaba 1996, van Bruinessen 1996). Through the indoctrination program called the *Pedoman Penghayatan dan Pengamalan Pancasila* (Guide to Comprehension and Practice of the Pancasila, P4), among other instruments, the Pancasila was systematically embedded in the minds of Indonesia's citizens. The spread of the Pancasila doctrine served to isolate dissidents from both the "left" and "right" and posed the constant threat of surveillance, in Foucauldian terms, replacing a less subtle form of control: domination of the body (Foucault 1979).

At the same time, the New Order attempted to domesticate the social force of *"ulama"* (religious Muslim scholars) by proposing the idea of the creation of a semi-governmental body, the Majelis Ulama Indonesia (Indonesian Council of *"Ulama"*), to which the function of issuing religious legal opinions *(fatwas)* and religious advice *(tausiyahs)* would be assigned. The idea was made known to the public during a national conference of Muslim preachers held in 1970 by the Pusat Dakwah Islam Indonesia (Centre for Indonesian Islamic Propagation), an institution established by the Ministry of Religious Affairs. Yet, it could not take hold immediately, partly because of criticism from a number of participants, notably Hamka, a leading modernist religious scholar, who saw in the idea certain Islamic political parties' attempts to mobilize support from other Islamic groups (Hosen 2004). Mukti Ali, a modernist Muslim scholar appointed as a minister of religious affairs in 1971, recalled the idea and facilitated another conference of Muslim preachers in 1974. Suharto came to deliver an opening address to this conference, in which he insisted the need for a nationwide body of *"ulama"* that can serve as, among other functions, as the translator of the concepts and activities of development as well as the mediator between the government and *"ulama"* (Ichwan 2005). It was also expected to be the representative of Muslims in inter-religious dialogues, a project launched by Mukti Ali in order to build what he frequently referred to as "the harmony of religious life," that i, peaceful co-existence of religious groups (Mujiburrahman 2006). The Majelis Ulama Indonesia was officially established a year later and Hamka was elected as its first chairman. The nature of the Majelis Ulama Indonesia as a body whose creation was instigated by the government was soon visible. It was involved in polemics and issued a number of (controversial) *fatwas* legitimizing government policies (Mudzhar 1993).

Suharto's endeavour to block access to power available to Islamic political forces triggered resistance in the form of uprisings in the name of Islam. A group called Komando Jihad (Jihad Commando), led by Ismail Pranoto, perpetrated bombing attacks in Java and Sumatra; another led by Abdul Qadir Djaelani and calling itself Pola Perjuangan Revolusioner Islam (the Model of Revolutionary Islamic Struggle) stormed the building of the

Majelis Permusyawaratan Rakyat (MPR, People's Consultative Council's Assembly) during its general session in March 1978. No less important was a series of murders and robberies committed by a band of radicals led by M. Warman, known as "Terror Warman," and the attacks of a group led by Imran M. Zein, aimed at a number of government facilities, that culminated in the hijacking of a Garuda Indonesia airplane on March 28 1981. Led by West Javanese Darul Islam veterans who had initially been employed by Murtopo's intelligence operators to destroy communism, these groups acted for a common cause: namely, to revolt against Suharto and establish an Islamic state (Santosa 1996, van Bruinessen 2002).

Yet Suharto remained undeterred and consistently wiped them out by force. Following the Tanjung Priok Affair on September 12 1984, which killed at least nine people and wounded more than fifty demonstrators who had gathered to demand the release of their colleagues, Suharto even applied the Mass Organization and Political Bill, which required all mass organizations and political parties to accept the Pancasila as the *asas tunggal* (the sole foundation), thus forbidding Islam from being used as the basis for any organization. This Bill was ratified in 1985. In reaction to this policy, the Nahdlatul Ulama, the Indonesia's largest organization of traditionalist Muslims, quickly declared its acceptance of the Pancasila, while the Muhammadiyah, a modernist-Muslim umbrella, took some time before doing the same (Ismail 1995).

It should be noted, however, at the end of the 1980s Suharto began to introduce a policy of accommodating Islam, focusing particularly on the accentuation of Islamic symbols in public discourse and accommodating religious socio-political powers. In this context, the Directorate General of Elementary and Secondary Education, for instance, issued a new regulation on student uniforms, allowing female students to wear *jilbab* while attending school. Suharto himself and his family went to Mecca to perform the *hajj* pilgrimage in 1991. Upon return from Mecca, Mbak Tutut, Suharto's eldest daughter and a popular figure, began to demonstrate her piety publicly by wearing colorful, elegant *jilbabs*. The model and the way she was wearing her *jilbab* provided the ultimate example for the whole nation (Marcoes-Natsir 2004). Since then cabinet members and high ranking officials have no longer hesitated to declare the Islamic greeting, *Assalamu'alaikum*, in the opening passage of their speeches and this greeting is becoming increasingly popular. They also sought to demonstrate their concern with various Islamic affairs by, for instance, participating in religious festivals and celebrations.

During the Ramadan month, they even competed to conduct the so-called "Safari Ramadan," a tour of mosques and participation in collective prayers across the country utilizing the heightened religious atmosphere of the fasting month of Muslims.

A number of organizations and institutions that made use of Islamic symbols appeared on the scene, including the Ikatan Cendekiawan Muslim se-Indonesia (Indonesian Muslim Intellectual Association, ICMI), which was led by Habibie and established under Suharto's patronage (Hefner 1993). The ruling party, Golongan Karya, began to align its cloak with Islam as more and more Muslim intellectuals were absorbed into its body. While thousands of mosques were built under the sponsorship of the state, the Islamic Court Bill was introduced, followed by the Presidential Decree on the Compilation of Islamic Law.[5] The Bank Muamalat Indonesia which holds as its slogan the words *pertama sesuai syariah*, or "the first [bank in Indonesia] in accordance with the *Sharia*" was set up and its establishment initiated the mushrooming of Islamic *Sharia* banks and insurance companies (Möller 2005). No doubt, these policies were part of Suharto's political strategy to hold onto power (Liddle 1996). In fact, various Islamic (opposition) groups saw the New Order's accommodation of Islam as a promising opportunity to enter the political arena of the state. They believed that through this way they would be able to change the fate of their society, their nation, and their state—not to mention bringing about changes at the personal level. In this sense, the strategy of the regime appeared to succeed in "subduing" pro-Islamist groups and indeed created "regimist Muslims," who did not recoil from showing themselves as a real partner of the state (Hefner 2000). Nasr (2001) refers to this sort of strategy as "Islamic leviathan" and perceives it as a facet of the state's drive to expand its power and control, which hardly bears any positive result.

Political Configuration after the New Order

The fall of Suharto seriously disturbed the political configuration in the final years of the New Order that was in favour of pro-Islamist groups. By the time he left office, the groups were still quite optimistic that the Islamized direction of the state would be maintained as Habibie, the main symbol of the Islamization of the state, was now in power. However, Habibie immediately had to confront strong opposition from different elements in society. In response to these challenges, he tried to convince the opposition about his commitment to reform by, among other measures, restructuring and strengthening the financial system and proposing an extraordinary session of the Majelis Permusyawaratan Rakyat with the primary aim of setting a new date for general elections (Anwar 1999). Despite these efforts, the opposition groups that did not support his ascendancy to power persistently protested against him and demanded his resignation. At one point, they threatened that if he was not prepared to step down at the Majelis Permusyawaratan Rakyat's extraordinary session in November 1999, "people power," a united front composed of leftist students and the Barisan Nasional (National Front), would force him out of his office (Schwarz 2000).

In reacting to this pressure, Habibie's supporters came out in force to stand behind him. They were mobilized by a number of influential Muslim figures, leaders of hard-line Islamic organizations associated with the Dewan Dakwah Islamiyah Indonesia (DDII, Indonesian Council of Islamic Propagation)[6] or Muslim parties, criticizing Habibie's rivals as the parties responsible for the political instability of the state. Fearful of the consequences of this instability, they supported the attempts made by certain military elites close to Habibie to mobilize thousands of massed forces armed with bamboo spears, known as Pam Swakarsa, from Jakarta, Bogor, Tangerang, Bekasi, and Banten. During the extraordinary session in November, this paramilitary force blocked the area around the headquarters of the Majelis Permusyawaratan Rakyat in Senayan to prevent the storm of anti-Habibie demonstrators (Van Dijk 2001). In the run-up to the general elections in June 1999 the challenge faced by Habibie mounted in relation to the candidacy for presidency of Megawati Sukarnoputri, the leader of the Partai Demokrasi Indonesia-Perjuangan (Indonesian Democratic Party of Struggle, PDI-P), known for her close relations with secular-nationalist and Christian politicians. Her candidacy immediately sparked a sharp rivalry between the pro-Islamist groups, on one side, and secular-nationalist groups, on another. Supporters of each camp attacked the other by exploiting ethnic, religious, and other primordial sentiments.

This rivalry has contributed to a surge in ethno-religious conflicts that had exploded in various regions of Indonesia, as mentioned before, and fuelled further tensions among different religious communities. It has even broken down the foundation of interfaith dialogue and tolerance—albeit artificial—that had been built by the state. In the context of the rivalry, a merciless debate emerged about, for instance, whether or not a woman could be president. The Kongres Umat Islam Indonesia (KUII, Congress of the Indonesian Muslim Community) in November 1998 passed a recommendation that the president should be male, according to Islamic injunctions (see Riddle 2002). As part of the rivalry, pictures of Megawati praying at a Balinese Hindu temple had appeared in Indonesian newspapers. Megawati's detractors immediately seized upon this image to suggest that she was a Hindu. A.M. Saefuddin, a Partai Persatuan Pembangunan minister in Habibie's cabinet, went even further, asking: are we ready to be led by a Hindu president? In an attempt to disqualify Megawati, and thus guarantee Habibie's victory, the Majelis Ulama Indonesia issued a *tausiya* just six days before the election suggesting Muslims vote for parties that "struggle for the aspiration and interests of the *umma*, nation and state" and not to vote for non-Muslim political leaders and parties dominated by non-Muslims (Ichwan 2005).

This campaign provoked reactions from Megawati's supporters, who felt the time had indeed come to stand behind her to win the election at all costs. Some pro-Megawati groups in Surabaya, for instance, stated their determination to die for Megawati, a pledge confirmed by a petition signed in blood. In their counter-arguments, Habibie's supporters insisted that to defend their candidate essentially meant to defend Islam and guarantee the state's continued progress toward Islamization. They continued to organize demonstrations against the opposition and echo religious sentiments, which was taken by his opposition as evidence of Habibie's incapability to cope with the situation and introduce fundamental reforms in the economy, political structure, and policy making. Here the state-run Islamization project apparently backfired. Instead of creating a greater harmony in state–society relations, it has facilitated ideologization of the public arena of political discourse and encouraged Islamist activism and militant attitudes.

Pro-Habibie groups did their very best to cut Megawati's feet out from under her, but they scarcely mounted a serious challenge. Thus the 35.7 million votes (34 percent) garnered by her PDI-P party won the election. This result indicated that the Islamization strategy supported by Habibie was narrowly based in the ruling party and hard-line Muslim supporters and certainly ignited discontent among his supporters, who then took to the streets to reject Megawati. Megawati supporters stood firm, supporting their leader. Prior to the general session of the Majelis Permusyawaratan Rakyat in October 1999, they demonstrated on Jakarta's streets to voice their support. These demonstrations were countered by Habibie's supporters, including those joined in the Front Jihad Bersatu (United Jihad Front) and the Laskar Fi Sabilillah (Holy Force for the Cause of God), who sent a message to take all the steps necessary to block Megawati's path to power (Feillard 2002, Meuleman 2002).

Though initially welcomed with euphoria, Abdurrahman Wahid's ascendancy to power to replace Habibie in October 1999 did not reduce tensions between the pro-Islamist and secular-nationalist camps. The leader of the Nahdlatul Ulama, Wahid had been known for not only his criticism of pro-Islamist groups, but also his close relations to secular-nationalists. Exacerbating matters, he began his term by declaring a willingness to establish commercial links with Israel and proposing to lift the thirty-four-year ban on the Partai Komunis Indonesia (PKI, Indonesian Communist Party). These controversial decisions provoked criticism from various quarters, particularly from hard-line Muslims who had long nurtured their hatred of Israel and the Partai Komunis Indonesia. The Majelis Ulama Indonesia, which also opposed Wahid, issued a *tausiyah* to remind Indonesians of the threat of communism depicted as an anti-God and anti-religion ideology that never dies and always endeavours to break down the Pancasila (Ichwan 2005). Partly as a result of these oppositions, Wahid's claim to political legitimacy faded and his popularity quickly plummeted (Mietzer 2000). Dissatisfaction with Wahid was also rife inside the military. He launched his ambitious plans to reduce the supremacy of an already demoralized and thinly stretched military (Mietzner 2002, Anwar *et al* 2002, Rinakit 2004). Against this background we can see why during his presidency, ethno-religious conflicts in the Moluccas and other Indonesian trouble spots culminated.

Rivalries and conflicts occurring at that time indicate that Indonesia's transition from an authoritative state to a fledgling democracy disturbed the nation's political equilibrium; consequently, proponents of the status quo tried hard to involve new political allies in their negotiations with the opposition. This problem was exacerbated by the fact that the emerging Indonesian democracy was still fragile, because of, among other causes, a serious lack of functional democratic traditions and the narrow interests of the political parties involved. As O'Donnell and Schmitter (1986) have argued, transition is typically a period during which regimented relations in a society become blurred and uncertain because the hegemonic discourse controlled by the state has undergone fragmentation. Many possibilities may be on the horizon, including the emergence of a chaotic situation that paves the way for the return of authoritarian rule. Even if democracy is to some extent manifested, it is frequently followed by uncertainty, since the rules of the game continue to change. The players in an era of transition do not strive simply to fulfil their temporary political ambitions but also to establish control over the state (Gill 2000). Within this context, transition often stimulates the formation of a coalitional structure linking "exemplary individuals" to societal organizations representing the masses.

Privatization of Violence

The complicated dynamics of Indonesia's transition towards electoral democracy sheds some light on the background of the rising tide of Islamic radicalism after the fall of Suharto. The demise of his secular regime, which was followed by the eruption of bloody communal conflicts in various regions of Indonesia, provided empirical credibility for the the militant Muslim groups to develop a strategy against the government system and thereby perpetrate anti-civilian violence. They demonstrated the failure of the existing secular system to cope with the financial and socio-political crises that resulted in instability, hostility, and conflict among the society—not to mention widespread vice and moral decadence. They stated their grievance in general terms, stressing that what happened in Indonesia might not be dissociated from the alleged Zionist-cum-Christian international coalition that attempts to undermine Islam in Indonesia. They argued that Indonesia has long been the target of destruction because it is the world's largest Muslim country, with a potential to challenge the hegemony of the Zionist-Crusader international forces. From their perspective the enemies of Islam have succeeded not only in perpetrating their evil plans through economic sabotage, the manipulation of human rights rhetoric, and other activities aimed at setting in motion the reformation process that resulted in the collapse of the New Order regime, but also in inflaming riots, turmoil, and communal conflicts in various regions, including Aceh, Papua, and the Moluccas. In such a situation, the government, they claimed, stood idly to the fate of Muslims and inclined instead toward sympathy for Zionists, Christians and communists.

The critical anti-government framework has resonated loudly and achieved wide currency through popular Islamist print media, such as the bi-weekly, *Sabili* and the monthly, *Suara Hidayatullah*. To some extent it has unified the militant Muslim groups and their sympathizers into one same concern, rhetoric and action. More importantly perhaps, it has facilitated their attempts to consolidate their cohorts and demand their commitment to defend Islam. By projecting that the contemporary crises and escalation of conflicts in various regions of Indonesia constitute a clear sign of the enemy's serious intent both to undermine Islam and eliminate the Republic of Indonesia, they combined religious rhetoric and national-ist sentiment perfectly. God and nation, state and Islam—these concepts were all blurred in their rhetoric. In this way, they shared incentives, thus enabling themselves to organize collective actions and emerge as heroes for their religion and religious fellows and, simultaneously, as patriots seeking to defend their beloved state.

In order to justify their action and provide it with an aura of righteous-ness the militant Muslim groups did not hesitate to call for jihad, perceived to be the only alternative to deal with the current situation. Imbued with symbols of martyrdom, jihad appeared to be a language which might func-tion as an identity marker crucial for acquiring as much social status and reputation as comradeship and excitement. In fact, by calling for jihad they conveyed the impression that they were the group most committed to defending the Muslim *umma* and thereby enhanced their identity and negotiated a place for themselves on the map of Indonesian Islam. Seen from this perspective, jihad might be better conceptualized as a drama. As I argue elsewhere in the case of the Laskar Jihad mission to fight jihad in the Moluccas (2006), this apparently frenzied action was motivated not so much by the hope for a resounding victory as by an ambition to fabricate an heroic image. The whole process began with the spectacular gathering at the Senayan Stadium, a strategic and prestigious site close to the political and business centres of Jakarta. Through the media, millions of Indonesians watched participants shout, cry, and laugh together, displaying their deter-mination and capacity to defend the Moluccan Muslims from the attacks of Christian enemies. There was near-hysteria. They wished to hypnotize the public by using the symbols of jihad.

Since anti-civilian violence constitutes part of the dynamic of mobiliza-tion, its longevity is largely the result of how long the political opportunity is available.[7] In fact, the shifts in the political landscape of Indonesia occur-ring after Megawati came to power to replace Wahid in July 2001 reduced the room to manoeuvre that had been available to the militant Muslim groups. The ascendancy of Megawati, who was known to have cordial ties with the senior military command, and Hamzah Haz, himself a supporter of hard-line Muslim groups who was chosen as vice-president, has to some extent stabilized the political configuration. Megawati's administration gave the military and security apparatus an opportunity to restore political stability. In the context of the global War on Terror launched by President George W. Bush in response to the terrorist attacks on September 11 2001, the government had no choice but to further reduce room for manoeuvre for the militant Muslim groups. At the same time, they tried to intensify dialogues with Muslim leaders and to bring the antagonists in the Moluccas and other Indonesian trouble spots to the negotiating table.

The government's endeavour to impede Islamic militancy went hand-in-hand with the attempt made by moderate Muslim forces, who had felt increasingly frustrated and hobbled by the spread of religious radicalism, to oppose the abuse of jihad and other Islamic symbols. The Jaringan Islam Liberal (JIL, Liberal Islam Network), established in March 2001 by young Muslim thinkers under the leadership of Ulil Absar Abdalla, led this opposition. They echoed the proliferation of liberal Islamic discourse in favour of democracy, human rights, gender equality, freedom of thought, and progressiveness, and rejected the concept of totality in Islam, the imposition of the *Shari'a* by the state, the identification of jihad with armed holy war, and gender inequality. The birth of the Jaringan Islam Liberal marked a widespread rise of consciousness among mainstream Muslim organizations, such as the Nahdlatul Ulama and the Muhammadiyah, that represent the majority of Indonesian Muslims and work to disseminate discourses advocating inter-religious harmony, democracy, egalitarianism, and gender equality. The leadership of both organizations sought to exercise a profoundly moderating and democratic influence on Islam and Indonesian politics through their campaigns asserting that Islam and democracy are compatible and their condemnation of Islamic radicalism.

Conclusion

I have demonstrated that political Islam, as a discursive and activist project that attempts to place Islam in the centre of the discursive field and within the circle of the state power, is contingent upon the political opportunity structure and very much determined by the context of power struggle. Its expansion naturally ensconces Islamic norms, symbols, and rhetoric in the public sphere, but the extent to which it informs the socio-political dynamic of society fluctuates, following the political direction taken by the state. No doubt, political Islam is a matter of the relationship between the state and society. In many cases, the state plays a key role in embedding Islam in politics. Yet, it is a multi-faceted relationship, which involves the state and diverse, sometimes competing, elements of Muslims. It sometimes triggers tensions and conflicts between the state and society, but another time promotes mutual-symbiosis, closeness and cooptation.

Instead of creating a greater harmony in state–society relations, the use of religion by the state has not infrequently facilitated ideologization of the public arena of political discourse and encouraged Islamist activism and militant attitudes. This seems to be the case when a political configuration in favour of pro-Islamist groups has experienced a tremendous transformation. One such example is the situation in Indonesia after the fall of Suharto in 1998 when militant Muslim groups emerged and engulfed the political arena of the country. In an endeavour to grasp a new foundation in the changing political configuration brought about by the transitional process towards electoral democracy, the groups do not hesitate to champion jihad, which is perceived as an effective means to deal with the current situation. Jihad emerges not only as a perfect identity marker crucial for acquiring social status and reputation which urges comradeship and loyalty, but also as a language of protest that has the capacity to transform marginality into centrality and frustration into heroism.

It should be noted, however, that the use of jihad by no means indicates that militant Muslim groups have successfully taken control of the Indonesian public sphere. This action ultimately served instead to highlight the marginal position of the groups and their unsuccessful efforts to popularize their discourse glorifying militancy and violence. In other words, it is more a sign of weakness than a harbinger of success for militant Muslim groups. Because such militants pursue their struggle through spectacular violence, *jihadi* Islam remains on the political periphery and may never succeed in changing the strategic landscape of the country. It certainly did not change the map of Indonesian Islam. Nor has it changed the secular system of the Indonesian nation-state. The majority of Indonesian Muslims remain tolerant and opposed to the use of violence, let alone terrorism. The militancy and violence that engulfed Indonesia in the early years of this new century actually spurred Indonesian Muslims to work more systematically in vocal support of democracy, gender equality, and human rights.

Notes

1. For further accounts on these conflicts, see, e.g., Van Klinken 2001, Aragon 2001, and Davidson 2003. It has been indicated that these conflicts are the result of an interaction between long-term "primordialist" social patterns and a short-term instrumentalization of those patterns in the context of intra-elite competition at the local level.
2. The Darul Islam was a rebellious movement led by Kartosuwirjo, who proclaimed an independent Islamic state in West Java in 1949. For a detailed discussion on this movement see Horikoshi 1975 and Van Dijk 1981.
3. The attempt made by Muslim leaders to include the seven words into the Indonesian Constitution was strongly challenged by secular *abangan* nationalists and like-minded leaders who preferred a secular republican model based on the Pancasila and the Constitution of 1945. As a result, many Muslim leaders felt betrayed. See Boland 1982.
4. There are a number of terms employed by scholars to denote this phenomenon. These include, among other terms, "Islamism," Islamic fundamentalism," "political Islam," "Islamic activism," and "new religious politics". Although I use the term "political Islam" in this paper, I do not mean that emphasis should be put on the political dimension of the phenomenon at the expense of the religious one.
5. The passing of this bill reinforced the existence of the Islamic courts within the Indonesian legal system. Previously, they ranked as second class courts after the public, military, and administrative courts.
6. DDII is a *da'wa* organization established in 1967 by former leaders of Masyumi as a strategy to deal with various political impasses that had blocked their ambition to play politics. On this organization see, e.g., Husin 1988.
7. On the discussion about the dimension of political opportunity in collective action, see Tarrow, e.g., 1998.

References

Ajami, Fouad. (1992) *The Arab Predicament: Arab Political Thought and Practice Since 1967.* Cambridge: Cambridge University Press.

Anwar, Dewi Fortuna (1999) "The Habibie Presidency". In *Post-Soeharto Indonesia: Renewal or Chaos?* Geoff Forrester, ed. Singapore: ISEAS, pp. 33–47.

Anwar, Dewi Fortuna *et al* (2002) *Gus Dur versus Militer: Studi tentang Hubungan Sipil-Militer di Era Transisi.* Jakarta: Gramedia.

Aragon, Lorraine V. (2001) "Communal violence in Poso, Central Sulawesi: where people eat fish and fish eat people," *Indonesia* 72(October): 45–79.

Ayubi, Nazih (1991) *Political Islam: Religion and Politics in the Arab World.* London: Routledge.

Bolland, B.J. (1982) *The Struggle of Islam in Modern Indonesia.* The Hague: Martinus Hijhoff.

Bruinessen, Martin van (1996) "Islamic state or state Islam? Fifty years of State–Islam relations in Indonesia," in *Indonesien Am Ende Des 20. Jahrhunderts,* Ingrid Wessel, ed. Hamburg: Abera, pp. 19–34.

—— (2002) "Genealogies of Islamic radicalism in post-Suharto Indonesia." *South East Asian Research* 10(2): 117–54.

Davidson, Jamie S. (2003) "The Politics of violence on an Indonesian periphery," *South East Asia Research* 11(1): 59–90.

Dijk, C. van (1981) *Rebellion under the Banner of Islam: the Darul Islam in Indonesia*. The Hague: Martinus Nijhoff.

—— *A Country in Despair: Indonesian Between 1997 and 2000*. Leiden: KITLV Press, 2001.

Feillard, Andree (2002) "Indonesian traditionalist Islam's Troubled experience with democracy (1999–2001)," *Archipel* 64: 117–44.

Foucault, Michel (1979) *Discipline and Punish: The Birth of the Prison*. New York: Vintage Books.

Gill, Graeme (2000) *The Dynamics of Democratization: Elites, Civil Society and the Transition Process*. Hampshire and London: Macmillan Press.

Hasan, Noorhaidi (2002) "Faith and politics: the rise of the Laskar Jihad in the era of transition in Indonesia", *Indonesia* 73: 145–69.

—— (2005) "September 11 and Islamic militancy in post-New Order Indonesia." In *Islam in Southeast Asia: Political, Social and Strategic Challenges for the 21st Century*, K.S. Nathan and Mohammad Hashim Kamali, eds. Singapore: ISEAS, pp. 301–322.

—— (2006) *Laskar Jihad: Islam, Militancy, and the Quest for Identity in Post-New Order Indonesia*. Cornell, N.Y.: Southeast Asia Program Publications, Cornell University.

Hefner, Robert W. (1993) "Islam, state, and civil society: ICMI and the struggle for the Indonesian middle class," *Indonesia* 56: 1–35.

—— *Civil Islam: Muslims and Democratization in Indonesia*. Princeton: Princeton University Press, 2000.

Horikoshi, Hiroko (1975) "The Dar-ul-Islam Movement of West Java (1942–62): an experience in the historical process," *Indonesia* 20: 59–86.

Hosen, Nadirsyah (2004) "Behind the Scenes: Fatwas of Mejelis Ulama Indonesia (1975–1998)," *Journal of Islamic Studies* 15(2): 147–79.

—— (2005) "Religion and the Indonesian Constitution: a recent debate," *Journal of Southeast Asian Studies* 36(3): 419–440.

Husin, Asna (1988) "Philosophical and sociological aspects of da'wah: a study of Dewan Dakwah Islamiyah Indonesia," PhD dissertation, Columbia University.

Ichwan, Moch. Nur (2005) "Ulama, state and politics: Majelis Ulama Indonesia after Suharto." *Islamic Law and Society* 15(1): 45–72.

Ismail, Faisal (1995) "Islam, Politics and Ideology in Indonesia: a Study of the Process of Muslim Acceptance of the Pancasila." PhD dissertation, McGill University.

Klinken, Gerry van (2001) "The Maluku Wars: bringing society back in." *Indonesia* 71(April): 1–26.

Lawrence, Bruce B (1995) *Defenders of God: The Fundamentalist Revolt Against the Modern Age*. London: I.B. Tauris.

Liddle, R. William (1996) "The Islamic turn in Indonesia: a political explanation," *Journal of Asian Studies* 55(3): 613–34.

Marcoes-Natsir, Lies. "Symbol of defiance or symbol of loyalty?" http://qantara.de/webcom/show_article.php/c-549/nr-5/p-/i.html. 18 September 2004.

Meuleman, Johan H (2002) "From New Order to national disintegration: the religious factor between reality, manipulation, and rationalization." *Archipel* 64: 81–99.

Mujiburrahman. (2006) *Feeling Threatened: Muslim-Christian Relations in Indonesia's New Order*. ISIM Dissertation. Amsterdam: Amsterdam University Press.

Mudzhar, Mohammad Atho (1993) *Fatwa-Fatwa Majelis Ulama Indonesia: Sebuah Studi tentang Pemikiran Hukum Islam di Indonesia 1975–1988*. Jakarta: INIS.

Mietzner, Marcus (2001) "Personal triumph and political turmoil: Abdurrahman Wahid and Indonesia's struggle for reform," in *The Presidency of Abdurrahman Wahid: an Assessment after the First Year*, Annual Indonesia Lecture Series No. 23, Damien Kingsbury, ed. Monash: Monash Asia Institute, Monash University, pp. 15–32.

—— (2002) "Politics of engagement: the Indonesian armed forced, Islamic extremism, and the "War on Terror." *The Brown Journal of World Affairs* 9(1): 71–84.

Möller, André (2005) *Ramadan in Java: The Joy and Jihad of Ritual Fasting*. Stockholm: Almqvist & Wiksell International.

Moussalli, Ahmad S., ed. (1998) *Islamic Fundamentalism: Myths and Realities*. Reading: Ithaca Press.

Nasr, Seyyed Vali Reza (2001) *Islamic Leviathan: Islam and the Making of State Power*. Oxford, New York: Oxford University Press.

O'Donnell, Gillermo and Philippe C. Schmitter (1986) *Transitions from Authoritarian Rule: Tentative Conclusions about Uncertain Democracies*. Baltimore and London: John Hopkins University Press.

Riddell, Peter G. (2002) "The diverse voices of political Islam in post-Suharto Indonesia." *Islam and Christian-Muslim Relations* 13(1): 65–84.

Rinakit, Sukardi (2004) *The Indonesian Military after the New Order*. Singapore: ISEAS.

Santosa, June Chandra (1996) "Modernization, utopia and the rise of Islamic radicalism in Indonesia." PhD dissertation, Boston University.

Schwarz, Adam (2000) *A Nation in Waiting: Indonesia's Search for Stability*, second edition. Colorado: Westview Press.

Tarrow, Sidney (1998) *Power in Movement: Social Movements and Contentious Politics*, second edition. Cambridge: Cambridge University Press.

Thaba, Abdul Aziz (1996) *Islam dan Negara dalam Politik Orde Baru*. Jakarta: Gema Insani Press.

6 British Muslims and the British State

Gabriele Marranci

Introduction: The Circle of Panic?

I was accompanying a Muslim friend to buy some fish and chips in a local shop in Aberdeen, Scotland. She could have been any ordinary Scottish girl, since she was born in Aberdeen, but her head scarf marked her visibly different. When we approached the shop, a lady dropped her package which her dog then tried to eat. My Muslim friend tried to reach the package in order to return it to the dog's owner. The lady finally succeeded in her battle to prevent the dog from eating it, and smiling to my friend said, "You see, he [the dog] is a real terrorist", and left. I am not sure whether the "lady of the dog" made such an observation purposely or it just slipped from her unconsciously; yet the fact is that today, in many people's minds, Muslims, head scarves and Islam are inevitably associated to terrorism.

I was speaking to Hassan, while coming back from the London Central Mosque, and he was quickly skimming *The Metro*, a free London newspaper. One of the articles reported the words of the Home Secretary, reminding the public that during the Christmas period there was a high chance of a terrorist attack in London. Hassan was upset because he felt that this would make people even more suspicious of Muslims and any problem during the Christmas period would have been blamed upon them. He, however, went on, adding that Christians were hypocritical because they only see the hedonistic side of their holy festivities. He added that England was certainly not a Christian place or a Christian society: they were all affected by *jahiliyya* (the time of ignorance before Islam). Of course, Muslims and Islam were attacked by the West because they represented the last outpost against *jahiliyya*. In other words, Hassan was arguing that the War on Terror was nothing else than the final attempt to impose *jahiliyya* on the entire world, including the Muslim one. Islam was the only antidote to the corruption of both Muslims and non-Muslims.

Analyzing these two stories, we can simply say that these attitudes and worldviews, apparently different but actually very similar in their essentialism, are the expressions of radical people. We can say that the mass media and propaganda mislead them to see in any "other" the enemy within, the assault on their own identity or lives. Yet, as I explain in this chapter, there is a process, which started in the 1979 Iranian Revolution but became globalized after 9/11, which can explain the polarization between Muslims and non-Muslims without referring to the misleading "Clash of civilizations theory" (Huntington 1996). I have named this process *the circle of panic*. The circle of panic is often engineered through the shift from stereotypes to what I shall call "chimerias". As I will explain below, chimerias have no "kernel of truth". They are easily spread to achieve political goals and they are also particularly difficult to control. It is my contention that under the leadership of Bush and Blair a simplistic vision of terrorism and Islamic fundamentalism has been promoted, leading to the formation, and reinforcement, of chimerias among both Muslims and non-Muslims, leaving the majority of people to face an increasing circle of panic.

Muslims in the United Kingdom

There are about 1.6 million Muslims in the UK. Although they account for only 2.7 percent of the overall population, Islam is the second largest religion of the country after Christianity and the first in growing populations (Census 2001). Furthermore, the highest concentration of Muslims in major English and Scottish cities, such as London (607,000), Birmingham (192,000), Greater Manchester (125,219), Bradford–Leeds (150,000), and Glasgow (33,000), make them an important and visible part of UK society; which is more than the statistical 2.7 percent may represent, in particular if we consider that Pakistani Muslims in Bradford are 14 percent of the entire city population. Nonetheless, it is important when we speak of Muslims in the UK to remember that they are not a monolithic entity, but rather highly variegated in ethnicity, nationality and religious affiliations. From the 2001 Census, it is evident, however, that in the UK the majority of Muslims (1.2 million out of 1.6 million) are of South Asian origin. Some relevant factors characterize the Muslim population in the UK. The Muslim population is very young when compared to other minority communities. For instance, 33.8 percent of Muslims are aged 0–15 years (national average is 20.2 percent), and 18.2 percent are aged 16–24 (national average is 10.9 percent). This explains why, after only fifty years of migration from their homelands, today 50 percent of the Muslim population were born in the United Kingdom. I will come back to this point further in this chapter since it has important implications between how the English and Scottish societies perceive their British-born Muslims. When we move to observe the statistical indicator which can reveal more about the economic and social status of the Muslim UK population, the overall picture cannot be defined other than grim.

The 2001 Census shows that Muslims are the most deprived section of the community, not only do they have the highest rate of unemployment, the poorest health, and the lowest level of education, but they were also the least likely to own their own homes.[1] In such a deprived status, after more than fifty years of living in and contributing to the UK society, should we be surprised, as some seem to be, that only 65 percent of Muslims were ready to define their national identity as British, English, Scottish or Welsh?

Indeed, to understand the disillusionment process which affects Muslims in the UK, we should understand from were they came from and the context in which the new generations have grown up. The historical relationship, given that the majority of Muslims are of South Asian origins, between them and the UK was marked by colonialism and colonial dynamics. India [Pakistan achieved independence from India in 1947], was the "Jewel in the Crown" of the British Empire. Racial ideologies and religious profiles were very common during that time, and the colonial power perceived the Hindu population as being more Western-oriented than the Muslims. Colonialism is embedded in the memories of the first, but also as we shall see, second generations. Even when they achieved independence in their own countries, the ties with the British Empire, or what was left of it, remained particularly strong. Thus, after the Second World War, Muslims coming from South Asian countries became part of the British proletariat. Yet the relationship between white workers and, in particular, Pakistani Muslims, was not easy.

Discrimination pushed these new migrants toward an increasing isolation within working-class neighborhoods depopulated of their white populations, which meanwhile could afford better locations (Lewis 1994). This facilitated the reconstruction of internal community dynamics and frictions that still today mark the South Asian Muslim community. The main division is between ethnic lines; however, they are also expressed through religious discourse as, for instance, the case of the Barelvis and Deobandis conflicting approaches to Islam (see, Werbner 2002).

Between Stereotypes and Chimerias

From the mid-1970s, both the Muslim communities and the rest of British society became aware that "the return" of these migrants to their homeland would remain what it was: a myth (Anwar 1979). This again shifted how the host society saw their South Asian populations. With the settlement of the guest workers, Islam became visible as part of the identity of these new communities. This changed also the way in which sociologists and anthropologists saw their informants. If ethnicity and nationality marked with few exceptions (e.g. Barclay 1969) the first studies, now an overwhelming majority of them started to feature the word "Muslim" in their titles and abstracts.[2] This does not mean that the focus on ethnicity and nationality completely disappeared. At the beginning of the 1980s, many studies were still referring to the ethnic-national identity of these immigrants and their social-economic status.[3] Nonetheless, the fact that these South Asians had started to define, in the new migration context, their identity as "Muslim" reinforced the centrality of Islam as their visible identity. Indeed, Islam progressively became also part of the landscape of main British cities, through the minarets and the oriental-styled mosques which, for the first time, left the pages of the *One Thousand and One Nights* to materialize in bricks and glass under the curious, or suspicious, looks of non-Muslim neighbors (Metcalf 1996). Unsurprisingly, nationality and ethnicity became less relevant to the understanding of the Muslim communities. New scholarly studies as well as popular press started to focus on "Muslims in Europe", "young Muslims", "Muslim communities", "Muslim girls", "Muslim women", and "Muslim teachers".[4] Thus, Islam became a keyword through which to make sense of the immigrants' *otherness*. The awareness that the, now redefined, Muslim immigration was a permanent feature of UK society, redirected the attention to the difficulties that Muslim immigrants had to face in the new environment to maintain their Muslim identity and community.

However, the tendency to see religion as the main element that could prevent Muslims from integrating within the "modern", "civilized" and "secular" western democracies increased at the end of 1980s. Two events, the less known Honeyford Affair (in 1984), and the evergreen Rushdie Affair (in 1989) seemed to confirm a previously alleged incompatibility between what were indicated as "western" and "Islamic" values. For the first time, in these "affairs" and in an exponential way, the western mass media played a central role in shaping the debate on Muslims in the West. Ray Honeyford did succeed in attracting both the mass media as well as the angry attention of the English Muslim community. In 1984, Ray Honeyford, who was the headmaster of Drummond Road Middle School in Bradford, England, published a controversial newspaper article (see Halstead 1998 and Lewis 1994 for the discussion of the article) asking for the rejection of "the multi-racial myth". At the centre of his call for the defence of an alleged Britishness was the rejection of "barbaric" Islamic customs, symbolized, in this case, by the Islamic slaughtering style. Honeyford mentioned it because of the *halal* meat his school had to provide to the Muslim pupils. According to him, the "barbaric" practice, which lacked any British sensitivity, was tolerated in the name of a dangerous politically-correct multiculturalism, which would finally kill what he perceived to be more civilized British values. By crying for the cruel destiny of British cows at the hands of Muslim butchers, he called for an assimilation policy that, through the denial of Muslim children's religious identity, could transform them into perfect "British subjects". Despite wide support from the right-wing press and various bourgeois members of the white middle classes, the South Asian protests, and the too visibly racially motivated argument forced him to take early retirement and to keep his opinions to himself.

The Honeyford affair highlighted the relevance that Islam as a religion and expression of identity had, not only for the immigrants, but also for their children (Halstead 1998 and Lewis 1994). In conclusion, if we analyze the Honeyford affair from an anthropological perspective, we can observe that four elements were part of it: religious identity, national identity, community affiliation, and, in particular, loyalty. The last one would play a fundamental role in the Rushdie affair. In 1989, *The Satanic Verses* was published, and on February 14, 1989, the Ayatollah Khomeini responded by issuing a *fatwa*, albeit an ineffective one, calling for the death of Rushdie, who ended up protected by the British Government. If the British Government could save Rushdie from hell, it could not avoid the global Muslim protests that the publication of the book triggered and culminated in the famous UK book-burning demonstration in Bradford, on January 14 1989. Journalists, politicians as well as ordinary non-Muslims questioned the "loyalty" of their host Muslim population. Yet, during my research ten years later, I was able to appreciate how some of the people who were involved in the riots and book-burning rituals, were unable to foresee the socio-political consequences of their acts of protest. One of my respondents, who took part in the protests, holding a placard asking the British government to sentence Rushdie to death, observed: "We had protested as we used to do in our country". Indeed, the protests organized in London and Manchester resembled those of Karachi or Tehran.

The act of protesting is culturally formed in that we learn what is socially acceptable in a protest, so that we can even decide consciously to break the rules to achieve the maximum impact and attention. Yet this was not a conscious decision in the case of the book-burning ritual organized that day in Manchester. To burn an object considered evil is not unusual among many Muslim societies; actually it is an appropriate behaviour to demonstrate the personal rejection of evil. So, those involved in the famous January protest had no real knowledge that for non-Muslim Europeans book-burning would be nothing less than a horrible historical déjà vu. Yet even the anthropologists who discussed *The Satanic Verses* Affair missed this simple observation. Many interpreted the Rushdie Affair as a symptom of the deep frustration of British Muslims and Muslims living in other parts of Europe. Others have emphasized the symbolic value of the event (Modood 1990, Asad 1990, Halliday 1995). Some have provided a cultural symbolic analysis which, on the one hand, has challenged the orientalistic stereotypes of the "uncivilized" Muslim, and on the other, has attempted to demonstrate that the reactions were not just visceral. Werbner has thus concluded that the British Muslim rebellion against *The Satanic Verses* was the product of the clash between two distinct aesthetics, and between two distinct moralities or worldviews, "the confrontation was between equal aesthetic communities, each defending its own high culture." (2002: 10)

The events of 9/11 have not facilitated the dialogue between the Muslim communities within the UK and the mainstream society. Rather, the perception of Muslims (seen and perceived as a monolithic entity) as an enemy within has affected the lives of young Muslims, as Hopkins (2004) has observed. I can report an experience I had in Glasgow. During one of my first research trips to Glasgow, I was looking for the central mosque. I reached the bus station and, equipped with Glasgow Mosque's address and postal code, reached the information desk of the bus company. First, my intention was to enquire which bus number I should take in order to reach the mosque. My previous experience with the same information desk was a very positive one. Indeed, the lady kindly directed me to the right number to reach Glasgow Barlinnie Prison. This time, however, to my standard question, I receive a non-standard answer. I found myself questioned, "Why are you going there?" "Are you Muslim?" "Which is your country?" and "What do you have in your bag?" I understood that I would never receive the information that I needed. There were many taxis outside the bus station, and for this reason, I decided to take a taxi. I approached one driver and told him the place and address I wished to reach. When, however, I said the words "Glasgow Mosque", he rudely opened his car door and said, "There is no taxi for Muslims." I insisted, "What about academics studying Muslims?" His answer changed in words but not in meaning: "There are no taxis going to the mosque." Before ending in a dangerous confrontation, I gave up. "Of course," I thought, "I have got the wrong guy." So I asked another driver of a different taxi company. This time the answer was even more sarcastic: "Are you a terrorist?" I found the situation anthropologically interesting but, at the same time, humanly upsetting. I decided to stop a police officer, who was walking nearby, and to report the facts. The answer let me wonder whether in Scotland Islamophobia is not more institutionalized than some scholars have argued. Indeed, the policeman briefly told me that he could not force a taxi driver to go to a location that made the driver feel uncomfortable, and, as far as the bus company's customer service desk was concerned, the policeman informed me that they had no obligation to know where the mosque was.

My interviews with some young Pakistanis in Glasgow have confirmed that to be discriminated against by some employees of the city transport companies is not an exception but rather the rule. Hopkins (2004: 259) has observed, "racism sees the reconstruction of the discourse of 'the Asian' reconstituted through the foregrounding of 'the Muslim'." We may wonder whether this religious-centric racism may have an impact on the integration process of both Muslim migrants and their children. Saeed *et al* (1999) have suggested that this may not be the case. Indeed, they have observed that the majority of Scottish young Muslims define themselves as "Scottish Muslims". From my research, I can confirm that the majority of my respondents defined themselves as "Scottish Muslims", and their parents were also proud to emphasize that their accent was becoming "more Scottish". Indeed, "Scottishness", as Kiely *et al* (2001: 36) have argued, could be formed by emphasizing different characteristics, such as place of birth, ancestry, place of residence, length of residence, upbringing and education, name, accent, physical appearance, dress and commitment to place. Indeed, while the Muslim children claimed "Scottishness" because of their place of birth, their parents emphasized the commitment to place. Although I agree that Muslims, in particular of Pakistani and Bangladeshi origin, have developed a certain social identity, which includes the category "Scottish". However, if being part of Scotland, or the UK in general, is relevant to the social identity-formation of my respondents, their being Muslim is essential to their personal identity. All the studies conducted in the UK concerning the Muslim community have confirmed the centrality that Islam has in the formation of identity of both Muslims locally born as well as migrants (cf. Saeed *et al* 1999, Hopkins 2004, Wardak 2002)

Yet this very identity, which is expressed in different ways, is perceived as dangerous, threatening, and destabilizing, not only by some ordinary members of the public but also politicians and members of the British clergies. Some politicians' comments, after the atrocity of 7/7, clearly aimed to increase public concerns and fear of Muslims and overall sense of suspicion, through raising particular sensitive issues in a very insensitive way. For instance, on 20th of September 2006, Home Secretary, Mr Reid, in his first speech to a Muslim audience in London, after noticing that "There is no nice way of saying this. These fanatics are looking to groom and brainwash children, including your children, for suicide bombings, grooming them to kill themselves in order to murder others", asked the Muslims parents to "keep an eye" on their children and report any suspicious behavior.[5] Despite the high level of security, one of the most notoriously controversial Muslim clerics in the UK, Abu Izzadeen, was allowed to attend the speech. Of course, the clash was inevitable, and Abu Izzadeen, in his classic rhetorical style, defined the Home Secretary an "enemy of Islam", and questioned him as to why he was coming to speak in a "Muslim area". Of course, we cannot believe that the police and security officers had not recognized Abu Izzadeen and that Mr Reid would not have expected his reaction. The Home Secretary's speech achieved two relevant results. To begin with, he further alienated moderate Muslims by implying that Muslim parents were not capable of managing their families, and that they had to even spy on their own children.[6] Secondly, by allowing the presence of a very famous extremist cleric, he has guaranteed that the mass media would have one more headline among the many which infer that Islam is a threat to our way of life as we know it.

We did not need to wait for an entire month before witnessing another unsolicited attack on the already tormented Muslim community. This time, on 21st of November 2006, Mr Straw, the Leader of the Commons, wrote an article in the *Lancashire Telegraph*, in which he argued that covering people's faces could make community relations more difficult, and this threatened community relationships. Consequentially, he would ask Muslim women attending his surgery to remove their veil (actually, he intended the *niqab*, the cloth covering the mouth and not the *hijab*, the head scarf). Mr Straw is the MP of a constituency with a large Muslim population. His comments triggered strong reactions among the Muslim community, although only two percent of Muslim women in the UK wear a *niqab*. The comments triggered a series of attacks on Muslim women in Liverpool and other cities. Even a student of mine, just wearing the *hijab*, was verbally abused more than once before reaching the University and my office.

The problem is not the debate in itself, but the continuous focus on Muslims as Muslims, as if they were a monolithic entity. This process, which involves politicians and in particular the mass media, risks not only to reinforce stereotypes but to create what Langmuir (1990) has called *chimerias*. Discussing anti-Semitism, Langmuir (1990) has coined the neologism chimeria[7] to define this characteristic of anti-Semitism. He pointed out that anti-Semitism is not just another form of xenophobia since "Chimerical assertions have no 'kernel of truth' while xenophobic have" (1990b: 334). In other words, xenophobic stereotypes manipulate real-life elements. To say that all Italians are "Mafiosi" is certainly xenophobic but it is not a chimeria, since there is a kernel of truth" in the fact that some Italians are "Mafiosi". For the same reason Langmuir has described the hostility against Jews in ancient Alexandria as xenophobic rather than anti-Semitic. By contrast, chimerical stereotypes formed the ideological Nazi anti-Semitism of the 1930s. Langmuir has suggested that these chimerias started and spread because of political interests and the use of "fear" as a political tool of mass control. It is my contention that with the start of the War on Terror, Muslims have started to suffer from a very similar process. An example of the new formation of chimerias concerning Muslims can be found in two authors, who, however, are becoming very representative of a certain type of political discourse.

Bat Ye'or (a pseudonym meaning "daughter of the Nile") is certainly a less romantic scholar than her name might suggest. She mixes concepts such as *jihad, dhimmitude* and anti-Semitism to form what we can read as anti-Muslim Protocols (see Ye'or 2004). To understand her "scholarly" production it is necessary to know that she is an independent Jewish scholar living in Switzerland who suffered the emotional experience of exile when in 1948 Egypt expelled, among others, her family. Reading her last production, less academic but increasingly influential in the discussion of Muslim anti-Semitism, we may get the impression that Bat Ye'or is crusading against Islam and Muslims. Her argument is popularly straightforward; Islam means submission, all contemporary Muslims dream of submitting non-Muslims and transforming them into *dhimmi*. In doing this, Muslims conduct two *jihads*, one violent and criminal, the other manipulative in trying to Islamicize the European political left. This is the gist of Bat Ye'or's main argument. Recently she has concluded,

> Europe's hidden war against Israel is wrapped in the Palestinian flag, and is part of a global movement that is transforming Europe into a new continent of dhimmitude within a world strategy of jihad and da'wa, the latter being the pacific method of Islamization. The implementation program [*sic*] of this policy of dhimmitude for the Euro-Arabian continent [*sic*] is set forth in the Rapport du Comité des Sages submitted to the European Commission President Romano Prodi in October 2003. This program, entitled "Dialogue between Peoples and Cultures in the Euro-Mediterranean region" was accepted by the European Union in December 2003. Unfortunately, the policy of "Dialogue" with Arab League nations, wilfully pursued by Europe for the past three decades, has promoted European dhimmitude and rabid Judeophobia. (Bat Ye'or 2004)

Not only does Bat Ye'or have to decontextualize the Islamic concept of *dhimmi* but she has also suggested that Muslims could use it in the same way they have done since the time of the first Caliph (*khalifa*). She has tried to create a new chimeria in which Muslims are the conspirators against the Judaeo-Christian civilized world.

Another example is Melanie Philips' book *Londonistan* (2006). Although Philips, in the first instance, seems to attack Muslims extremists, it becomes evident that Muslims in general[8] are under charge, either because they "refuse to accept *minority status* and insisted instead that their values must trump those of the majority" (2006: 28, italics mine), or because "playing on the pathological fear of prejudice created by victim culture, leading Muslims refuse to *accept responsibility* for Islamist violence, blame the British government instead for siding with America over Afghanistan and Iraq, and denounce any resistance to the imposition of an Islamic perspective as 'Islamophobia.'" (2006: 28). So, in conclusion, here is the chimeria, "The West is under threat from an enemy that has shrewdly observed the decadence and disarray in Europe, where Western civilization first began. And the greatest disarray of all is in Britain, the very cradle of Western liberty and democracy, but whose cultural confusion is now plain for all to see in Londonistan ... Whether it will finally pull itself together and stop sleepwalking into cultural oblivion is a question on which the future of the West may now depend" (2006: 285). Unfortunately, another country, in 1930s, finally pulled itself together and stopped sleepwalking into cultural oblivion; the result was 6,000,000 people killed. This, of course, is a provocative observation, but the process through which Europeans discriminated against Jews as the enemy within and then persecuted them does not appear to be so different from the ways in which some scholars, politicians and journalists have demonized Muslims as the "anti-civilizing" force attacking our democracies.

The Circle of Panic

Wolfendale (2007), as well as many Liberal Democratic MPs, have argued that the New Labour Government has increasingly played the card of "fear" to find support among the public for controversial policies challenging civil liberties and European human rights legislation. It needs a very simple reflection to understand how the fear of falling victim to terrorist activities is exaggerated if compared with other, more commonplace dangers that we face in the world: 500,000 people who are killed every year by light weapons and the 3.9 million annual deaths from diseases like influenza, 2.9 million annual deaths from HIV-AIDS, 2.1 million annual deaths because of diarrhoea and 1.7 million annual deaths from tuberculosis (see Jackson 2005). Nonetheless, the mass media tends to reinforce the "official" position of government (Cram 2006) and provide a sensationalistic as well as simplistic view of the involvement of young Muslims in terrorist activities. Yet, these controversial headlines and such an overemphasis on young British Muslims being involved in suicide operations have achieved a dangerous effect: the spreading of panic among non-Muslims and Muslims alike. On the one hand, non-Muslims, but also Muslims, fear becoming victims of *jihad*, on the other, however, only Muslims fear becoming victims of Islamophobic attacks and inaccurate intelligence leading to home raids and arrests.[9] Yet Muslims in the UK, particularly when of Pakistani origin, remain the dangerous stereotyped *other* per-definition within an emotionally scarred mainstream society.

Bhabha (1994) has suggested that stereotyping is not only a fixed representation of the subject in the construction of the colonial "other", but also a process similar to fetishism. "The fetish or stereotype gives access to an 'identity' which is predicated as much on mastery and pleasure as it is on anxiety and defence, for it is a form of multiple and contradictory beliefs in its recognition of difference and the disavowal of it" (1994: 75). In this complex process, contradictions between the known and imagined become the reality of representation. In other words, the object is understood not in its integrity but as metonymy. Bhabha has emphasized how the identity of the "other" becomes fetishized not for the sake of false representation which may become "the scapegoat of discrimination", but for "the fantasy that dramatizes the impossible desire for a pure, undifferentiated origin" of the colonizer (1994: 81). The rhetorical question "Are you ... or Muslim?", this metonymical re-imagination of Muslim identity through stereotypes, emotionally destabilizes young Muslims' identities. The young Muslims find themselves projected into parallel dimensions in which ethical and moral, as well as political, values may become cacophonic, almost schizophrenic. For some Western societies, such as Britain, these Western-born Muslims represent the materialization of an unwanted and unplanned post-colonial present, as their parents represented the objectification—this time, desired and wished for—of a glorious colonial empire (see Doty 2003: 44–57). The colonizer's resistance to the self-determination of the colonized used to repeat "you belong to us". Now, in an inverted performance of power, the former colonizer feels colonized and asks "are you one of us?" Bhabha has discussed this process under the label of "mimicry". "Mimicry is the desire for a reformed, recognizable Other, as subject of a difference that is almost the same, but not quite, which is to say, that the discourse of mimicry is constructed around an ambivalence; in order to be effective mimicry it must continually produce its slippage, its excess, its difference" (1994: 86). The colonized, through mimicry, become part of the process that defines the colonizer. In other words, the colonized claim power by being the "Other" of him/herself. Mimicry is a form of political and identity mockery that may leave the subject personal self because, as Bhabha has observed, he/she is "almost the same but not white: the visibility of mimicry is always produced at the site of interdiction. It is a form of colonial discourse at the crossroads of what is known and permissible and that which though known must be kept concealed" (1994: 89). Almost the same but not British, the denial of authenticity became, for some of my respondents, the trap of their "I" set in a difficult ubiquity, a form of eternal questioning that if they wanted to become "real" they had to answer.

It is also true that an increasing number of Muslims in the UK are highly concerned about their future and the possibility of being victims of the anti-terrorist legislation which was supposed to protect them, as British citizens. Islam becomes something more than just a religion (Marranci 2006). We have seen that British Muslims are certainly not monolithic as far as ethnicity and nationality are concerned. Furthermore, there are also internal divisions expressed through religious affiliations, such as, in the case of the South Asians, Deobandi and Barelvi. Notwithstanding these divisions, Muslims in the UK have often pointed to the discourse of the *umma* (the community of believers) as a metaphysical place of unity. The concept of *umma* has been explained and analyzed from different viewpoints: theological, historical, sociological and anthropological. While the theological approach has highlighted the different ideas of *umma* in the Islamic sources, the historical approach has explored the first experiences of the Muslim community, in particular the case of Medina, in reference to the theological conceptualization of *umma*. The majority of anthropologists have based their understanding of *umma* through the emic interpretations provided during ethnographic research (see for instance Lukens-Bull 2005), while sociologists have preferred to focus on the aspects of social belonging to the group and social identities. Yet none of these approaches has been free from essentialism. One of the reasons for this essentialism is the lack of attention to the divisions, religious sectarianism, and even racism existing among Muslims. This leads to a paradox: Muslims acknowledge the divisions, but do not see them as a factual denial of the *umma* beyond a general religious rhetoric. Social scientists also have evidence that a certain collective sense of belonging is visible among Muslims, in particular during times of crisis, such as the Rushdie Affair or the more recent Danish Cartoons. In order to avoid essentialism but at the same time explaining this trans-national, trans-ethnical, and often trans-sectarian (Sunni versus Shi'a) sense of belonging, I have suggested that we need to reconsider the role that emotions and feelings have in it.

Notwithstanding the visible antagonisms existing among Muslims, a vivid rhetoric of a single, united, *umma* is, from an emic viewpoint, acknowledged. Evidence of global reactions to local incidents involving offences to Islam, its Prophet, or Muslims in general, confirm that in certain circumstances, Muslims are able to put aside differences in order to find a unity behind the concept of *umma* as the physical body of Islam, instead of regrouping around a single charismatic leader. Maffesoli (1996) has suggested that communities are not based on rational, but rather emotional processes producing a sense of ethos, which can be shared among members who are connected not merely through physicality but by empathy. If we observe how Muslims discuss and represent the conceptualization of the *umma*, it is not difficult to recognize a strong similarity to Maffesoli's "community of emotions". Indeed, although different forms of sectarianisms exist among Muslims, they can be considered as part of an internal dynamic, which, however, does not contradict or deny the shared, and fundamental, basic ethos. Whenever, as in the case of the Rushdie Affair, Palestinian Intifada, Danish Cartoons, and other less known or minor incidents, the *umma* is threatened by external forces, the shared ethos is, or seems to be that the internal dynamic is suspended in favour of a visible unity.

We have to notice now, that a very similar process is starting among people living in the West since 9/11. Politicians, the mass media, and commentators have increasingly referred to the "civilized West", the West as a monolithically "Judeo-Christian" entity as well as terrorism, or in the case of some right-wing politicians and commentators (see Phillips 2006), Islam itself, the anti-western force, the anti-civilizing enemy. To use an allegory, we may say that they represent the West represented as a secular God and secular civilization (i.e. secularism) his religion (Asad 2003). In an expression, we can represent the essentialization of both the West and the *umma* as well as Islam and secularism in this equation the West :: *Umma* = Secularization :: Islam. The events of the War on Terror have radicalized not just the viewpoint of some Muslims but also the viewpoint of many people living in the so-called western world. On the one hand, the misleading concept of civilization, at the very heart of the British Empire's colonial missions, (Van Krieken 1999), is today recycled within a new rhetoric of good and evil, in which the evil is the rebellious Other. On the other, extremists, dreaming of Hollywood-style *jihads* against crusaders, recycle *hadiths* and decontextualized Qur'an verses to transform the holy concept of martyrdom into a philosophy of violence against "the western Satan".

Recently, even the director of public prosecutions, Sir Ken Macdonald, "warned of the pernicious risk that a "fear-driven and inappropriate" response to the threat could lead Britain to abandon respect for fair trials and the due process of law" (Clare Dyer 2004, *The Guardian*, Wednesday, January 24, *There is no war on terror*). This process resembles a vicious circle in which the over use of emotional appeals, megaphoned through the power of the mass media, has affected mainstream societies as well as host communities. The panic is created through the lack of meaning associated to symbols and stereotypes concerning a particular group seen as dangerous but also mysterious. Bhabha (1994) has described this process through the analysis of the 1857 Uprising in British India. Rumors started concerning the new Lee-Enfield Rifle used by the troops, among both Muslims and Hindus. The rumors suggested that the water-resistant paper used to load the rifle was greased in pig and cow fats. Since soldiers had to tear it with their teeth, this severely offended both Muslim and Brahmin soldiers in the Company army. Finally, after the British officers punished their Indian, Muslim and Hindu, soldiers for refusing to use the rifle, on May 10, 1857, the whole regiment mutinied and killed their British commanders. So, Bhabha has suggested that circles of panic are caused by "the indeterminate circulation of meaning as rumor or conspiracy, with its perverse, physical affects of panic" (1994: 200).

It is my contention that the circle of panic is affecting both the Muslim communities and mainstream British society. This creates a dangerous misunderstanding of each other, which, however, politicians are exploiting for their own propaganda purposes. A recent example can confirm the perverse logic of increasing the circle of panic as a method of mass control. As the BBC online announced, MI5 has recently introduced a new public service, which in future will send text messages to inform British citizens of the terrorist threat level, and when this reaches "imminent" level.[10] Since terrorist threats today are connoted as Islamic, such a service can only enhance the fear of Muslims, and increase Islamophobia and discrimination, but I suppose it cannot save one life from a recondite terrorist attack (unless people will renounce their everyday activities upon receiving the MI5 text message). It is clear how this new service, paid for by the British taxpayer, is only useful to increase paranoia and fear. Yet the circle of panic is exactly what the knights of the political War on Terror and the *jihadis* of global terror without politics envisage.

Conclusions

The War on Terror is continuing on as well as the terrorist threats. Ordinary everyday life is often counterpointed by news of explosions, killed people, plots and assassinations, of invasions and enemies within. As the director of public prosecutions, Sir Ken Macdonald has pointed out, the New Labour policies, such as allowing the indefinite detention of suspected terrorists without trial (which was then rejected by the courts,) and the replacement law that permits suspects to be placed under control orders instead of being brought to trial as well as the government's temptations to opt-out from the European Convention on Human Rights, can increase, instead of reduce, the risk of terrorism in the UK because of the alienating effect that these legislations can have on young Muslims. In other words, what the critical voices, from within the parliament to civil society, seems to suggest is that the British Government is actually facilitating the spread of the circle of panic instead of preventing it. However, what the government cannot control is the formation of chimerias that the panic may produce.

Muslim communities within the UK (and the rest of Europe) are not just suffering from xenophobia, racism, Islamophobia, discrimination and an intolerable intrusion in all aspects of Muslim life from the mass media, but also witnessing the formation of dangerous chimerias, not very dissimilar from those accusing Jewish people in the infamous *Protocols of Zion*. In this chapter, we have observed some of these chimerias; the commonest of which is the claim that Islam is a dangerous and violent religion aiming to subject non-Muslims and the great "superior" Western Judeo-Christian civilization to *dhimmitude* through *jihad*. The discourse on civilization reinforces the idea that barbaric people are pushing, with their barbaric rudimental weapons, on the physical and metaphysical border of our democratic civilized lands. The tensions which these chimerias have created have pushed the Muslim community in the UK into a defensive position, isolated and mistrusted, facing delegitimizing and dehumanizing campaigns. Of course, an increasing number of Muslims have entered the circle of panic and are questioning whether there will be a future for them in their own country, the UK.

The reactions to the circle of panic, however, can be also varied, as I have explained in my recent book *Jihad Beyond Islam* (Marranci 2006). In some Muslims, the circle of panic can lead them to develop what I have defined as a rhetoric of *jihad*, a way to express their identity in a context which is constantly denied. In few cases, as with the members of the 7/7 attacks, the rhetoric can give away to action, a self-destruction in which killing oneself in the act of killing others exorcize, at the same time, the suicide-bomber's fear by materializing the fear on his or her victims. Indeed, nobody can any more alienate or deny the chosen identity of the 7/7 perpetrators. The blood of their victims and their own has written an indelible page of tragic history. They knew that the "civilized West" can kill thousands of innocent lives in their War on Terror (as in Iraq or recently in Somalia), and both the killer and the killed will remain invisible, unknown to the majority. Yet they knew that the "civilized West" stop minutes for their own victims, remember the victims and do not forget the executioners. Rather, their action will reinforce the panic and the chimerias affecting the Muslim community. This is exactly what, for different reasons, both the Muslim extremists and the British Government want. However, are the reasons so different when we reduce them to the minimum? The British Government has been accused by Liberal Democrats of trying to achieve a political and social hegemony among its citizens by maintaining a continuous sense of insecurity and danger. Through the circle of panic, the violent extremists want to achieve a political and social hegemony among Muslims. Indeed, these violent extremists are still a tiny minority and have no hope of taking emotional control of the *umma*. Yet the actions and counter actions between them and the British Government, with the consequent circles of panics, can alienate the majority of Muslims and facilitate that rhetoric of *jihad* which the violent extremists need in order to have a chance to develop from a inconsiderable minority into a formidable and threatening majority.

Notes

1. For more information see *The Guardian*, 12/10.2004 http://www.guardian.co.uk/uk_news/story/0,3604,1324962,00.html
2. Sometimes maintaining in the titles, the ethnic or national denomination as in "Muslim Pakistanis".

3. See, for instance, Bhatti 1981, Werbner 1980 and 1981, as well as Wilson 1981.

4. Just to cite some examples, see Anwar 1982 and 1984, Barton 1986, Mildenberger 1982, Nielsen 1981, Qureshi 1983.

5. See BBC Wednesday, 20 September 2006 http://news.bbc.co.uk/1/hi/uk/5362052. stm as well as *The Guardian*, Thursday September 21, 2006 "Defiant Reid clashes with Islamist radicals".

6. Yet the Home Secretary has certainly not required non-Muslim white families the same surveillance as far as drugs, violent crime, and anti-social behaviour is concerned.

7. The Chimera is a mythological monster.

8. With some clear exceptions, based on what she called the "Israel-Zionism" test, i.e. if a Muslim accepts Israel as a legitimate state and Zionism as a democratic and civilizing force in the region.

9. See *The Guardian*, "Two brothers held in armed raid on home released without charge" Saturday June 10, 2006.

10. See BBC News, Tuesday, 9 January 2007 http://news.bbc.co.uk/1/hi/uk/6242883. stm.

References

Anwar, M. (1979) *The Myth of Return: Pakistanis in Britain*, London: Heinemann.

—— (1982) *Young Muslims in a Multi-Cultural Society: Their Educational Needs and Policy Implications*. London: The Islamic Foundation.

—— (1984) "Employment patterns of Muslims in Western Europe," *Journal: Institute of Muslim Minority Affairs* 5(1): 99–122.

Barton, S. (1986) *The Bengali Muslims of Bradford*. Leeds: University of Leeds.

Bhabha, H. (1994) *The Location of Culture*. London and New York: Routledge.

Bhatti, F. M. (1981) "Turkish Cypriots in London," *Research Papers: Muslims in Europe* 11, Birmingham: Centre for the Study of Islam and Christian–Muslim Relations, pp. 1–20.

Cram, I. (2006) "Regulating the media: some neglected freedom of expression issues in the United Kingdom's counter-terrorism strategy," *Terrorism and Political Violence* 18: 335–355.

Doty, R. L. (2003) *Anti-Immigrantism in Western Democracies*. London and New York: Routledge.

Halliday, F. (1995) "Islam is in Danger: Authority, Rushdie and the struggle for the migrant soul", in *The Next Threat: Western perceptions of Islam*, J. Hippler and A. Lueg, eds. London: Pluto, pp. 71–81.

Halstead, M. (1988) *Education, Justice And Cultural Diversity: An Examination of the Honeyford Affair 1984–85*, London: Falmer.

Hopkins, P. E. (2004) "Everyday racism in Scotland: a case study of East Pollokshields in Glasgow", *Scottish Affairs* 49(3).

Huntington, S. (1996) *The Clash of Civilizations*. New York: Simon and Schuster.

Jackson, R, (2005) *Writing the War on Terror: Language, Politics and Counter-terrorism*. Manchester: Manchester University Press,.

Kiely, R., F. Bechhofer, R. Stewart and D. McCrone (2001) "The markers and rules of Scottish national identity", *Sociological Review* 49(1): 33–55.

Langmuir, G. (1990) *Toward a Definition of Antisemitism*. Berkeley: University of California Press.

Lewis, B. and Schnapper, D., eds. (1994) *Muslims in Europe.* London: Pinter.

Lukens-Bull , R. A. (2005) *A Peaceful Jihad.* New York: Palgrave Macmillan.

Maffesoli, M. (1996) *The Time of the Tribes.* London: Sage.

Marranci, G. (2006) *Jihad Beyond Islam.* Oxford: Berg.

Metcalf, B. D., ed. (1996) *Making Muslim Space in Northern America and Europe.* Berkeley: California University Press.

Mildenberger, M. (1982) "What place for Europe's Muslims? Integration or segregation?", Research Papers: Muslims in Europe, No 13, Birmingham: Centre for the Study of Islam and Christian-Muslim Relations.

Modood, T. (1990) "The British Asian Muslims and the Rushdie affair", *The Political Quarterly* 62(2): 143–60.

Nielsen, J. S. (1981) "Muslims in Europe: an overview", Research Papers: Muslims in Europe, No 12, Birmingham: Centre for the Study of Islam and Christian-Muslim Relations.

Philips, M. (2006) *Londonistan: How Britain is Creating a Terror State Within.* London: Gibson Sqare.

Qureshi, R. B. (ed.) (1983) *The Muslim Community in North America.* Edmonton: University of Alberta Press.

Saeed, A., N. Blain and D. Forbes (1999) "New ethnic and national questions in Scotland: post-British identities among Glasgow Pakistani teenagers", *Ethnic and Racial Studies* 22(5): 821–844.

Talal, A. (1990) "Ethnography, Literature, and Politics: Some Readings and Uses of Salman Rushdie's *The Satanic Verses*", *Cultural Anthropology* 5(3): 239–69.

—— (2003) *Formations of the Secular: Christianty, Islam, Modernity,* Stanford: Stanford University Press.

Van Krieken, R. (1999) "The barbarism of civilization: cultural genocide and the 'stolen generations'," *British Journal of Sociology* 50(2): 297–315.

Wardak A. (2002) "The Mosque and Social Control in Edinburgh's Muslim Community", *Culture and Religion* 3(2): 201–219.

Werbner, P. (1980) "Rich man, poor man, or a community of suffering: heroic motifs in Manchester Pakistanis' life histories", *Oral History* 8: 43–48.

—— (1981) "From rags to riches: Manchester Pakistanis in the textile trade", *New Community* 9: 216– 29.

—— (2002) *Imagined Diaspora among Manchester Muslims.* Oxford: James Curry.

Wilson, A. (1981) *Finding a Voice: Asian Women in Britain.* London: Virago.

Wolfendale, J. (2007) "Terrorism, security, and the threat of counterterrorism," *Studies in Conflict & Terrorism* 30: 75–92.

Ye'or, B. (1978) *Dhimmi People: Oppressed Nations.* Geneva: World Organization of Jews from Arab Countries.

7 Education and Social Cohesion in Malaysia and Indonesia

Julie Chernov Hwang

Introduction

How can education foster social cohesion and improve social order? When states provide public and religious education, they encourage peaceful coexistence among ethnic and religious groups by reducing inequalities amongst groups and providing access to the channels for social mobility through increased job skills. States also utilize education to reduce the likelihood of conflict by employing the education system to spread values of tolerance, mutual aid, and understanding through their set curricular standards for both public and religious education. Furthermore, in providing education, the state gains a measure of legitimacy for being effective and capable.

However, the government is not alone in using education as a means of increasing pluralism and improving inter-communal relations. Religious education providers also play a role, especially in the Islamic world. This may come as a surprise to some scholars and politicians. Today, many studies of Islamic education highlight the role played by a minority of radical *madrasas* in violent conflicts and sectarian strife. However, the role of radical *madrasas* is grossly overstated. Even in Pakistan, where the state has retrenched substantially in the provision of education, ceding the sphere to Islamic and private education providers, it is estimated that only 10–15 per cent of all boarding schools are highly sectarian or radical.[1] In Indonesia and

Malaysia, there are only a handful of radical schools in operation. Indeed, Islamic educational institutions often are a positive force in the community. Islamic education providers often teach their students in a manner that emphasizes tolerance of different religious perspectives, interpretations, and communities. They may foster social cohesion by providing community development assistance in surrounding towns. Finally, given that the head-masters of Islamic boarding schools are often community leaders, Islamic boarding schools also have the capacity to lead efforts in conflict resolution and mediation, thus reducing sectarian violence and inter-communal conflict. This speaks to the great potential for education in Muslim countries.

In real terms, how is the Muslim world faring in the provision of education? Muslim nations are lagging behind the developing and developed world in the provision of higher education and prioritization of research and development funding (Hassan 2006). This is indeed true, as statistics from the *Times Higher Education Supplement* indicate (*ibid*). However, the picture is not so bleak. For the past three decades, Malaysia and Indonesia have made the improvement of primary, secondary and tertiary education a top government priority. This study contends that the Malaysian and Indonesian Governments recognized the utility of investing in education to promote national unity, improve social mobility, reduce poverty and increase social cohesion. In their efforts, they have been assisted by Islamic organizations, most notably the Malaysian Islamic Youth Movement (ABIM) in Malaysia and Nahdlatul Ulama (NU) in Indonesia. In both countries, impressive strides have been made. This chapter will highlight those accomplishments.

First, this study will analyze the underlying mechanisms through which education can be an engine for social integration. Then, it will outline the advances in the governments' provision of education as a means of promoting social mobility and economic prosperity. Third, it will assess how Indonesia and Malaysia provide for primary and secondary education to strengthen national unity, stability and cohesion. Next, it will examine how major Islamic organizations have assisted in the provision of Islamic education. Finally, it will address those groups that seek to undermine social cohesion and examine the potential threats they pose.

Before proceeding further, it is necessary to define what is meant by social cohesion and establish the boundaries of education. Robert Putnam explains social cohesion as a term that encompasses "issues of social justice, tolerance, inclusion and social integration" (Putnam 2005: 2). To instill these values in young people, education is becoming a crucial link between government and youth. Putnam notes that as governments are becoming more concerned with social cohesion, due to increased ethno-religious diversity and socio-economic inequality, education has become the single most effective means of increasing that sense of national unity and inter-cultural tolerance (*ibid*: 5). This is especially true in primary and secondary education. As a result, this study will focus primarily on primary and secondary education. While Malaysia and Indonesia are strong providers of tertiary education vis-à-vis their fellow majority Muslim nations, this study will only briefly touch on university education.

Education as Mechanism for Social Cohesion

Education's socio-economic benefits have been well established. Investment in education by states can be an important force for reducing poverty. When Indonesia and Malaysia began expanding access to education in the 1970s and 1980s in tandem with other economic development programs, poverty rates dropped significantly. Poverty decreased in Indonesia from 60 per cent in 1965 to 16 per cent in 1996[2] and in Malaysia from 74 per cent in 1970 to 6 per cent in 1994 (Abuza 2003: 50). Increased opportunity for primary, secondary and tertiary education bears partial responsibility for these substantial shifts.

However, education provides more than economic opportunity. Education has a direct impact on social cohesion and civic engagement (Putnam 2005: 5, Mujani 2003: 159). Mujani contends that educated people are less likely to be intolerant toward disliked groups, and more likely to be supportive of values such as equality, freedom, and tolerance (2003: 247). Putnam concurs, noting that the learning process can inculcate students with factual information about public life and can instill norms of open-mindedness and skills such as cooperation (2005: 6). However, this is not simply a passive mechanism through which students are taught these desirable values. There is also an element of active learning. In the classroom and outside it, students can interact with students of diverse backgrounds and viewpoints. By working in groups, they learn the value of collaboration and of resolving differences peaceably. There is also considerable evidence that more educated people are more likely to form networks and work through those groups to achieve their goals, rather than resort to violence and anti-system activities (Putnam 2005: 6, Mujani 2003: 159). If one examines those groups working for an Islamic state in Indonesia today, the ones with an educated membership eschew violence and work through political channels to achieve that goal.[3] These include Hizbut Tahrir, the Crescent and Star Party and the Prosperous Justice Party. Groups like the Islamic Defenders Front, which tend to employ strategies of violence, including rioting and property damage, have a far less educated membership.

Mujani notes, however, that if states teach intolerance toward least liked groups in the classroom, for example, communists, this will undermine the ability of education to be a positive force in supporting social cohesion (Mujani 2003: 183–184). Likewise, Indonesian researcher I.G. Wilakuda, a scholar of radical Islamic boarding schools, explains that education alone may not foster national integration; it is important for students to study civic education to instill the values of national unity and a powerful national identity.[4] He advocates that the government encourage all Islamic boarding schools, especially radical *pesantren* like Al Mu'mim and Al Mujihideen in Solo to add courses in civic education to promote a strong national identity among *pesantren* youth.[5]

In sum, education is a powerful force for promoting social cohesion. It fosters norms of tolerance and pluralism in the classroom, while providing opportunities for students of to collaborate through assignments and extra-curricular activities. Schools may also play an important role in creating a strong national identity among young people. Educated youths are more likely to grow into adults that participate in civil society networks and work constructively through political and community channels to achieve their goals, rather than resort to strategies of violence and intimidation, which would undermine cohesion. All of this is positive for states. For decades, Indonesia and Malaysia realized the benefits brought by investing in education and have sought to do so to encourage values of national unity, integration, and tolerance.

Indonesia

Given Indonesia's ethnic, linguistic, economic and religious heterogeneity, it is imperative that institutions of national education provide opportunities for social mobility across ethno-religious and cultural groups and reinforce social cohesion. Indonesia is home to four of the five major world religions—Islam, Christianity, Hinduism and Buddhism. It has over 325 different ethnic groups and 300 different linguistic communities. The Suharto

Government understood the potential for instability that could result from the ethnically and religiously fragmented nature of the archipelago. With that in mind, the Indonesian Government, beginning in the 1970s, prioritized education with the goals of strengthening national integration; reducing poverty; and improving social welfare.

In a short time, primary education enrollment ratios rose from 62 per cent in 1973 to 97 per cent in 1985 (Van Zorge 2006: 1). Primary education levels enrollment ratios have stayed almost constant, fluctuating minimally between 95 per cent and 97 per cent over the past two decades (*ibid*). The institution of universal primary education was one of the most significant accomplishments of the New Order regime (Liddle 1996: 26). The government under Suharto established six years of compulsory education covering primary school and lower-secondary school. This was extended to nine years in 2003 with the passage of the National Education Act (RUU Sidiknas 20: 2003). However, despite the new law, enrollment ratios for secondary school remain low vis-à-vis primary school (see Table 1).[6]

The educational reforms were encapsulated in a set of policies labeled INPRES (Presidential Instruction), which provided development assistance to local governments. By the mid-1980s, the state had built health care clinics in every sub-district and paved roads to connect remote regions to urban centers (Liddle 1996: 6). The government sought to ensure that all children, even those living in the most remote areas, had access to inexpensive primary education and built thousands of new elementary schools to fill the demand for education (*ibid*). This investment in education was one important reason for the decline in poverty that began in the 1970s.

Table 1: *Enrollment and Education Duration in Indonesia 1985–2004*

	1985	1990	1995	2000	2004
Net Enrollment Ratio %					
Primary Level	97.2	96.7	95.4	93.9	94.3
Secondary Level		51.7	47.8	41.5	40.1
Duration of Education (Years)					
Primary level	6	6	6	6	6
Secondary Level	6	6	6	6	6
Compulsory Schooling				9	9

EDSTATS Summary Education Profile: Indonesia. http://devdata.worldbank.org/edstats/SummaryEducationPrifiles/CountryData/GetShowData.asp?sCtry=IDN, Indonesia.

However, the government focused on primary education to the detriment of secondary education. In the post-Suharto era, the government has taken steps to remedy this problem. In 2002, a clause was inserted into the constitution requiring the government to spend 20 per cent of its annual budget on education in addition to paying teacher salaries (Van Zorge 2006). Since 2002, education budgets have risen each year to a height in 2006 of RP 38 trillion (US$ 4.13 billion) or 10 per cent of the annual budget (*ibid*). This is a significant accomplishment but is still short of the 20 per cent marker. In 2005, the government sought to make basic education free for all children, but the program faced implementation problems due to inadequate monitoring mechanisms. The majority of public schools are still making children pay entrance fees and building maintenance fees (Khalik 2005). Thus, we can assert that Indonesia's achievements in education have been notable, but more work needs to be done.

Education for Values

The Suharto regime not only prioritized education for reasons of reducing poverty but also to inculcate students with a set of values that would promote stability within an ethnically and religiously heterogeneous nation. The government perceived these values as being encapsulated in the five principles of *Pancasila* (belief in one god, social justice, humanitarianism, unity in diversity and democracy through deliberation and consensus), so it enforced *Pancasila* as a common rallying point for national unity. Beginning in 1975, the state required students to take courses, which taught them how to apply the five principles of *Pancasila* to their daily lives. Classes in *Pancasila* (P4) and Morals Education (PMP) emphasized the virtues and values of respect for authority and hierarchy, harmony in social relations, patriotism and commitment to economic development, all of which the state felt were necessary to ensure stability (Porter 2002: 39). These values sought to cement national cohesion and to indoctrinate young Indonesians to support the government's developmentalist ideology. The state's philosophy about the role and responsibility of education as productive of social order and national identity was not just restricted to state-funded public education but also extended to Islamic education.

The government sought to ensure that Islamic education providers would also teach *Pancasila* values. To that end, the New Order began a lengthy and complicated process of setting a common standard for education that would promote national unity and patriotism for the sake of stability and development (Porter 2002: 52). This included providing incentives for Islamic schools to include general coursework in their curriculums and ensuring that all public schools include periods of state-approved religious education. However, it has been difficult for the state to integrate the two education systems, since they are run out of different government ministries; the Ministry of Religious Affairs oversees Islamic education and the Ministry of Education and Culture manages public education.

The state was most successful in influencing the development of *madrasa* education. Under Suharto, the state extended control over the *madrasa* sector to ensure compliance with P4 and PMP instruction to ensure the spread of *Pancasila* values and support for the government's development policies. They reoriented Islamic education at the *madrasas* to emphasize rationalist and comparative-scientific approaches, as a replacement for the static methods of the traditionalist schools, and standardized the *madrasa* curriculum (Pohl 2006: 4). Furthermore, new state-run *madrasas* were established with a specified curriculum of 70 per cent general studies and 30 per cent religious subjects (Murray 1998: 903). The government sought to make the diploma a student received from the *madrasa* equal to one received from a public school to increase the prestige of a *madrasa* education so that *madrasa* graduates would be accepted to institutions of higher education (*ibid*). This improved the opportunities for *madrasa* graduates to become more socially mobile and achieve a degree of economic prosperity.

The state also sought to play a role in the development and training of future *pesantren* teachers to ensure that the Islam they taught was in compliance with *Pancasila* values and the state's developmentalist goals. To that end, they expanded the State Islamic University (IAIN) consortium to 14 National Islamic Institutes, and 33 Islamic Senior Schools. The IAIN system has produced a highly educated cadre of graduates trained in Islamic theology, law and pedagogy, yet also exposed to theories of social science, philosophy, and other non-Islamic intellectual influences (Hefner 1997: 88, Van Bruinessen 2004: 6). The existence of the IAINs aided Indonesia in reducing the problem of unemployed *pesantren* graduates that is so acute throughout Muslim Asia and the Middle East. Furthermore, as a result of the changes to and improvements in the IAIN system, the caliber and educational sophistication of the *pesantren* teachers has improved, and from this, *pesantrens* gained new strength.

Under Suharto, the hard push for *Pancasila* values generated controversy among Islamic education providers due to the passage and enforcement of *Undang-Undang Keormasan* (Mass Organizations Law) in 1985. The law required all organizations to adopt *Pancasila* as their *asas tunggal* (sole foundation). This meant that organizations that previously had *Pancasila* and Islam in their charters had to, in effect, abandon Islam. Thus, the issue of *Pancasila* indoctrination in education was a controversial one that could have undermined social cohesion due to the authoritarian manner in which it was carried out and enforced. There could be no other publicly affirmed ideologies.

Despite misgivings, the state was successful in the Suharto period in using *Pancasila* in education as a unifying concept. This was due, in part, to the efforts of Munawir Sjadzali, Minister of Education from 1983–1993. He stepped up efforts to win over Muslim adherence to *Pancasila* ideology by working to persuade the Muslim political community that *Pancasila* was not antithetical to Islam (Porter 2002: 59). He contended that the government's approach to *Pancasila* was not to avoid teaching religion or to negate the teaching of religion (*ibid*). Rather, it was to use education as a means of increasing people's understanding of the "substance" of religion, while ensuring it did not take an "extremist" turn that would undermine unity and stability. In the post- Suharto period, the state still uses *Pancasila* as a rallying point in education to foster social cohesion. However, it no longer imposes it in an authoritarian manner that constrains all other viewpoints.

The Role Shared by Islamic Organizations: Supporting Cohesion

Throughout the Suharto and post-Suharto periods, the state has been a key provider of public education, but never dominated religious education. Instead, it shared it with the Nahdlatul Ulama, an Islamic mass organization with approximately 40 million members and numerous other Islamic organizations.[7] Nahdlatul Ulama runs an extensive network of *pesantren* (Islamic boarding schools) centered in rural areas and small towns, which comprise 69.28 per cent of all Islamic boarding schools in Indonesia (Yunanto and Harun 2005: 30). Since education at NU schools is typically cheaper than government school fees, many poor families choose to send their children to these schools. Education quality at NU *pesantren* varies. Some *pesantren* like Sunan Pandanaran in Yogyakarta, Salafiyah Syafiiyah

Sukorejo in Situbondo are renowned for the high quality education they provide. For example, Pesantren Salafiyah Syafiiyah Sukorejo in Situbondo has as many as 9,000 students and a university campus on its grounds. Others were quite small with poor facilities and only a few hundred members. As a result of this variation, *pesantren* are often criticized for providing sub-standard education due, in large part, to insufficient resources (Suparto 2004). *Pesantren*, however, play a vital role in supplementing the state's efforts to provide education and promote social cohesion.

Nahdlatul Ulama as an organization accepted *Pancasila* as sole foundation in 1985, and thus, *Pancasila* values were taught in the *pesantren*. However, these values did not run counter to the NU's culture, which emphasized consensus and pluralistic living within one's community environs. The New Order regime attempted to co-opt the *pesantren* by providing financial incentives for them to adopt the government's curricular recommendations to facilitate greater social mobility and economic viability among *pesantren* graduates. However, NU schools and *kyai* have a long tradition of independence. Thus, they varied in the extent to which they would adopt the state's curricular instructions. Some schools agreed to adopt the state's recommended curriculum and accept state funding after NU had a difficult time meeting funding obligations (Feillard 1997: 141–2). Other *kyai* accepted state patronage but retained the existing NU standard curriculum (Porter 2002: 113). Still others accepted state funding and modernized their teaching methods to an extent.

Over time, many *pesantren* have recognized the need to ensure their students have employment prospects so they can achieve economic stability and viability. NU saw no reason why its graduates should be condemned to poverty. Therefore, numerous *pesantren* have opened their own *madrasas* as part of their school system to obtain government funding or modified their daily study routines to permit their students to visit public schools outside of the *pesantren* during the day (Pohl 2006: 3). Other *pesantren* began teaching vocational classes in one of many trades, including farming, animal husbandry, forestry, small scale entrepreneurship, home based industry, garment making and handicrafts (Directorate of Religious Education and Pondok Pesantren 2005: 5). Some *pesantren* that wish to retain an independent curriculum also take part in a government program that offers students the opportunity to take national certification exams by providing them with study guides to prepare for those exams.[8] If they obtain these certifications, they too can go on to university education. This is yet another way that *pesantren* are seeking to provide students with a sound Islamic education, while enabling students to have access to channels for higher education and employment.

The picture of NU *pesantren* is a complicated one, but it is extremely important for understanding how education has contributed to social cohesion in Indonesia. As stated earlier, *pesantren* are often found in rural communities and small towns. Their *kyai* are often key figures in those communities. Thus, they play important roles in community development, social and the maintenance of harmonious inter-religious relations (*ibid*). *Pesantren* may function as centers for community health services, applied technological development for rural communities, natural resource conservation, community-based economic empowerment, and religious, social and cultural counseling (*ibid*: 5–6). *Pesantren* students go into the local communities providing agricultural and medical training (*ibid*). The work of the *pesantren kyai* and students serve to promote cohesive community relations and economic viability at the local level.

Furthermore, many *pesantren* have begun to shift in their roles to focus not only on community development but also on support for a democratic civil society. Some *pesantren* have begun to see their educational and social activities closely connected with raising critical political awareness on issues of social justice, pluralism, religious tolerance, and human rights (Pohl 2006: 5). In doing this, they are utilizing classical Islamic texts and their primary text, the *kitab kuning* (yellow book) to teach the importance of non-violence, civility, and justice from an Islamic perspective (*ibid*). These *pesantren* have been assisted in their efforts by numerous NGOs which were established in and around the *pesantren* communities in the 1970s and 1980s. At that time, these organizations focused on community development. However, with the changing political climate in the 1990s, many of these organizations, most notably the P3M and the LKIS, began to shift focus. According to Zuhairi Misrawi,[9] Coordinator of the Emancipatorist Islam Program of P3M,

> we hold trainings and provide education for *pesantren* on issues of clean government, democracy and human rights. We do trainings by combining *kitab kuning* and citizenship, sociology, anthropology, political science, hermeneutics, etc. … We choose these subjects because they can be studied by using the *kitab kuning*. They dealt with these issues back in ancient days. We can use these methods to talk about today's issues.

In effect, they are empowering students not only to understand the importance of tolerance, non-violence and social cohesion in theory but also in practice as Muslim members of a diverse, multi-ethnic and multi-religious society.

In the post-Suharto era, it is clear that the government sees *pesantren* as partners in community development and social cohesion. This can be seen in RUU Sidiknas (National Education Law 20: 2003), which notes that *pesantren* have a legal-formal basis to participate in ensuring a civilized community (Directorate of Religious Education and Pondok *Pesantren*. 2005). A majority of *pesantren* have become cooperative institutions within the national education system and in civil society, especially in the post-Suharto era (Pohl 2006: 5). We have also seen some *pesantren* working to make their contribution on critical domestic issues by working with Islamic organizations. The most notable work in this manner has been done by P3M. According to Zuhairi Misrawi[10],

> We have a forum with leaders in *pesantren* to solve problems like poverty and environmental problems. We have a network of over 6000 *pesantren*. The *pesantren* can choose one of many issues to adopt. Some choose to work on gender issues. Others on environmental issues or anti-corruption.

Pesantren Al Muayyad, near Solo, is a notable example of a *pesantren* that works on democratization issues with an eye toward inter-religious tolerance, inter-religious dialogue and gender issues. In its education and community efforts, it cooperates with many NGOs, including P3M, LKIS, Rahima (the Center for Education and Information on Islam and Women's Right's Issues), CePDes (Center for Pesantren and Democracy Studies), Interfidei (Institute for Inter-Clerical Dialogue), FPUB (Yogyakarta Interfaith Forum) and Percik (Institute for Social Research, Democracy and Social Justice) (Pohl 2006: 5). Pesantren Darul Tawhid in Cirebon is renowned for its work on improving women's rights at the local level, through the *pesantren*-based NGO, Fahmina and the tireless efforts of their headmaster, Kyai Hussin (*ibid*).

Some *pesantren* have also been forces for conflict-resolution, prevention, and peace-building in their communities. Some have actively engaged in inter-religious dialogues, others have maintained strong communications networks with other religious communities, and still others have actively sought to protect minority groups from threats to their person or property (Sholeh 2005: 3). Members of the NU *pesantren* communities actively work to protect churches at Christmas together with NU and Muhammadiyah militias and the Indonesian police.

Pesantren have also played important roles in conflict resolution following outbreaks of riots and violence in local communities, including the Situbondo and Tasikmalaya riots in 1996 and the Mataram Riots in 2000. It is important to note that the Situbondo and Tasikmalaya riots were largely caused by socio-economic grievances and resentment against the government (Bertrand 2004: 102). However, the clashes became viewed through the lens of religion.

Pesantren kyai played a key role in reducing the impact of the violence on the communities and in working to repair relations in inter-religious communities. For example, in the case of the Situbondo riots, Kyai Fawa'id of Pesantren Salafiah Syafi'iyah Sukorejo coordinated with other *kyai* to persuade the rioters to cease their actions toward Christian churches, and following the riots, he facilitated meetings among Muslim and Christian community leaders and the riot victims, which served to improve interreligious relations and inter-community communications.[11] *Kyai* played a similar role in the aftermath of the Tasikmalaya riots in West Java a few months later. Some *kyai* participated in meetings with security forces, local government officials and religious leaders to restore peace and order to the area (Sholeh 2005: 14). Some *pesantren* also played important roles in conflict resolution in Maluku and Poso and in preventing further escalation of the Mataram riots in 2000.

In sum, just as the state has sought to promote social cohesion through the educational system, so too have Islamic educational providers played a role, most notably the Nahdlatul Ulama. NU *kyai* and *pesantren* graduates have played key roles in the development of non-governmental organizations that have promoted democracy, pluralism, non-violence, social justice, and women's rights from an Islamic perspective. They have been key providers of community assistance, which has reinforced the norms of tolerance and unity in the communities in which they operate. Furthermore, certain *pesantren* have also participated in conflict resolution efforts following the outbreak of riots or communal violence. Thus, together with the state's efforts, *pesantren* are also doing their part to ensure national unity and stability.

Pesantren that Undermine Cohesion

Not all *pesantren* are active players in promoting pluralism; many Islamic boarding schools focus their attentions on training the next generation of *ulama*. However, there is a small third group that bears mention. A minority of *pesantren* with links to underground remnants of the *Darul Islam* movement of the 1950s, and in certain cases, the terrorist group, Jemaah Islamiyah (JI) undermine social cohesion. They oppose the concept of pluralism and the practice of inter-religious dialogues as a method for maintaining favorable inter-communal relations. Wahyuddin, chairman of the Al Mu'mim *pesantren*, explained that he sees pluralism as running contrary to the code of conduct in the Qur'an that states: *Lakum Dinukum Waliyadin*—your religion is yours and mine is mine (Sholeh 2005: 16). In this view, religions can coexist peacefully, but there is no reason for dialogue on religious matters. Instead, each religious group should stay apart. In this short term, this solution may bring peace, but it will not build tolerance. In the long-term, it undermines social cohesion by impeding communication among religious groups at critical times.

For example, when communal conflicts broke out in the provinces of Maluku and Central Sulawesi in 1999, the radical *pesantren* took a narrow view. Al Mu'mim in Solo and Darul Istiqamah in Maros not only employed the term "*jihad*" to characterize the conflicts but also encouraged their members to participate in that *jihad* (*ibid*). By contrast, NU *pesantren* refused to use the term "*jihad*" to describe the conflicts, maintaining that jihad in the Indonesian context referred to improving education and eradicating poverty (*ibid*: 17). Hasyim Muzadi, Chairman of Nahdlatul Ulama recognized the root causes of the conflicts were economic in nature, not religious.[12]

One may speculate that their views on the priority of social cohesion spilled over into their perceptions of the conflicts. The radical *pesantren* saw Muslims in Maluku and Poso as under attack by Christian secessionists and, therefore, it was their duty to defend the Muslims against further victimization. Their priority was the safeguarding of Muslim lives and interests. Former NU Chairman and then Indonesian President Abdurrahman Wahid, on a visit to Maluku, called for an end to conflict, appealing to open-minds, the rule of law, and the spirit of brotherhood. (McCarthy 2000). These divergent perspectives may explain why NU *kyai* worked to reduce conflict in Maluku and Poso, whereas the *kyai* from the radical *pesantren* did not. They did not see the different religious communities in Indonesia as part of a single unified brotherhood but as separate communities with incompatible differences.

In sum, the Indonesian government in the Suharto and post-Suharto eras has invested heavily in education to promote social mobility, stability, national unity and social cohesion. This is very important given the multi-ethnic and multi-religious character of the nation. The government has been aided significantly in these efforts by Islamic organizations, most notably the Nahdlatul Ulama and its network of *pesantren* and affiliated NGOs, which have been key players in movements to promote pluralism, democratization, tolerance, non-violence, and social justice. In addition, they have been important actors in community development and conflict resolution efforts, which have improved inter-religious and inter-ethnic relations at the local level. Thus, we see the key role of NU in reinforcing the state's vision and in complementing it with its own vision of tolerance and dialogue. A minority of *pesantren* focus instead on the establishment of an Islamic state under a strict interpretation of *Shari'a* and contend that each religious group within Indonesia should concern themselves with their own affairs, as is stated in the Qur'an. Any interactions between religious groups should be minimal. This viewpoint is not productive of social cohesion in the Indonesian context. What is important to note, however, is that this viewpoint is not the majority perspective. That belongs to groups like NU, which prioritizes social cohesion, reducing poverty and achieving consensus.

Malaysia

In Indonesia, the government and Islamic civil society groups play key roles in providing education. However, in Malaysia, the state is the dominant provider of education and Islamic organizations play supporting roles. Thus, this section will focus primarily in the role of the state in the provision of education and how it uses that education to promote national unity, social mobility, and order. Malaysia is 65 per cent *bumiputera* (Malays + Indigenous groups), 26 per cent Chinese and 7.7 per cent Indian.[13] This heterogeneous ethnic construction makes social cohesion imperative for national stability. This has, in turn, impacted the development of education and social policy.

Furthermore, the 1969 race riots had a profound impact on policymaking and on the political culture today. In the aftermath of the clashes between Malays and Chinese, the government enacted a series of policies to address the economic inequality between Malays and Chinese and poverty among Malays, which it perceived to be the root of the problem. In 1971, the government enacted the New Economic Policy (NEP) as a program that would eliminate poverty among Malays, especially the rural poor. It sought to improve Malay social and economic standing through a system of quotas for Malays in education, employment and government contracts; to enable Malays to have easier access to bank loans and business licenses; and to increase Malay ownership of corporate equity (Nasr 2001: 71).

The National Education Policy was developed as a key component and compliment of the NEP. It dramatically expanded educational opportunities. By the end of the 1970s, almost 90 per cent of children were attending primary school; by 1980, 75.3 per cent of children were attending lower secondary school and 41.1 per cent were attending upper secondary school (Crouch 1996: 185). These numbers have continued to increase, most notably for secondary school so that today, 92.75 per cent of all students attend primary school; 82 per cent proceed on to lower secondary school and 72.45 per cent to upper secondary school.[14] With the adoption of the integrated curriculum in 1998, the state also increased the number of compulsory years of education from 6 years to 11 years (six years of primary school and 5 years of secondary school).[15]

The state has shown increasing commitment to ensuring that all have access to primary and secondary education by controlling costs and improving infrastructure. Education in Malaysia is inexpensive. Students pay yearly entrance and exam fees, but this does not amount to a serious amount of money.[16] Moreover, school fees can be waived for children of the poor.[17] The state provides several programs of aid to offset the cost of education for poor families, including free breakfast and lunch, free uniforms, free textbooks and free hostels for students to live if their family's residence is far from a secondary school.[18] The state has also improved public transportation in rural areas to facilitate higher attendance in secondary schools.

The National Education Policy also increased educational opportunities at the tertiary level for Malays by initiating university quotas for Malays, starting new universities and increasing the number of scholarships available for Malays to attend higher education abroad (Nasr 2001: 84). The number of Malay students studying abroad rose by 65 per cent between 1970 and 1975 and by 1979, 66.4 per cent of all university students were Malay (*ibid*). By 1989, Malays accounted for 83.2 per cent of all students enrolled in science and technology degree programs and 62.8 per cent of all arts enrollments

(Daud 1989: 97). As a result of the combined effects of the New Economic Policy and National Education Policy, poverty dropped in Malaysia from 74 per cent in 1970 to 6 per cent in 1994 (Abuza 2003: 50). The result of these policies was the advancement of a Malay middle class and significant opportunities for social mobility among Malays.

The government has taken a keen interest in developing the state religious education sector as an alternative to private *madrasas* to ensure that a pro-development Islam that emphasizes the uniqueness of the Malaysian context is taught. There are five types of primary and secondary religious schools in Malaysia: *sekolah agama persekutan* (federal religious schools-SAP); *sekolah agama negeri* (state religious schools-SAN); schools run by a state's Council of Islamic religion; *sekolah agama rakyat* (community religious schools-SAR) and *sekolah agama swasta* (private religious schools-SAS) (Hamid 2005: 173). The state has a centralized standard curriculum for all Federal SAP schools, state SAN schools and community SAR schools, although the SARs do not consistently apply it.[19]

The state is also a leading funder of Islamic schools. Federal religious schools are federally funded; state religious schools are funded by the individual state governments; and the community religious schools are partially funded by the federal governments according to per capita per child grants.[20] Private religious schools are eligible for government grants if they agree to register and adhere to national curricular recommendations.

Education for Values

In 1987, Malaysia formulated a national education philosophy, which highlighted the critical importance of social cohesion in the Malaysian context. It aimed to create Malaysian citizens who were intellectually, spiritually, emotionally and physically balanced and harmonious, with a strong belief in God (Hashim 1996: 8). The state has a clear vision of the purpose of education, which is rooted in ideas of tolerance and mutual coexistence.

> Education is viewed as a vehicle for promoting national unity, social equality and economic development. It strengthens national integration by inculcating a common and shared destiny among different ethnic groups, removing racial prejudices, encouraging cultural tolerance, and fostering the use of a common language. Economically, education supplies much needed human resources for economic growth ... As an

agent of social equality, education promotes social mobility and in the process creates avenues for income redistribution and restructures social relations (Lee 2004: 437).

It is clear that the state sees education as a crucial means to foster social cohesion and national unity. The government's educational philosophy and perceptions about the proper role of education would significantly impact the direction of the education reforms it undertook two years later.

In 1989, the government channeled its educational philosophy into curricular reforms and launched an integrated curriculum for secondary schools, the *Kurikulum Bersepadu Sekolah Menegah*. The state increased the number of classes devoted to Islamic studies for Muslim students, required courses in morals education for non-Muslims and living skills courses for all students. The goal of the integrated curriculum was to inculcate all young people with universal religious values (Hashim 1996: 8). Among Muslims, the government sought to increase their understanding of fundamental Islamic values that would compliment the state's integrative vision and teach them how to practice their faith in an informed manner. This would keep them from falling prey to *dakwah songsang* or "deviant" Islamic groups that might adopt divisive, cult-like, or anti-government perspectives. Taken in total, the purpose of the integrated curriculum was fundamentally rooted in values. It sought to create well-rounded students able to balance faith and the modern world and able to coexist peacefully and constructively in a multi-ethnic and multi-religious society. These curricular reforms were met with approval by the major national religious groups.

Role Shared by Islamic Organizations: Supporting Cohesion

The Malaysian government clearly dominated in the provision of education and Islamic groups subscribed to the government's curriculums in their own schools so that their students could sit for government exams and go on to tertiary education. Therefore, the role of Islamic education providers is far smaller compared to Indonesia. However, certain groups, most notably the Malaysian Islamic Youth Association (ABIM), took on a complementary vision and role and sought to help those Muslims who had not benefited from National Education Policy programs. ABIM is a *dakwa* (Islamic propagation) organization that seeks to Islamize the nation by making the society more pious. ABIM was founded at the University of Malaysia under the tutelage of noted Islamic scholar, Dr. Syed Naguib Ali Al Attas and is influenced by and respectful of Malaysian culture, Malay nationalism and the heterogeneous Malaysian context.

ABIM members tend to be middle class, young professionals with university education backgrounds. They benefited from the National Education Policy, which enabled them to attend university and they became middle class as a result of the New Economic Policy. As a result, they have been willing to work within the state's parameters in providing education services to their fellow Muslims. This was especially true after 1982, when Anwar Ibrahim, president of ABIM, joined the government. Many of his fellow members of ABIM became influential in the Ministry of Education, the Department of Islamic Development (JAKIM), and in the development of the International Islamic University of Malaysia (IIUM). Through their various educational programs, ABIM works not only to increase Islamic knowledge but also to compliment the state's goals of providing Malay Muslims with channels for upward social mobility and economic viability.

ABIM's work is focused on educating the Muslim community and helping them to achieve a better standard of living through their education programs. ABIM runs primary and secondary schools, which are registered with the Ministry of Education and state level ministries of religion. They follow the government curriculum so that they can obtain government funding and their students can attend Malaysian universities. However, they also extend the school day to make sufficient time for Islamic studies.[21] ABIM's private schools are run according to the idea of an integrated curriculum that Islamizes the philosophy of education and civic concepts.[22] Through this method, one can fulfill the state's curricular requirements, while teaching students about Islam's practical applications and while staying firmly grounded in pluralistic nature of the Malaysian context. In this way, ABIM works to reinforce national social cohesion.

In addition to their schools, ABIM also runs programs to assist drop-outs, provides tutoring for students who failed the national exams but want to retake them, and holds several short courses in Islamic banking, Islamic politics and Arabic (Abdullah 2003: 95). These programs for drop-outs and struggling students are a very important part of Malaysia's economic development. By targeting these vulnerable populations, ABIM helps to ensure that all Malays have access to channels for social mobility, even if they have faltered or failed in the past.

Groups That May Undermine Social Cohesion

Darul Arqam was a prosperous ultraconservative Islamic organization that advocated self-reliance and had established numerous communes, businesses and schools throughout Malaysia. Although Darul Arqam committed no violent act, it was banned in 1994 for allegedly training armed warriors and for its increasing cultism. Darul Arqam members isolated themselves from the larger Malaysian population, preferring to live in communes and restrict their interactions to fellow members of the organization. This undermined social cohesion in the country because its ideology served to segregate them from the larger multi-ethnic, multi-religious society.

As opposed to those schools run by ABIM, Darul Arqam schools did not adopt the national recommended curriculum and were not formally registered with the Ministry of Education (Abdullah 2003: 108). Instead, their curriculum focused solely on Islam. The Malaysian education system is highly centralized, which is seen as desirable so that all students have access to educational services of reasonable quality (Lee 2004: 440). There is no tradition of independent mass Islamic educational institutions as exist in Indonesia. Therefore, Darul Arqam's rejection of the state system was very alarming to Malaysian officials because the organization presided over a rapidly growing network of schools. Darul Arqam had 257 schools in Malaysia with a total enrollment of 9,541 in 1994 (Abdullah 2003: 108). There was no way to provide Arqam graduates with access to tertiary education and the channels of upward social mobility. Since they rejected the government's educational ideology and developmentalist vision, Arqam was seen as a threat to social cohesion.

The state also began to see the *sekolah agama rakyat* (community religious schools-SARs) as a threat to national unity and stability because it believed they were teaching politicized and extreme forms of Islam that ran counter to the government's developmentalist and pluralistic vision. As a result, they temporarily withdrew federal aid from those schools and provided financial incentives for students and teachers from the SARs to join the national education system. This hurt the *rakyat* (community) schools, which depended on government aid. Fearing that SARs were indoctrinating their children in radical Islamism, parents pulled their children out. The government then launched an investigation into those schools to identify which ones were teaching extremist and intolerant forms of Islam and then close them.

There is some controversy over whether the SARs undermine national stability and social cohesion. It is commonly believed that SAR graduates are more likely to support the opposition party, Partai Islam Se Malaysia (PAS). Thus, one can interpret the withdrawal of funding for the SARs as a political gesture. However, others contend that a minority, perhaps 1–2 per cent of those schools teach radical Islam. Abdul Razak Baginda, Director of the independent Malaysian Strategic and Research Center, noted specifically that PAS-affiliated SARs had become centers of extremism and intolerance toward other faiths (Nathan 2003: 248). To date, the state has closed only one SAR in Johor for teaching radical Islam. This school was quite unique, for it was started by Abu Bakar Basyir and Abdullah Sungkar, two Indonesian exiles and the founders of Jemaah Islamiyah.[23] Thus, the threat posed by SARs to social cohesion is ambiguous.

In sum, the Malaysian government invested heavily in education to foster tolerance, social cohesion, stability, and opportunities for social mobility and economic prosperity. The Malaysian educational system is rooted in these values, and it is imperative that it continues to stay that way, given the multi-ethnic and multi-religious nature of society. As a result of the Malaysian government's policies, there has been a dramatic expansion of the Malay middle class and a reduction in poverty levels, especially among Malays. In helping to ensure that Muslims have access to the channels of social mobility, the government is assisted by *dakwah* organizations, most notably, ABIM, which has a network of primary and secondary schools as well as a series of programs to help dropouts re-enter the education system and assist students in preparing for their exams. The prioritization of social cohesion and economic development has become part of the socio-political culture in Malaysia. Those schools that are seen as teaching intolerance risk losing funding and closure. However, from the government's own investigation, there seem to be very few of those schools in operation.

Conclusion

Education is an important force in promoting social cohesion, stability, and opportunities for social mobility. The state has an important role in the provision of that education and in spreading of values of harmony in social relations that underpin it. Furthermore, it is a key force in ensuring that citizens possess a strong sense of national identity in multi-ethnic and multi-religious societies. However, the state is not alone in the provision of education and the teaching of these values. Instead, Islamic education providers can play an important reinforcing role for Muslims living in these countries.

The complimentary role of the state and Islamic education providers is clear in examining the cases of Indonesia and Malaysia. In both of these countries, the state's provision of education contributed to dramatic reductions in poverty and an increase in the number of people in the middle class. Furthermore, each state prioritized the spread of cohesive values to keep order and maintain that prosperity. In Indonesia, the Nahdlatul Ulama played a very significant role in reinforcing social cohesion at the local level by improving community relations and providing local development programs, social services and educational training workshops. Furthermore, in the aftermath of riots targeting Chinese and Christian minorities, NU *kyai* worked to resolve conflicts and rebuild inter-religious ties through sponsoring dialogues and discussions and through the physical protection of churches at Christmas.

Malaysian Islamic organizations played a subordinate role to the state but an important one nonetheless. While the New Economic Policy and National Education Policy aimed to assist all Malays, not all were reached. Some children dropped out of school or failed their examinations. ABIM assisted the government by running their own schools, providing study skills workshops and programs to help dropouts prepare to re-enter school or prepare for pertinent exams. This evidence indicates clearly that Islamic education providers are an important force for community and national cohesion.

In both Malaysia and Indonesia, there are some Islamic schools on the fringes of society that advocate religious separation and teach intolerance. However, it is important that we do not overestimate the danger they pose. Perhaps state governments should keep a watchful eye on these groups. However, it is important that we recognize the complementary contributions that Islamic education providers and governments play in helping to develop young Muslims with keen minds, sound values, and a fundamental understanding of the necessity of preserving social cohesion in heterogeneous societies.

Notes

1. "Pakistan: Madrasas, Extremism and the Military." ICG Asia Report, No. 36 Islamabad/ Brussels 2002, p. 2.

2. "Survey Indonesia: time to deliver," *The Economist*. <http://www.economist.com/sur-veys/displayStory.cfm?story_id=3444238> December 9, 2004.

3. Interview, Dr. Saiful Mujani, Professor, State Islamic University-Syarif Hidayatullah, March 2006, Jakarta, Indonesia.

4. Interview, I.G. Wilakuda, researcher on radical *pesantren* and radical Islamism, April 2006, Solo, Indonesia.

5. *Ibid.*

6. Van Zorge, Heffernan and Associates, "Grade Point Average." Van Zorge Report. vol. 8, no. 12 July 2006. The Van Zorge report breaks down the secondary school level enrollment ratios into junior and senior secondary levels and still there is a significant decrease from primary school. In 2003, primary enrollment ratio was at 94.6 percent; this decreased to 60.2 percent enrollment for junior secondary school, *sekolah menegah pertama* (SMP) and decreases further at the senior secondary level, *sekolah menegah atas* (SMA).

7. These include Muhammadiyah, which runs urban private schools, *madrasas*, and a consortium of universities. Numerous smaller Islamic organizations run their own schools including Persis, DDII, Mathlaul, Al Khairat, Nahdlatul Wathan, Perti and LDII. Yunanto, S. and Harun, Badrudin. 2005 "Terminology, History and Categorization." In *Islamic Education in South and Southeast Asia*. S. Yunanto *et al*, eds. Jakarta: Ridep Institute, p. 30.

8. *Ibid.*

9. Interview, Zuhairi Misrawi, Coordinator of the Emancipatorist Islam Program of P3M of the Association of Pesantren and Community Development, March 2006, Jakarta, Indonesia.

10. *Ibid.*

11. Interview, Kyai Mudzakkir Abdul Fattah, Secretary Chairman of Pesantren Salafiah Syafi'iyah Sukorejo as quoted in Sholeh, Badrus, "Pluralism and Islamist Ideas in Contemporary Indonesian Pesantren." Conference on Political Legitimacy in Islamic Asia. Organized by the Asia Research Institute. National University of Singapore 25–26, April 2006.

12. Interview, Kyai Hj Hasyim Muzadi, Chairman of Nahdlatul Ulama, Jakarta, Indonesia, April 2006.

13. Malaysian Census Report 2000. http://www.statistics.gov.my/english/frameset_census. php?file=pressdemo.

14. Interview, Dr. Rosnani Hashim, Professor at International Islamic University of Malaysia, Gombak Malaysia, February 2006.

15. *Ibid.*

16. Interview, Jagdeesh Gul, Ministry of Education, Putra Jaya, Malaysia, February 2006.

17. Interview, Dr. Rosnani Hashim, Professor at International Islamic University of Malaysia, Gombak Malaysia, February 2006.

18. *Ibid.*

19. Interview, Dr. Rosnani Hashim, Professor at International Islamic University of Malaysia, Gombak Malaysia, February 2006.

20. Interview, Abdul Halim Bin Mohd Naam, Assistant Director, Curriculum Division, Department of Islam and Moral Education, JAPIM, Kuala Lumpur, Malaysia February 2006.

21. Interview, Shahran Kasim, former Secretary General of ABIM, ABIM Headquarters, February 2006, Gombak, Malaysia. Due to the influence of Anwar Ibrahim, the

government responded favorably to these ideas and adopted them into the state's curricular recommendations.

22. Interview, Professor Dato Osman Bakar, ISTAC, Kuala Lumpur, Malaysia, January 2006.

23. Interview, Abdul Halim Bin Mohd Naam, Assistant Director, Curriculum Division, Department of Islam and Moral Education, JAPIM, Kuala Lumpur, Malaysia February 2006.

References

Abdullah, Kamarulnizam (2003) *The Politics of Islam in Contemporary Malaysia*. Bangi: Penerbit Universiti Kebangsaan Malaysia.

Abuza, Zachary.(2003) *Militant Islam in Southeast Asia: Crucible of Terror*. Boulder: Lynne Reinner.

Bertrand, Jacques (2004) *Nationalism and Ethnic Conflict in Indonesia*. Cambridge: Cambridge University Press.

Crouch, Harold (1996) *Government and Society in Malaysia*. Singapore: Talisman.

Dhofier, Zamakhsyari (1999) *The Pesantren Tradition: The Role of the Kyai in the Maintenance of Traditional Islam in Java*. Monograph Series Press. Program for Southeast Asian Studies. Arizona State University.

Feillard, Andree (1997) "Traditionalist Islam and the state in Indonesia: the road to legitimacy and renewal," in *Islam in an Era of Nation State: Politics and Religious Renewal in Muslim Southeast Asia*, Robert W. Hefner and Patricia Horavitch, eds. Honolulu: Hawaii University Press, pp. 129–153.

Hamid, Ahmad, Fauzi Abdul (2005) "The strategy of Islamic education in Malaysia: Aan Islamic movement's experience." In *Islamic Education in South and Southeast Asia*. S. Yunanto *et al*, eds. Jakarta: Ridep Institute, pp. 171–204.

Hashim, Rosnani (1996) *Educational Dualism in Malaysia: Implications for Theory and Practice* Southeast Asia Social Science Monographs. Oxford: Oxford University Press.

Hassan, Riaz (2006) "View: challenge of intellectual stagnation" *Daily Times*. Monday, October 16.

Hefner, Robert (1997) "Islamization and democratization in Indonesia," in *Islam in an Era of Nation States*. Robert Hefner and Patricia Horavitch, eds. Honolulu: University of Hawaii Press, pp. 75–127.

Khalik, Abdul (2005) "State still fails to provide free basic education." *Jakarta Post*, July 17.

Lee, Molly, N. N. (2004) "Education reforms during the mahathir era: global trends and U turns." In *Reflections: The Mahathir Years*, Bridget Welsh, ed. Washington DC: Southeast Asian Studies Program, Johns Hopkins SAIS, pp. 437–449.

Liddle, R, William (1996) *Leadership and Culture in Indonesian Politics*. Sydney: Allen and Unwin.

Malaysian Census Report (2000) http://www.statistics.gov.my/english/frameset_census.php?file=pressdemo, January 10, 2007.

McCarthy, Terry (2000) "Time for leadership." *Time Magazine*, July 3, Vol 155 No.26.

Mujani, Saiful (2003) "Religious democrats: democratic culture and Muslim political participation in post-Suharto Indonesia." Dissertation, Ohio State University.

Nasr, Seyyed, Vali Reza (2001) *Islamic Leviathan: Islam and the Making of State Power*. Oxford: Oxford University Press.

Nathan, K.S. (2003) "Counter-terror cooperation in a complex security environment." In *After Bali: The Threat of Terrorism in Southeast Asia*, Kumar Ramakrishna and See Seng Tan, eds. Singapore: Institute of Defense and Strategic Studies. pp. 241–257.

Pohl, Florian (2006) *"Pesantren* and global integration." Paper given at informal talk held at Center for Religion and Cross-Cultural Studies, Yogyakarta, Indonesia, May 6.

Porter, Donald, J. (2002) *Managing Politics and Islam in Indonesia.* London: Routledge Curzon.

Putnam, Robert (2005) "Education, diversity, social cohesion and social capital." Meeting of OECD Education Ministers: Raising the Quality of Learning for All. Dublin. 18–19 March.

Sholeh, Badrus (2005) "Pluralism and Islamist ideas in contemporary Indonesian pesantren." Conference on Political Legitimacy in Islamic Asia. Organized by the Asia Research Institute. National University of Singapore. 25–26 April.

Suparto (2004) "Reforming pesantren: while reform of Islamic Education is necessary, secularization is not." *Inside Indonesia.* January–March.

The Dynamics of Pondok Pesantren in Indonesia. (2005) Directorate of Religious Education and Pondok Pesantren. Directorate General of Islamic Institutions. Department of Religious Affairs. Republic of Indonesia.

The Economist (2004) Survey Indonesia: time to deliver. *The Economist.* <http://www.economist.com/surveys/displayStory.cfm?story_id=3444238> December 9.

Van Bruinessen, Martin (2004) "Traditionalist and Islamist *pesantren* in contemporary Indonesia. Paper presented at the ISIM workshop on 'the Madrasa in Asia', Netherlands May 23–24.

Van Zorge, Heffernan and Associates (2006) "Grade Point Average." *Van Zorge Report.* vol. 8, no. 12. July.

Wan Daud, Wan Mohamad Nor (1989) *The Concept of Knowledge in Islam and Its Implications for Education in a Developing Country.* London: Mansell.

Yunanto, S. and Harun, Badrudin (2005) "Terminology, History and Categorization." In *Islamic Education in South and Southeast Asia: Diversity, Problems and Strategies.* Eds. Yunanto et.al. Jakarta: Ridep Institute, pp. 19–36.

The Poetics of Religious Philanthropy:
Buddhist Welfarism in Singapore[1]

Kuah-Pearce Khun Eng

Introduction

In a globalizing world and especially in recent years when there is a resurgence of religious fundamentalism and militancy, there is an urgent need by many governments to tackle these issues to avert inter-ethnic and inter-faith violence in our society. As we consider the role of religion in a globalized world, it is important for us to understand the continued significance of religion in modern society. It is often easier to portray religion in a negative light given the current level of violence and negative emotions attached to the more militant religious groups and cults that have recently made inroads into our society. Apart from the actual violence associated with religious extremists, primarily with so-called militant Islam, negative attitudes are often directed at religious groups and cults that have embarked on aggressive programmes of proselytization, thereby alienating many established religious traditions and increasing tensions in existing communities.

In contrast to these perceptions, this chapter examines how religion continues to play a positive and supportive role in modern society through a case study of the role of Buddhism in contemporary Singapore. Specifically, it explores the role of Buddhism (as represented by the Buddhist institution, Sangha and Reformist Buddhists) in creating a welfare niche and in the delivery of welfare services to the less privileged sector of the population.

In this discussion, the convergence of the state–religion ideology will be explored to understand the intersection of the political and religious goals resulting in the creation of a religious philanthropic culture cum welfare niche as an essential part of modern Singaporean Buddhism. At the same time, it looks at the reasons behind the active participation of these Buddhist institutions.

The close relationship between politics and religion is instrumental here as we seek to unravel how the Singaporean state identifies, encourages and seeks partnerships with the religious institutions to harness the religious and moral teachings of compassion, transforming them into tangible social and welfare services to cater to the needs of Singapore's multi-ethnic community. In so doing, both the Singaporean state and the religious institutions have indirectly established and expanded a religious philanthropic culture and enhanced a localized religious identity.

Religion and Its Search for a Modern Role in Singapore

In my earlier studies of the tripartite relationship between the state, society and Sangha (Kuah-Pearce 2003), culminating in a movement towards a Reformist Buddhism in Singaporean society, I outlined the various reasons explaining the need for religious modernisation as a secular Singapore evolves towards a post-industrial globalized society. As Singapore moved away from its colonial status into a nation-state and multicultural society, there emerged new needs and wants on the one hand and a shifting ideological orientation on the other. As a new nation-state, Singapore embarked on a path towards nationhood through rigorous nation-building and the formation of a Singaporean citizenry and identity. In this process of nation-building, the key platform that governed the nation is one of multi-ethnicity, multiculturalism and multi-religiosity. From these foundations, the so-called CMIO-BDIHC model emerged (Kuah-Pearce 2003: 136).

In this model, the CMIO stands for the four official ethnic categories of Chinese, Malay, Indian and Others as recognized within the Singapore Constitution. Furthermore, there is a close correlation between ethno-linguistic and ethno-religious boundaries. Thus, in the official parlance, there are four official languages namely Chinese (as represented by Mandarin), Malay, Indian and English which correlate with the ethno-linguistic boundary of its four main ethnic groups. Since the establishment of the bilingual policy in 1965, the English language was considered as an important functional global language and taught to all school going students. In addition, mother-tongue languages would be taught to students of the respective ethnic groups, unless the parents opted out of the scheme. Thus, the Chinese is assumed to speak the Chinese language (Mandarin, although many continue to use various dialects such as Fujianese, Chapzhouese, Cantonese, Hakkaese and others), Malays speak the Malay language, Indians speak Tamil (although many continue to use Malayaese, Gujerati, Urdu, Arabi, Hindi and others) and Others (Caucasians and Eurasians) speak the English language.

Likewise, the official assumption is there is also a close correlation between the ethno-religious boundary where the Chinese are assumed to be practicing Chinese religions (as represented by a composite of Buddhism, Daoism and Confucianism or as separate entities), the Malays hold on to their Islamic faith, Indians are Hindus and Others practice Christianity (of various denominations). Thus, the CMIO-BDIHC model represents the correlation of Chinese as having the Buddhist-Daoist faith, the Malays have the Islamic faith, Indians have the Hindu faith and the Others are Christians. This ethno-religious boundary has served the nation well in terms of decision-making and policy formulation. However, such a neat categorization obscures the actual religious representations found within each ethnic group. There are now over ten per cent of the Chinese population who proclaim the Christian faith of various denominations with more converting into the fold of Christendom on a daily basis. Likewise, there is also a sizeable number of Indians who are Christians. Others do not necessarily uphold Christianity as their religious faith. Some are Buddhists and there are also a very small number of Muslim converts. Among the Malays, very few belong to other faiths and almost all of them are Muslims. Today, the official census has recognized religious movements across ethnic boundaries.

Within the Chinese community, the traditional Chinese religious practices with elaborate ritual contents no longer fulfilled the spiritual needs of the Chinese community and especially the younger generation of Singaporeans who have been much influenced by the secular education system. To many of them, traditional Chinese rituals which are more concerned with practices than reasoning are less appealing than the canonically based religions. Often they regarded ritual practices such as the Seventh Lunar Month Hungry Ghost festival as "superstitious", *mixin* (迷信), practices.

Of course today, there have been attempts to redefine these mass religious practices as part of traditional Chinese cultural practices. This is another aspect that warrants further studies within the paradigm of the reinvention of tradition.

In my earlier study, I argued that the Singaporean State played an important role in pushing for religious modernisation through encouraging and directing the religious institutions (including the monastic order, the temple and the laity) to embark on social, educational, heath and welfare activities through various legislative policies including fiscal benefits to the religious institutions. At the same time, I explored how the Sangha and the laity have felt the need to transform and recast their roles in order to become socially relevant to its adherents as well as the wider society in order that they do not become redundant in the face of challenges both within and without. It is to be noted that religious conversion to Christianity among the Chinese has increased rapidly during the last two decades. Thus, the challenge facing the Sangha and the lay community is how to arrest this outward flow. This has resulted in competing claims of modernity and status among the various religious groups in Singapore, particularly between the Reformist Buddhists and the various Christian groups.[2]

At the forefront in this process of religious modernisation are various issues that concern the Sangha, the Buddhist organization and Buddhist members and laity. Within the Sangha order, the key concern is how to transform the Sangha into a modern entity with a global outlook on the one hand, and enmesh it with appropriate skills that are demanded by the young Singaporeans on the other. Such skills include the ability of the Sangha members to transmit *dharma* knowledge and new forms of religious practice, such as various forms of meditation, and to discharge non-religious leisure, recreational and welfare works. To supplement existing religious practices, essentially those that focused on liturgy and rituals that cater primarily to the elderly adherents, by creating more trendy or fashionable practices demanded by the younger Singaporean Chinese, there is a need to revitalize the Sangha order through the recruitment of progressive young Sangha members. The trend is towards recruiting and training a monastic order that is reformist, humanist and socially-engaged in orientation. Only through this transformation can the Sangha become socially relevant and be able to attract the younger generation. Owing to the dearth of a younger Singapore-born educated monks and nuns, it becomes clear that the Sangha order needs to recruit from overseas in order to replace the falling numbers of monks and nuns in the local community.

A second trend is the development of lay Buddhist organizations and lay Sangha among the laity. Among the laity, and especially among the younger generation, there is a movement away from a dependence on the Sangha to self-discovery and self-reliance. This has resulted in the development of lay Sangha and lay Buddhist organizations where the lay Buddhists organize this-worldly religious, social and other activities in order to attain their other-worldly spiritualism. The development of the lay movement resulted in the emergence of a group of reformist Buddhists in Singapore that has gained prominence during the last two decades.

The reformist Buddhists are of the younger age group. About 85% belong to 20–29 and 30–39 age groups. They tend to be better educated with 48% with ten years of education, 37% with 12 years of education and 13% with tertiary education. They are also the product of the post-colonial education system with half English-educated and English-speaking and half Chinese-educated and Chinese-speaking, but most are bilingual. Many of them are also of a higher social status; 73% of English-educated and English speaking considered themselves middle class and 52% Chinese-educated and Chinese-speaking considered themselves lower middle class.

The reformist Buddhist movement focused on the following aspects: (a) non-sectarian ideological and scriptural purity; (b) this-worldly socially engaged humanistic practices (c) individualized spirituality where individual awareness is the key focus (d) minimal ritualism (e) proselytization and (f) the creation of a lay Buddhist order. Thus, the search for a modern role resulted in the development of a lay Buddhist reformist movement which is socially engaged and humanistic in orientation.

From Compassion to Religious Philanthropy

This development of a socially engaged and humanistic reformist Buddhism in modern Singapore has become increasingly urgent in the face of stiff competition from the ever-increasing number of religious organizations in a global religious supermarket. Singaporeans, like their counterparts else-where, are spoilt for choices and could shop and hop around for one religious brand to another according to their socio-spiritual needs. The strategy that the reformist Buddhists adopted is one that would reach out to the wider Chinese population (in particular those that practice traditional Chinese religion and passive Buddhists) by offering a socially engaged humanistic brand of Buddhism that focused on the cultivation of personal spirituality and compassion. To articulate the cultivation of compassion, the Reformist Buddhists established a niche as a provider of welfare services for the wider community, cutting across ethnic and religious boundaries.

Establishing a welfare niche is often seen as a natural progression of the teachings of most religions. Within Buddhism, one of the key Buddhist tenets, the Bodhisattva Ideal of the Mahayana Buddhist tradition, is commonly seen to embody compassion towards all sentient beings. It is this doctrine of compassion that helped to propel the Buddhist community to establish a religious philanthropic culture, similar to that of the Christian and Islamic community. Unlike the Islamic community where a system of tithes is well-established, these philanthropic institutions are in their infancy within some of the reformist Buddhist organizations and not practiced among others. While tithing in Islam is collected from all members on a regular basis, the Buddhist philanthropic culture is one that is highly contextualized and Buddhists are often counted upon to dig deep into their pockets for various types of humanistic projects that the Buddhist community is engaged in at different points in time. Within the Singaporean context, Buddhist philanthropy reaches out to all Buddhists and is not confined to a specific or localized Buddhist organization, thereby defying the traditional argument that such acts only confine themselves to a localized parish's community of the faithful. It is the goal that governs the act that governs the attitude towards the contribution. Thus, in terms of priorities, temple building and welfare works feature prominently, followed by education, social and recreational activities. This development of Buddhist religious philanthropy is closely tied to the Buddhist teaching on *karma* and merit-making. Thus, the rank order of the different activities and hence contributions to them are dependent on how the Buddhists view their acts and contributions. Temple-building, welfare works and education are regarded as accruing more merit and hence Buddhists are more willing to contribute to these activities compared to others.

Buddhist philanthropy extends beyond the ethnic and political boundary where such activities increasingly cater to a multi-ethnic Singapore society as well as in a transnational context, resulting in the emergence of a transnational religious philanthropic culture.

In exploring the development of a welfare niche by Buddhist or other religious communities in Singapore, it is also significant to explore the proactive role played by the Singaporean State from the 1980s onwards. To begin with, it is important to note here that the Singapore Government does not subscribe to the theory of a welfare state and hence only those in dire situations can expect to receive welfare handouts from the state. As part of the state ideology of self-reliance, the government channels its resources into education, training, housing, public works and other ends that aim to create a citizenry that is self-reliant, productive and independent. However, it also recognizes that there are individuals that might require social welfare aid. As such, the Singaporean State systematically encourages and provides various fiscal and other incentives to community groups, including the religious groups to take on the challenges of providing social and welfare services to the wider community.

The roles of community organizations in charity and welfare work have been enshrined in the *Shared Values* White Paper. The White Paper states that:

> We are seeking a balance between the community and the individual, not promoting one to the exclusion of the other … The need for the community to support the individual, and especially show compassion to the less fortunate, surfaced repeatedly in the discussions on Shared Values.
>
> One way Singaporeans can put society above self and show concern for others is by participating personally in this effort. Many Singaporeans volunteer to do community work. Many more contribute to community and welfare programmes. Such community efforts not only help in a practical way to solve the problems of the poor, but also strengthen the sense of togetherness, cohesion, and self-reliance of the society (*Shared Values* 1991: 7).

The Reach of Buddhist Welfarism

Buddhist organizations in Singapore have since their inception taken on an active interest in providing for the socially less privileged sector of the Chinese community and the rest of the population on an ad hoc basis. It was only in the 1980s that the Buddhist community identified itself as an important welfare provider and institutionalized its delivery of the welfare services. Thus, it is possible for us to identify three phases in the development of welfare and charity works as Buddhists embarked on a Weberian process of "rational adjustment to the world". The first phase stretched from the post Second World War to post-independence years, coinciding with the economic and social restructuring of the Singaporean nation-state from pre-industrial to industrial. The second phase coincided with rapid industrialization and development from the early 1970s to the 1980s, and the third phase started from the 1990s until the present with Singapore evolving from a newly industrialized nation to a post-industrial global nation.

Each phase of development was tied to the sociopolitical and socio-economic development of Singapore society and the Chinese community. In the first phase of welfare development from after World War Two to 1965 poverty was rife among the migrant population from the impact of underdeveloped economic institutions in a colonial context. Poverty and poor living conditions were a common experience of a sojourner population. The Buddhist community was also not well developed nor were they well-endowed financially and materially. Nevertheless, they provided ad hoc welfare services in times of need and urgency.

During this period, members of the Sangha, especially the monks, also provided some form of counseling to those in need of a sympathetic ear. This was especially important in an immigrant society where there was an absence of facilities for this. The Sangha, as a neutral party, served this important role. To a certain degree, the temple and the Sangha can be seen as the predecessors of the modern day Chinese welfare system in Singapore. Temples also provided temporary shelter or a home for those who where homeless or without kin or had no means to meet their basic needs in situations where the needy were too old to work. Temples routinely took them in, resulting in the emergence of the first homes for the aged with rudimentary facilities. Furthermore, it was not uncommon that the Chinese temple also served as a kind of "tea house" where the poor, the destitute and social misfits could be assured of some kind of material support. The temple rarely turned away anyone who needed a bowl of rice or a cup of tea. They often relied on temples for food, and sometimes, for shelter. During the early years, when poverty was still an issue, there were many instances when workers and pedestrians could not afford drink or food during their course of travel from one part of town to the next. It was not uncommon for temples to open their doors and provide refreshment to these needy people. Women especially benefited from this gesture, as virtuous women continued to be regarded as those who did not "expose themselves" in public places, thereby psychologically preventing them from entering coffee-shops on their own. Visiting a temple for worship and accepting some refreshment there, however, was different.

In addition to these routine activities, the temple also provided relief aid in emergency situations. This was especially true during the immediate post-independence years. From the 1950s to the early 1970s, the temples and the Sangha were involved in emergency work, providing funds, food, clothing and shelter to victims of natural disasters, especially floods and fires. The temple also provides relief aid in emergency situations. This was especially the case during the immediate post-independence years. Singapore has a tropical monsoon climate. During the monsoon season, heavy downpours result in massive flooding in low-lying areas. Prior to the construction of a comprehensive drainage system in the 1970s, flooding was a frequent occurrence. Many families, in both rural and urban areas, were affected. Fire was the other major hazard. As late as the 1960s, residential buildings, especially those in rural villages, were built primarily of wood and palm-leaves. It was not uncommon that a whole village would be burned to the ground as a result of fire. In the urban centres, badly connected electrical circuits of old pre-war shop-houses were the main causes of fire, and it was a frequent sight to witness rows of shop-houses ablaze resulting from these faulty connections. These fire victims needed relief aid to help them through their difficult moments. While the state provided some kinds of emergency relief for these victims, it was insufficient. Much relief was left to private organizations. The temple played its role by rounding up its supporters and helping these victims. The temple and the Sangha rarely offered cash, which was often given by the state or large charitable institutions. They co-ordinated the devotees of the temple and prepared communal meals for the victims. Sometimes, its devotees would help collect used clothing and food items from the public and distribute them to the victims. Likewise, temples were also used as temporary shelters, along with schools and community centres.

Another welfare role played by the temple was that it acted as a benevolence hall (*shan-tang*), a prelude to modern Buddhist Free Clinic. The benevolence hall functioned as a clinic where Chinese physicians treated and dispensed herbal medicine. Some Sangha members were also trained as physicians. The benevolence hall was known as *shan-tang* because its aim was charity. Patients were treated by a trained physician, who could either be a Buddhist monk, a Daoist priest or a lay person. In some temples qualified physician monks treated patients. Otherwise, a trained physician

Daoist priest or a lay physician would be invited to treat patients on a voluntary basis.

During the second phase, Buddhist involvement in welfare activities shifted along with the changing political landscape from one of a colonial society to an independent nation-state, a sojourner mentality gave way to one of permanent settlement and citizenship in a new nation-state. During this phase, a new political and settlement landscape led to the institutionalization of welfare works and activities from the 1970s to 1980s. To begin with, the benevolence halls were replaced with Buddhist Free Clinics which continued to treat patients using the traditional Chinese medicine. These clinics, with their bureaucratic organizational management structure, employed updated technological knowledge, used modern equipment and expanded services. They now provide alternative health care treatment to Singaporeans. In the future, the Sangha intends to establish a hospital based on the Chinese medical system of health care and treatment, employing natural cures and medicines, in accordance with the present global trend towards alternative medicine such as herbal medicine, acupuncture, naturopathy and homeopathy.

The transition from *shan-tang* to free clinic indicates a move from an informal to a formal structure as dictated by the bureaucratic requirement set down in legislation and the expanding needs of the population. As a non-profit charitable institution, it has formally to register with the Registrar of Companies. As such, it is required to have a constitution spelling out its objectives and its trusteeship, executive council and administrative structure. Thus, the primary objective of the clinics is to "work for the welfare of the poor and sick. Patients, irrespective of sex, race and creed, who are in a strained financial condition may be given Chinese medicine and treatment, free of charge". In line with Buddhist morality, the clinics do "not treat patients with venereal or infectious diseases or patients injured or wounded because of fighting" (Buddhist Federation Free Clinic Constitution).

The first Buddhist Free Clinic was established in 1969. During the early days, patients were given free treatment, and the needy were given free medicine as well. Today, patients are charged a nominal registration fee of $1 with the fee waived for those who request it. Likewise a nominal charge has been levied for the medicine which was waived for those who request it. The number of patients using this clinic increased overwhelmingly from a mere 2,510 in 1969 to over 200,000 in 1974 and to over 400,000 patients in 1982. This increase has been viewed as a positive indication of the need to provide alternative medical care to the general population. This high demand has prompted the Singapore Buddhist Free Clinics to open up more branches. Today in organizational terms, the Singapore Buddhist Free Clinic has six branches (five clinics and one rehabilitation centre) under the central management of the Singapore Buddhist Free Clinic. From its formation until the present time, it has treated over twelve million patients. Patients go there for acupuncture treatment as well as traditional Chinese medicine (www.sbfc.org.sg).

Because of the need for public accountability, the state has systematically encouraged the formalization of institutional structures among voluntary, benevolence, welfare and religious institutions. All Buddhist temples and the Sangha Council are now public institutions. The monks and nuns are often consulted on religious and moral matters. They can also be physicians if they are trained and qualified to be so. However, today they are not involved in temple administration. During the early years, monks were decisive in the management of the *shan-tang*, but this is not so presently. This check on the influence, strength and power of the Sangha is deliberate, because the state regards religion as a sensitive element and is cautious about its roles and activities. In encouraging religious institutions to provide welfare facilities and charity to the less privileged, the state is careful to ensure that the powers of religious institutions are confined within a stipulated boundary.

As the government encourages private and religious institutions to contribute to charity and the welfare of its population, it also provides incentives for them. The Charities Act of 1982 provided fiscal privileges. An institution registered as a charitable organization under the Societies Act (cao 262) before 1 January 1983 is entitled to tax exemption, including property tax as well as government subsidy.

As non-profit charities, the clinics operate on private funds generated mostly from public donations, and individual temples, monks and nuns often appeal to their adherents for donations. A handful of wealthy philanthropists are often counted on to give large donations to worthy causes of this nature. However, small sums ($5 to $200) usually form a constant pool of ready resources for operating and maintaining these clinics. Most temples organize an annual drive for donations for the clinics. Lay people also help to raise funds through personal ties and social networks with friends, colleagues and employers. Apart from this, the Singapore Buddhist Free Clinic raised funds from various events, such as walks, their banquets and other celebrations. They also issued charity vouchers and these can be used as presents or condolences in place of cash or a wreath (www. sbfc.org.sg). Since 1997, the Singapore Buddhist Free Clinic has become a member of the Health Endowment Fund under the Ministry of Health and it is now entitled to generous grants from the government to help run its welfare projects.

During this period, there was also a rapid expansion of Buddhist welfare homes for the aged. The government thus encouraged temples to build and to run welfare homes not only for the aged but also the handicapped children. In an attempt to streamline welfare policies, some temple-based welfare homes now work in collaboration with the Social Welfare Department and only take in recommended inmates. These temples are provided with a subsidy by the state. Several Chinese Buddhist temples have established welfare homes for the aged. They include the Tai Pei Old Folks' Home, attached to Tai Pei Temple; Evergreen Old Folks' Home, attached to Phor Khar See Temple (the largest temple in Singapore); and Singapore Buddhist Welfare Services Old Folks' Home. All three admit elderly men and women on the recommendation of the Social Welfare Department and do not take in any on their own. These welfare homes conform to the guidelines laid down for voluntary welfare homes. The homes provide spacious accommodation (four to a room), and are equipped with a gymnasium and/or a recreation room. A trained nurse is on service on a daily basis. The homes also organize handicraft sessions to help inmates utilize their time productively. Religious services are conducted to cater to their spiritual development and the elderly are encouraged to attend and participate in prayer services. At the Tai Pei Old Folks' Home there is an in-house clinic to take care of general medical needs. For the other two, voluntary medical practitioners make weekly rounds to check on inmates. Those who are in need of specialist services are taken to hospital. Likewise, qualified nurses, doctors, physiotherapists and teachers are recruited to help with the elderly and the autistic children in the homes and centres run by Metta Welfare Associations.

The third phase, from the 1990s onwards, coincided with a society that had become politically stable with a mature economy shifting towards a post-industrial society. During this phase, the development of Buddhist philanthropic culture moved from local to transnational sites. Since the 1990s, many Buddhist organizations have formalized their role as provider of various types of welfare facilities and services to the general public. Today, there are sixty Buddhist organizations involved in such provisions.

The welfare facilities and services can be broadly divided into three main types. The first include community homes and centres that provide home care facilities for the elderly and needy. These include homes for the aged (as illustrated above), homes and services for the socially marginalized groups in the community such as drop-in centres for recovered and recovering drug addicts, residential homes and services. They also provide services for the sick, elderly, destitute female elderly and the needy. The second includes the provision of centres and services in the area of health services and education such as dialysis centres for kidney patients, day activity centres for the intellectually disabled. These centres provide counseling, rehabilitation services, physiotherapy, occupational therapy services and support for patients affected by an array of illnesses, including stroke, arthritis and other diseases, as well as the chronically ill. They also provide loans of medical equipment for patients from low income groups. The third area includes the provision of education facilities and services to the general community. Some Buddhist organizations run child care and student care centres in various housing estates as part of Buddhist involvement in community care.

One poignant development in recent years is the development of Buddhist welfare corporatism. Here, the key characteristic of the large Buddhist organizations in their role as welfare providers is that each one of these organizations is involved in the provision of a variety of welfare services. This development is in contrast to the earlier Buddhist organizations which generally only provide one type of welfare service. An example is the Golden Pagoda Temple, which operates the Metta Welfare Association. Under the umbrella of the Metta Welfare Association, there are nine affiliated centres that provide an array of services and facilities. In 1995, it established the Metta Day Care Activity Centre for the Intellectually Diasbled. In 1998, it established the Metta Day Rehabilitation Centre for the Elderly and a neighbourhood Yu Neng Metta Student Care Centre One for the South East district. In 2000, it established the Metta Home for the intellectually disabled and Metta Hospice Care. In 2001, it further established the Metta School for Students with Learning Disabilities and another neighbourhood Metta Student Care Centre in North East district. In 2002, a second Yu Neng Metta Student Care Centre Two was established. The Association has 136 staff with an annual expenditure of $4.3 million, funded primarily by government grants, sponsorships and donations (Metta Welfare Association Annual Report 2001). Apart from this, the Association, in conjunction with the temple, organized fund raising activities, such as the sale of Chinese New Year Cakes, Mooncakes and Christmas cakes, the Metta Charity Walk, Charity Draw, I-Charity golf and charity banquets.

Another example is the Foo Hai Ch'an Monastery which established the Foo Hai Buddhist Cultural and Welfare Association which manages four welfare centres and facilities. There is the Aspiration Child Care Centre in Tampines, Marine Parade Aspiration Elderly Lodge, Marine Parade Aspiration Child Care and Student Care Centre in Bedok North, and Wan Qing Lodge Day Centre for the Elderly. Another initiative is its establishment of the Buddhist Ren Ci Hospital in 1994, initiated by one of its abbots, Venerable Shi Ming Yi. This is the first hospital that is operated by the Buddhist community in Singapore.

What motivates these Buddhist organizations to expand their delivery of welfare services and facilities and to become comprehensive in reaching out to the socially less privileged and marginalized population is the vision of the monastic leaders and their interpretation of religious doctrine. For example, the abbot of the Foo Hai Ch'an Monastery, Venerable Shi Ming Yi said that:

> Buddhism talks about compassion, and compassion should not just be a theoretical thing but it should be put into practice. So putting it into practice through doing some social work, I believe, is also a way for people to get to know Buddhism ... to cultivate compassion in us.

Another characteristic of the present Buddhist philanthropic culture is the move towards transnational welfare works. In the early years, some of the wealthier Buddhist organizations would provide financial assistance to overseas Buddhist organizations or to poverty-stricken or natural disaster stricken countries on an ad hoc and based on needs basis. Today, some of these Buddhist organizations have formalized their welfare roles on a transnational basis. For example, the Foo Hai Ch'an Monastery has extended their religious compassion to Sri Lanka. It is in the process of building a welfare home called the "Village of Compassion" and training Sri Lankans to care for and manage people. Venerable Shi Ming Yi also started Buddhist counseling services in Hong Kong. Likewise, the abbot of the Golden Pagoda, Venerable Shi Fazhao has also been actively involved in transnational charity, welfare works and helped with temple rebuilding in Thailand, Myanmar, Cambodia, China, Nepal and Sri Lanka.

On the home front, the Buddhist philanthropic culture is becoming more all encompassing and moving towards non ethnic welfarism, thereby cutting across ethnic boundary and reaching out to other ethnic groups. Today, many of these welfare homes and facilities are accessible by people and children from different ethnic and social backgrounds. This is in contrast to the earlier welfare homes that generally admitted only the Chinese. At the same time, the workers and volunteers also come from different ethnic backgrounds. For example, in the Metta Welfare Associations, the supervisor of the Metta Hospice Care and a senior staff nurse of the Metta Home are Muslim. Likewise the principal of the Metta School is a Christian and the Vice-principal is a Muslim. This fits neatly into the government's push for a multi-religious and multi-cultural Singapore work and social environment.

State–Religion Partnership

While the proliferation of welfare facilities and services organized by the Buddhist organizations can be attributed to the Buddhist understanding of compassion and enacting upon this ideology, it can also be argued that the actions of the state has facilitated the formalization and the expansion of such facilities and services by these organizations.

Within the religious landscape, it is possible to argue that what we might call the poetics of religious philanthropy in Singapore has become a way for wealthy Chinese to gain social recognition and an elevation of their social status, and it is a common practice for welfare institutions to acknowledge large contributions by naming rooms and buildings after the donors. For example, the Buddhist Federation recognizes those who contribute more than $5,000 annually as life members, while those who donate over $100 are ordinary members. Donors are often mentioned in the newsletters of the respective Buddhist organizations for public consumption.

On the other hand, it is also possible to argue that through the years, the state and religious organizations have developed a strategic partnership in the delivery of welfare services and facilities to the general public in Singapore. In general, the Singaporean government has mapped out areas where welfare services and facilities are required and encouraged the religious institutions to take up the role as welfare providers. At the same time, the state laid out guidelines to ensure that homes and facilities meet the requirement of the state and to protect the interests of the elderly, the children and the socially disadvantaged Singaporeans. For example, Metta School operates under the

Ministry of Education Special Education guidelines. Hence, there is a need for a proper school management committee and the curriculum needs to be approved by the Ministry of Education.

To establish welfare homes and facilities and provide welfare services requires both human and financial resources. While it is often easy to encourage volunteers to perform community works, welfare homes and services required both full-time working personnel as well as sizeable financial resources. While there are a very small number of wealthy Buddhist organizations and temples, many religious organizations, on their own, found it hard to have sufficient financial resources to start up these services. Given the fact that the state has actively encouraged these institutions to provide welfare facilities and services to the less privileged group of the population, it established legislation to provide financial assistance to assist these religious organizations who run welfare homes, facilities and services to the public.

Religious organizations who run welfare homes, facilities and services could apply for an annual grant from the government to help defray the running costs of these homes. The amount of grant given varies from institution to institution. One example is the Metta School for the intellectually disabled where part of their funding comes from Ministry of Education and the National Council of Social Services (NCSS). Likewise, NCSS provides a grant to many welfare homes run by the religious organizations. At the same time, these religious organizations also become members of the NCSS. Membership in the NCSS provides them with legitimacy in the eyes of the State and facilitates their applications for financial grants to run these homes. At the same time, it legitimizes their activities in the eyes of the general public. As such, many of these Buddhist organizations have become affiliated to this state bureaucracy, facilitating a workable state–religion partnership.

This state–religion partnership has its advantages and disadvantages. The key advantage is that the strict guidelines laid down by the government will ensure quality assurance in the delivery of care and prevent mistreatment and exploitation of the young, elderly and intellectually disabled people. This is very important to ease the anxiety of parents and related kin of these people. However, one of the drawbacks is that these religious-based welfare centres and homes have to observe the tight guidelines laid down by the NCSS or the relevant government authorities. For example, the religious-based dialysis centres for kidney patients cannot accept patients over the age of 60 years which is the guideline lay down by the National Kidney Foundation. As a result, elderly patients are known to be rejected from such services and have to pay a huge bill for their dialysis treatment in private clinics or government hospitals.

Apart from government grants given to run the homes and centres, the government also provides land at nominal prices to religious institutions who want to build welfare homes and service centres, but the religious institutions need to raise funds for the construction costs and internal furnishing. Depending on the size and scale of the home, it could be a hefty sum of several million or more dollars and funds raising by these institutions become crucial to ensure the fruition of these projects. Likewise, they also charge nominal rent in housing estates for the various centres run by religious institutions as part of their community care projects. This partnership has enabled the Buddhist community to consolidate its role as welfare provider, and render religion an integral partner in the development of modern Singapore.

Conclusion

As I have already stated in the opening sections of this chapter, I have examined the positive and contributive roles of religion, as illustrated through the case study of Buddhism. As Singapore matures as a nation-state and as it moves towards integration into a global economic environment, it is also inevitably drawn into a global world interconnected with other social and humanitarian goals, aspirations and movements. In this respect, while local secular NGOs are attempting to keep up with their western counterparts, the religious institutions have quietly carved out a niche as both local and transnational welfare providers. At home, these religious institutions have already enmeshed fully into the welfare sector and as illustrated by the Buddhist community, the emerging religious philanthropic culture has taken root, moving quickly towards a comprehensive welfare strategy. Given its reach towards other ethnic groups within both the local and transnational communities, it is possible to argue that this development would lead to the establishment of a closer dialogue among the various religious groups thereby fostering a truly multi-ethnic religious welfare platform for both local and transnational needs. In this sense, religion could be seen as an adhesive, bringing social cohesion to a plural society. At the same time, religious institutions are also fast becoming important organizations in an expanding Singaporean civil society. The Buddhist institution in our case study could be seen as playing such a crucial role in Singapore society.

Notes

1. Part of this paper is derived from the chapter titled "Delivering Welfare Services in Singapore: A Strategic Partnership between Buddhism and the State" that will be published in a forthcoming edited book titled, *Religious Harmony and Diversities in Singapore*, to be edited by Lai Ah Eng.
2. For a fuller discussion on the competition for adherents between Buddhist and Christian groups (see Kuah-Pearce 2003: 265–286).

References

Buddhist Federation Free Clinic Constitution, n.d., Singapore: Singapore Buddhist Federation,.

Chua, Beng Huat (1982) "Singapore in 1981: problems in new beginning," *Southeast Asian Affairs*. Singapore: Institute of Southeast Asian Studies: 315–335.

Dayal, Har (1978) *The Bodhisattva Doctrine in Buddhist Sanskrit Literature*. Delhi: Motilal Banardidass.

De Bary, William Theodore (1972) *The Buddhist Tradition*. New York: Vintage Books.

Goh, Chok Tong (1992) Speeches: A Bimonthly Selection of Ministerial Speeches vol.16, Singapore: Publicity Division, Ministry of Information and the Arts.

Kuah, Khun Eng (1998) "Maintaining ethno-religious harmony in Singapore," *Journal of Contemporary Asia*, 28(1): 103–121.

—— (1991) "Buddhism, moral education and nation-building in Singapore," *Pacific Viewpoint*, 32(1): 24–42.

—— (1992) "Confucian ideology and social engineering in Singapore," *Journal of Contemporary Asia* 20(3): 371–382,.

—— (2002) "Buddhism in Singapore", in *Religions of the World: A Comprehensive Encyclopedia of Beliefs and Practices*, vol. 4, J. Gordon Melton and Martin Baumann, eds. Santa Barbara, California: ABC-Clio, pp. 1184–1185.

—— (2003) *State, Society and Religious Engineering: Towards A Reformist Buddhism*. Singapore: Eastern Universities Press.

Ling, Trevor (1989) "Religion" in, *Management of Success: The Moulding of Modern Singapore*, ed. Kernial Singh Sandhu and Paul Wheatley, Singapore: Institute of Southeast Asian Studies, 692–709.

Matthews, Bruce and Judith Nagata (1986) *Religion, Values and Development in Southeast Asia*. Singapore: Institute of Southeast Asian Studies.

Metta Welfare Association (2001) *Annual Report*. Singapore: Metta Welfare Association.

Obeyesekere, Gananath (1968) "Theodicy, sin and salvation in a sociology of Buddhism," in *Dialectic in Practical Religion*, Edmund R. Leach, ed. Cambridge: Cambridge University Press.

Singapore Department of Statistics (1994) *Singapore Census of Population 1990: Religion, Childcare and Leisure Activities*. Singapore: Department of Statistics. Statistical Release 6.

Smith, Bardwell L. (1979) *Religion and the Legitimation of Power in Southeast Asia*. Leiden: E.J. Brill.

Spiro, Melford E. (1979) *Buddhism and Society*. New York: Harper and Rows.

Tan, Chee Beng (1995) "The study of Chinese religions in Southeast Asia: some views," in *Southeast Asian Chinese: The Socio-Cultural Dimension*, Leo Suryadinata, ed. Singapore: Times Academic Press.

Weber, Max (1951) *The Religion of China*. New York: The Free Press.
—— (1996) *The Sociology of Religion*. London: Associated Book.
Wee, Vivienne (1976) "'Buddhism' in Singapore," in *Singapore: Society in Transition*, Riaz Hassan, ed. Kuala Lumpur: Oxford University Press.
White Paper on Maintenance of Religious Harmony. Singapore: Singapore Government, 1989.
White Paper on Shared Values 1990. Singapore: Singapore Government, 1991.

Newsletters and magazines of the following Buddhist organizations in Singapore

Singapore Buddhist Federation. *Singapore Buddhist Free Clinic.*
Mangala Vihara Buddhist Temple. *Echo.*
Buddha Sasana, *White Conch.*
National University of Singapore Buddhist Society. *One Wheel.*
Ngee Ann Polytechnic Buddhist Society. *The Golden Link.*
Golden Pagoda Temple. *Vaidurya*, ([琉璃坊] 佛教生活杂 +).
Metta Buddhist Welfare Association, *Metta News.*

Websites

DharmaLink. http://www.aloha.net/~horaku/dharmalink.html. (date accessed 5 December 2006).
Singapore DharmaNet. http://www.singapore-dharmanet.per.sg. (date accessed 6 December 2006).
Singapore Buddhist Free Clinic. http://www.sbfc.org.sg/. (date accessed 5 December 2006)

Index